STAR WARS®

KNIGHTS OF THE OLD REPUBLIC

VOLUME FOUR
DAZE OF HATE,
KNIGHTS OF SUFFERING

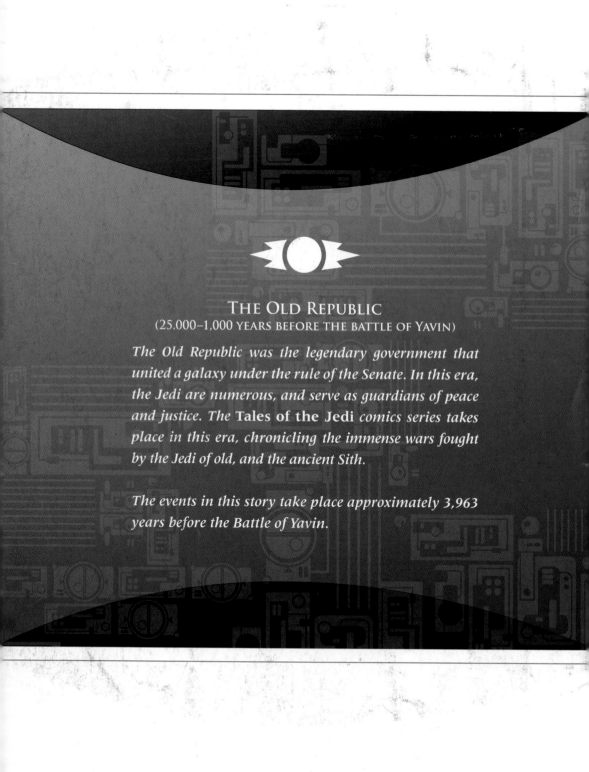

THE OLD REPUBLIC
(25,000–1,000 YEARS BEFORE THE BATTLE OF YAVIN)

The Old Republic was the legendary government that united a galaxy under the rule of the Senate. In this era, the Jedi are numerous, and serve as guardians of peace and justice. The **Tales of the Jedi** comics series takes place in this era, chronicling the immense wars fought by the Jedi of old, and the ancient Sith.

The events in this story take place approximately 3,963 years before the Battle of Yavin.

STAR WARS®

KNIGHTS OF THE OLD REPUBLIC

VOLUME FOUR
DAZE OF HATE, KNIGHTS OF SUFFERING

SCRIPT JOHN JACKSON MILLER

ART BONG DAZO, DUSTIN WEAVER & DAN PARSONS

COLORS MICHAEL ATIYEH

LETTERING MICHAEL HEISLER

FRONT COVER ART COLIN WILSON

BACK COVER ART CHRIS WARNER & KELSEY SHANNON

Dark Horse Books®

PUBLISHER MIKE RICHARDSON

COLLECTION DESIGNER KRYSTAL HENNES

ART DIRECTOR LIA RIBACCHI

ASSISTANT EDITORS FREDDYE LINS & DAVE MARSHALL

SERIES EDITOR JEREMY BARLOW

EDITOR RANDY STRADLEY

Special thanks to Elaine Mederer, Jann Moorhead, David Anderman, Leland Chee, Sue Rostoni, and Carol Roeder at Lucas Licensing.

STAR WARS: KNIGHTS OF THE OLD REPUBLIC VOLUME FOUR—DAZE OF HATE, KNIGHTS OF SUFFERING

This volume collects issues nineteen through twenty-four of the Dark Horse comic-book series *Star Wars: Knights of the Old Republic*.

Published by
Dark Horse Books
A division of Dark Horse Comics, Inc.
10956 SE Main Street
Milwaukie, OR 97222

darkhorse.com
starwars.com

To find a comics shop in your area,
call the Comic Shop Locator Service toll-free at 1-888-266-4226

First edition: September 2008
ISBN: 978-1-59582-208-6

1 3 5 7 9 10 8 6 4 2
Printed in China

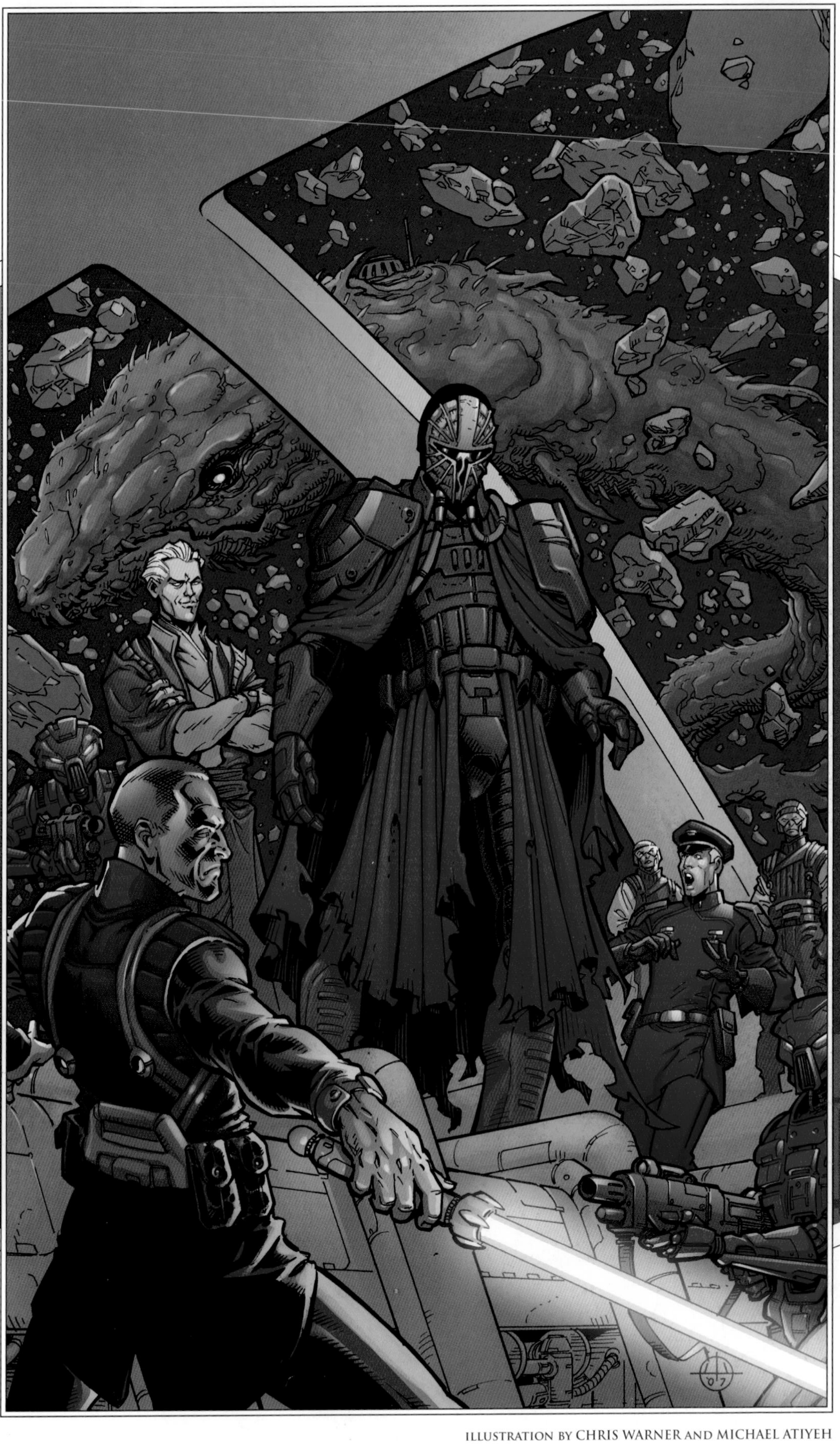

ILLUSTRATION BY CHRIS WARNER AND MICHAEL ATIYEH

DAZE OF HATE

art by Bong Dazo

With their love for biotechnology, the Arkanians consider themselves the scientific center of the Republic. Now, with the Mandalorians approaching their space, the charismatic Lord Adasca seeks to secure—and perhaps improve—his people's place by offering a new super-weapon to the highest bidder.

Aboard the ship *Arkanian Legacy*, Adasca sends invitations to potential buyers, including one to Republic Admiral Karath, who has fugitive Padawan Zayne Carrick in his custody. Also held captive on the ship are Adasca's former employee Gorman Vandrayk—also known as Zayne's friend Camper—and Camper's protector, the mysterious female warrior Jarael, another of Zayne's friends . . .

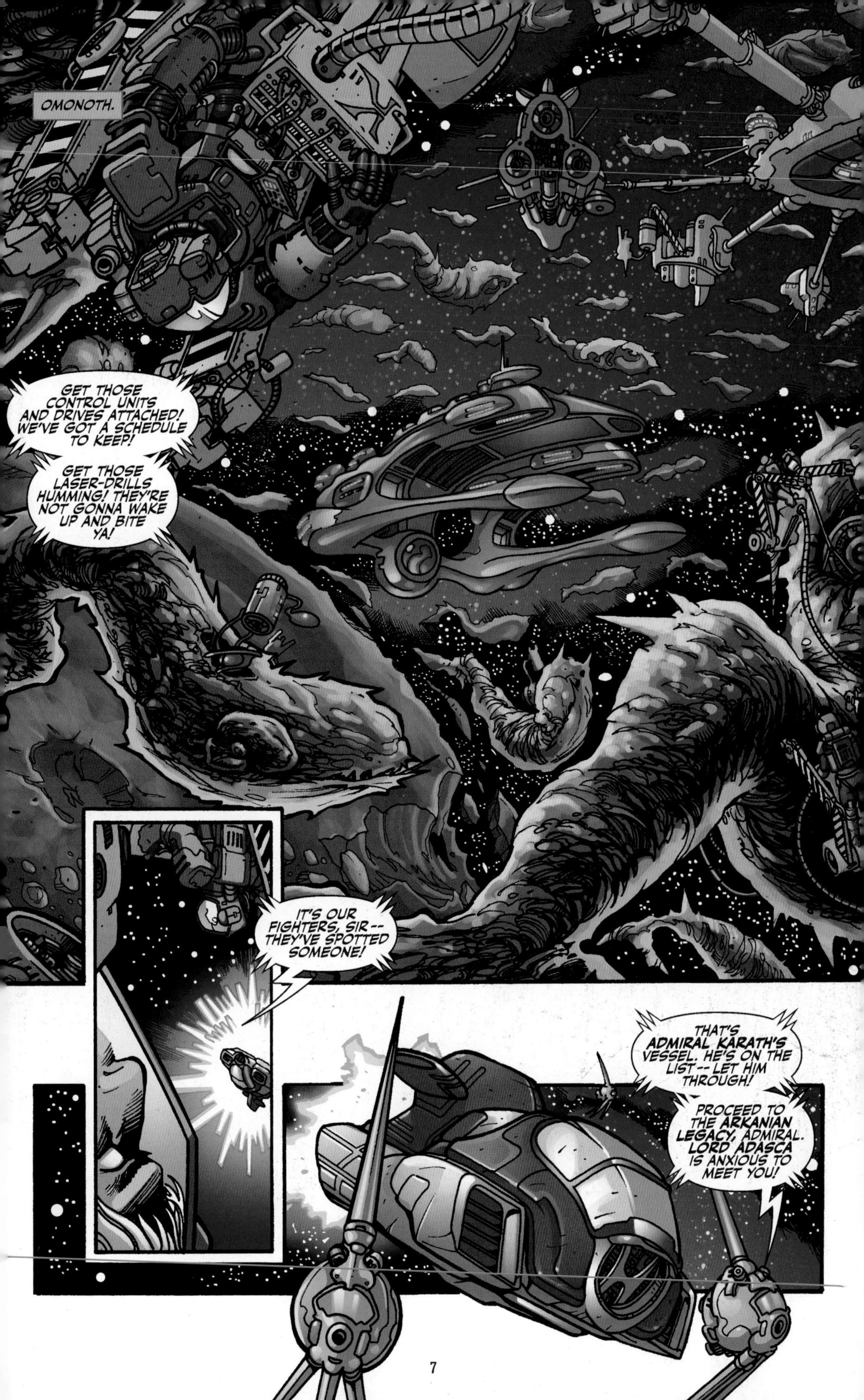
OMONOTH.
GET THOSE CONTROL UNITS AND DRIVES ATTACHED! WE'VE GOT A SCHEDULE TO KEEP!
GET THOSE LASER-DRILLS HUMMING! THEY'RE NOT GONNA WAKE UP AND BITE YA!
IT'S OUR FIGHTERS, SIR-- THEY'VE SPOTTED SOMEONE!
THAT'S ADMIRAL KARATH'S VESSEL. HE'S ON THE LIST -- LET HIM THROUGH!
PROCEED TO THE ARKANIAN LEGACY, ADMIRAL. LORD ADASCA IS ANXIOUS TO MEET YOU!

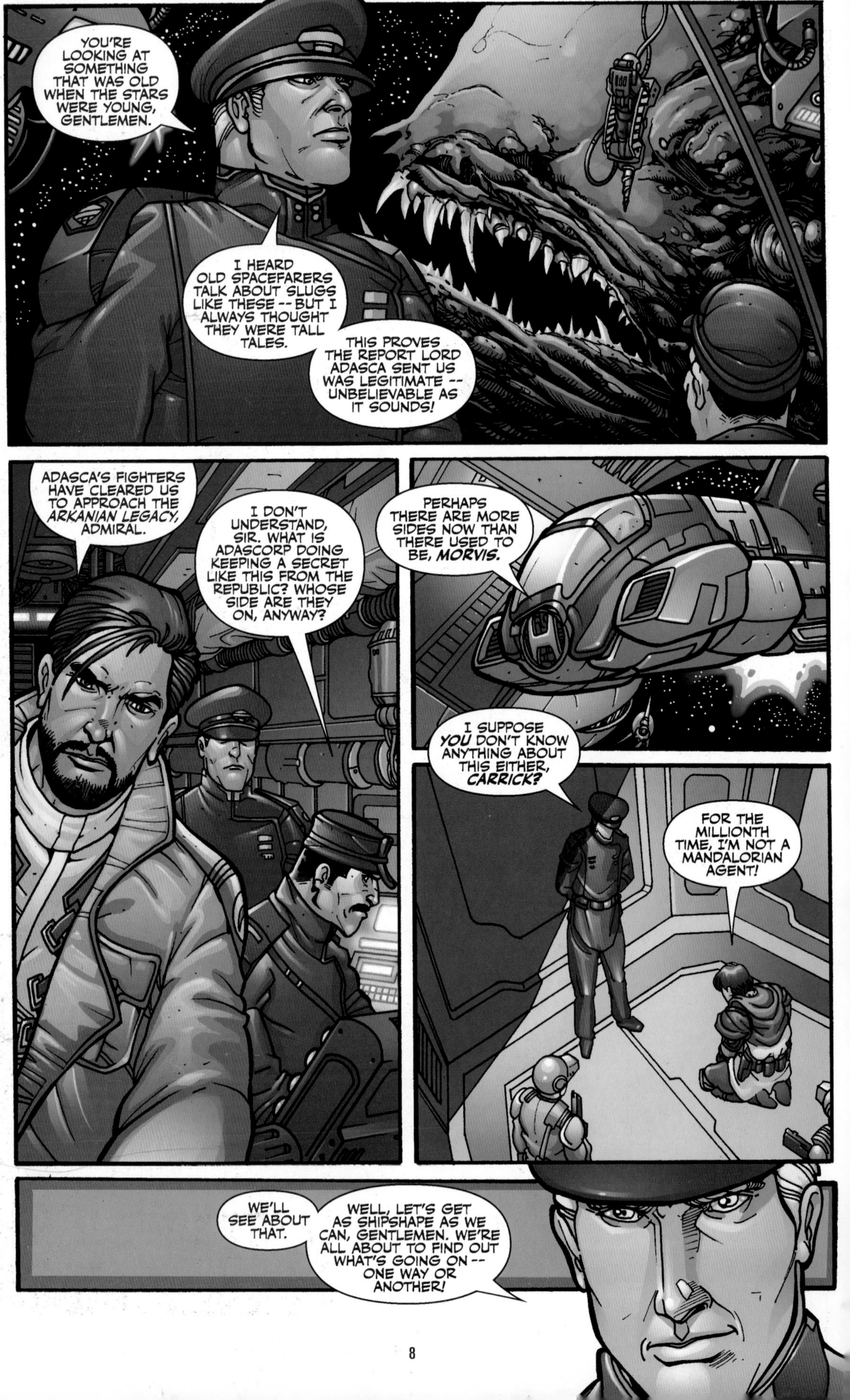
YOU'RE LOOKING AT SOMETHING THAT WAS OLD WHEN THE STARS WERE YOUNG, GENTLEMEN.
I HEARD OLD SPACEFARERS TALK ABOUT SLUGS LIKE THESE -- BUT I ALWAYS THOUGHT THEY WERE TALL TALES.
THIS PROVES THE REPORT LORD ADASCA SENT US WAS LEGITIMATE -- UNBELIEVABLE AS IT SOUNDS!
ADASCA'S FIGHTERS HAVE CLEARED US TO APPROACH THE *ARKANIAN LEGACY,* ADMIRAL.
I DON'T UNDERSTAND, SIR. WHAT IS ADASCORP DOING KEEPING A SECRET LIKE THIS FROM THE REPUBLIC? WHOSE SIDE ARE THEY ON, ANYWAY?
PERHAPS THERE ARE MORE SIDES NOW THAN THERE USED TO BE, ***MORVIS.***
I SUPPOSE ***YOU*** DON'T KNOW ANYTHING ABOUT THIS EITHER, ***CARRICK?***
FOR THE MILLIONTH TIME, I'M NOT A MANDALORIAN AGENT!
WE'LL SEE ABOUT THAT.
WELL, LET'S GET AS SHIPSHAPE AS WE CAN, GENTLEMEN. WE'RE ALL ABOUT TO FIND OUT WHAT'S GOING ON -- ONE WAY OR ANOTHER!

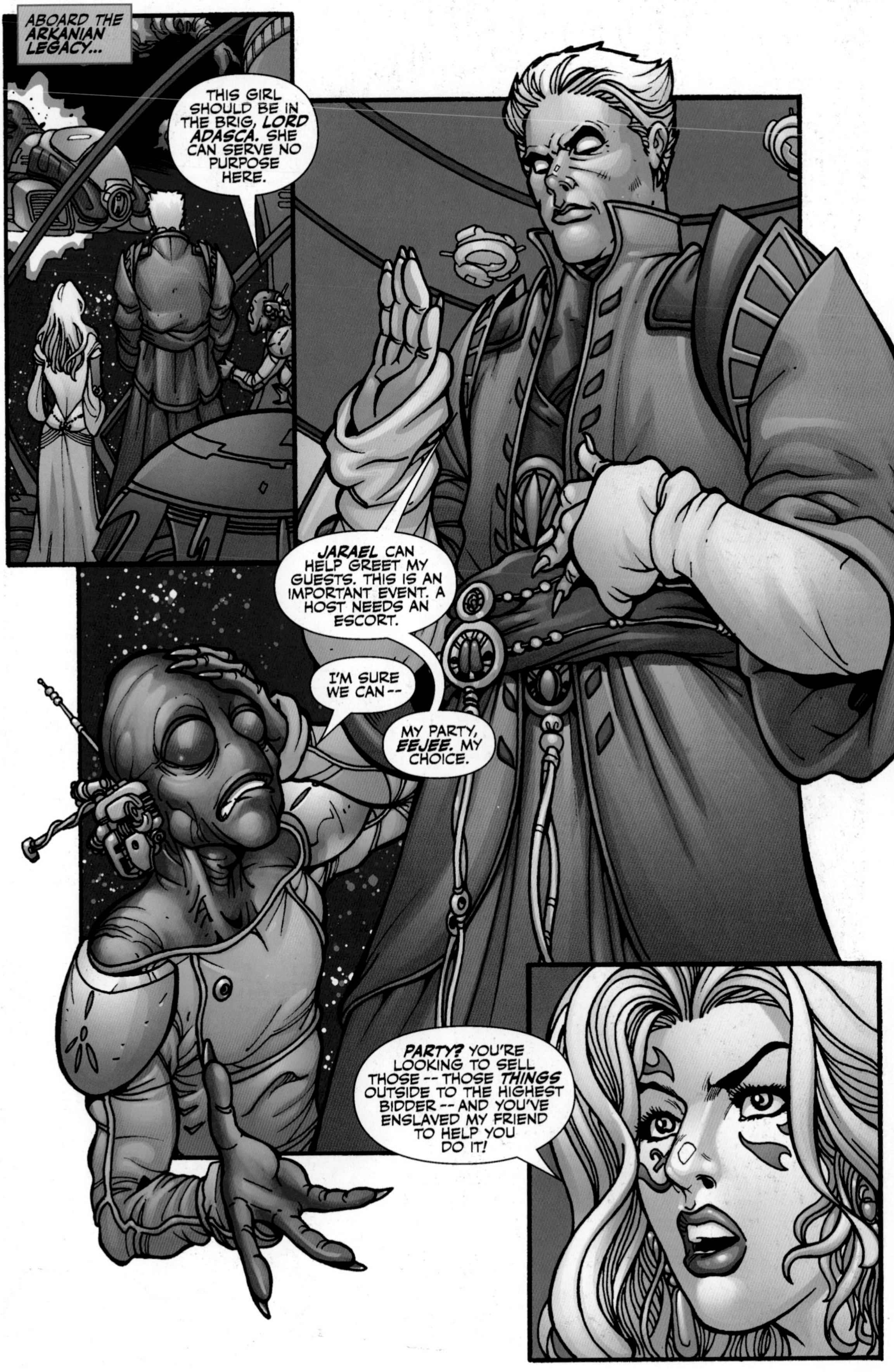

ABOARD THE ARKANIAN LEGACY...
THIS GIRL SHOULD BE IN THE BRIG, LORD ADASCA. SHE CAN SERVE NO PURPOSE HERE.
JARAEL CAN HELP GREET MY GUESTS. THIS IS AN IMPORTANT EVENT. A HOST NEEDS AN ESCORT.
I'M SURE WE CAN--
MY PARTY, EEJEE. MY CHOICE.
PARTY? YOU'RE LOOKING TO SELL THOSE -- THOSE THINGS OUTSIDE TO THE HIGHEST BIDDER -- AND YOU'VE ENSLAVED MY FRIEND TO HELP YOU DO IT!

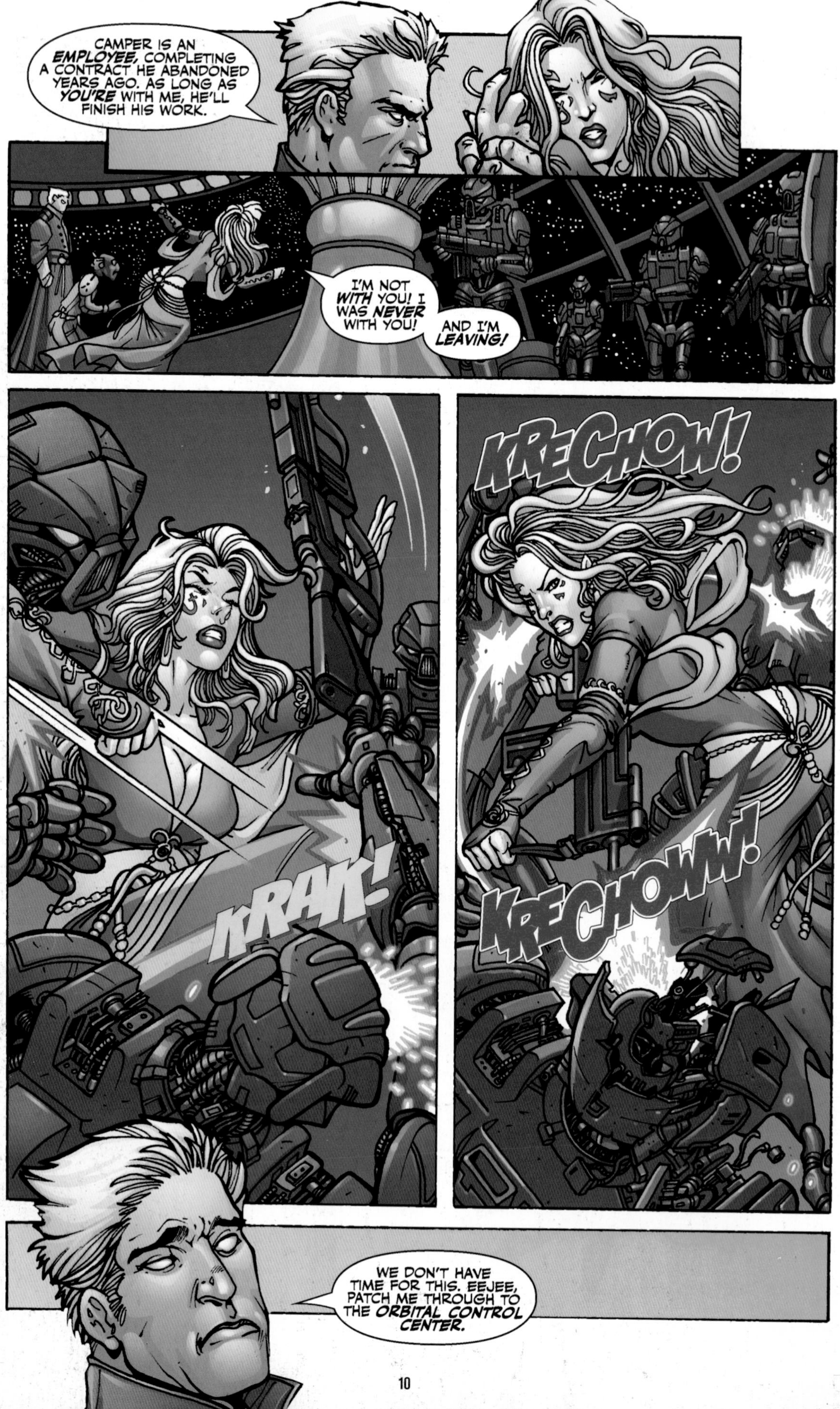

CAMPER IS AN EMPLOYEE, COMPLETING A CONTRACT HE ABANDONED YEARS AGO. AS LONG AS YOU'RE WITH ME, HE'LL FINISH HIS WORK.
I'M NOT WITH YOU! I WAS NEVER WITH YOU!
AND I'M LEAVING!
KRAK!
KRECHOW!
KRECHOWW!
WE DON'T HAVE TIME FOR THIS. EEJEE, PATCH ME THROUGH TO THE ORBITAL CONTROL CENTER.

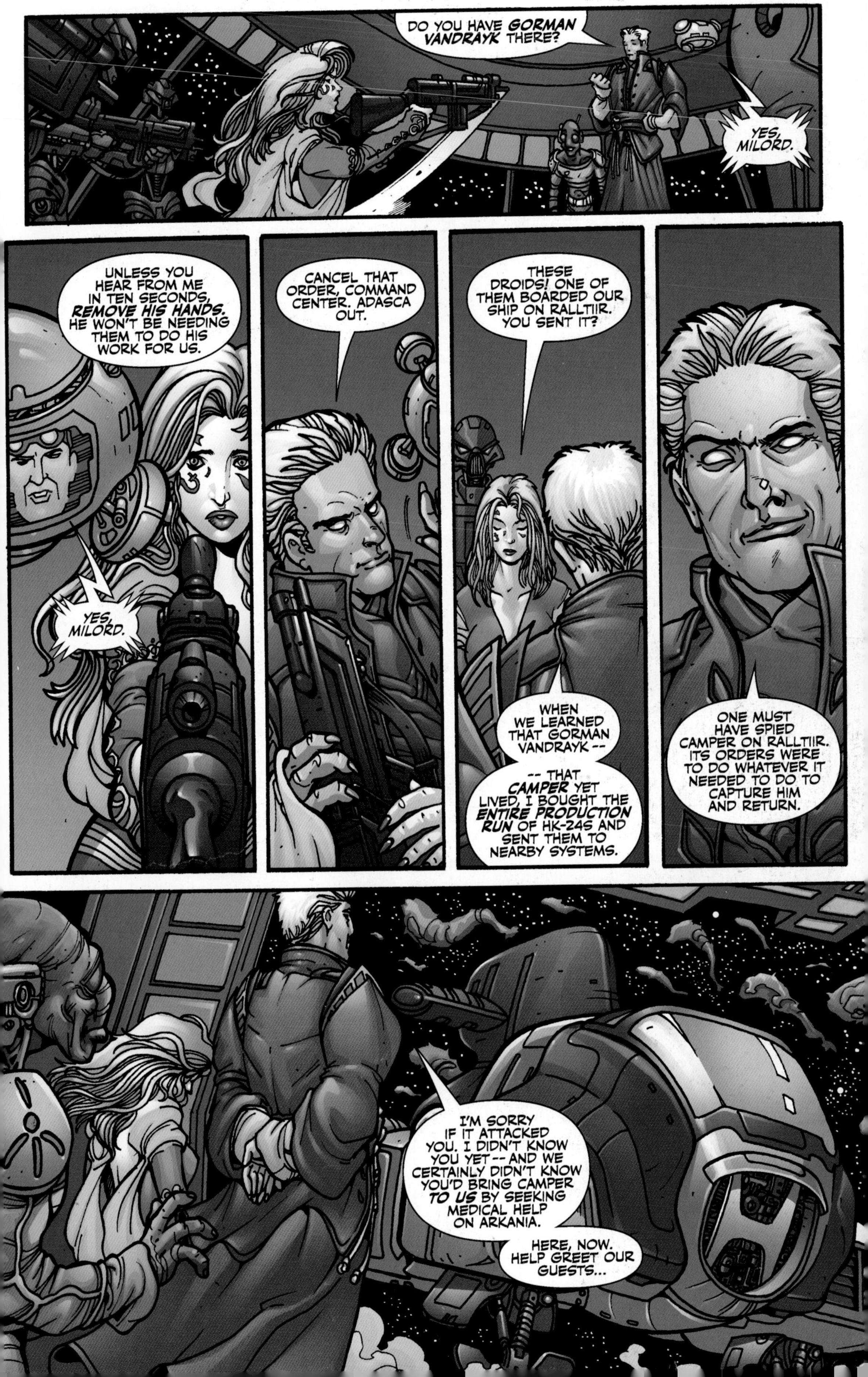
DO YOU HAVE GORMAN VANDRAYK THERE?
YES, MILORD.
UNLESS YOU HEAR FROM ME IN TEN SECONDS, REMOVE HIS HANDS. HE WON'T BE NEEDING THEM TO DO HIS WORK FOR US.
YES, MILORD.
CANCEL THAT ORDER, COMMAND CENTER. ADASCA OUT.
THESE DROIDS! ONE OF THEM BOARDED OUR SHIP ON RALLTIIR. YOU SENT IT?
WHEN WE LEARNED THAT GORMAN VANDRAYK --
-- THAT CAMPER YET LIVED, I BOUGHT THE ENTIRE PRODUCTION RUN OF HK-24S AND SENT THEM TO NEARBY SYSTEMS.
ONE MUST HAVE SPIED CAMPER ON RALLTIIR. ITS ORDERS WERE TO DO WHATEVER IT NEEDED TO DO TO CAPTURE HIM AND RETURN.
I'M SORRY IF IT ATTACKED YOU. I DIDN'T KNOW YOU YET -- AND WE CERTAINLY DIDN'T KNOW YOU'D BRING CAMPER TO US BY SEEKING MEDICAL HELP ON ARKANIA.
HERE, NOW. HELP GREET OUR GUESTS...

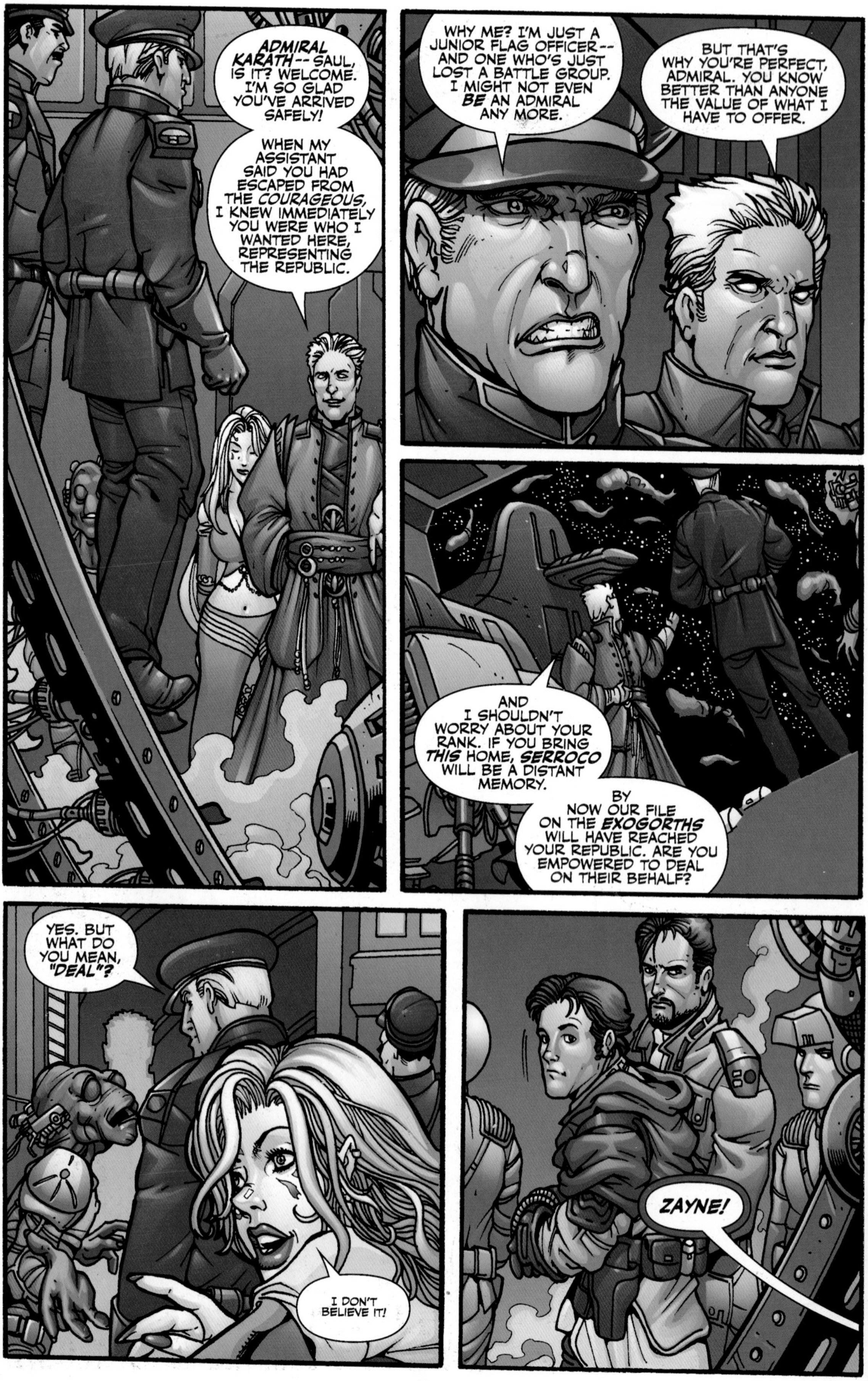
ADMIRAL KARATH-- SAUL, IS IT? WELCOME. I'M SO GLAD YOU'VE ARRIVED SAFELY!
WHEN MY ASSISTANT SAID YOU HAD ESCAPED FROM THE COURAGEOUS, I KNEW IMMEDIATELY YOU WERE WHO I WANTED HERE, REPRESENTING THE REPUBLIC.
WHY ME? I'M JUST A JUNIOR FLAG OFFICER-- AND ONE WHO'S JUST LOST A BATTLE GROUP. I MIGHT NOT EVEN BE AN ADMIRAL ANY MORE.
BUT THAT'S WHY YOU'RE PERFECT, ADMIRAL. YOU KNOW BETTER THAN ANYONE THE VALUE OF WHAT I HAVE TO OFFER.
AND I SHOULDN'T WORRY ABOUT YOUR RANK. IF YOU BRING THIS HOME, SERROCO WILL BE A DISTANT MEMORY.
BY NOW OUR FILE ON THE EXOGORTHS WILL HAVE REACHED YOUR REPUBLIC. ARE YOU EMPOWERED TO DEAL ON THEIR BEHALF?
YES. BUT WHAT DO YOU MEAN, "DEAL"?
I DON'T BELIEVE IT!
ZAYNE!

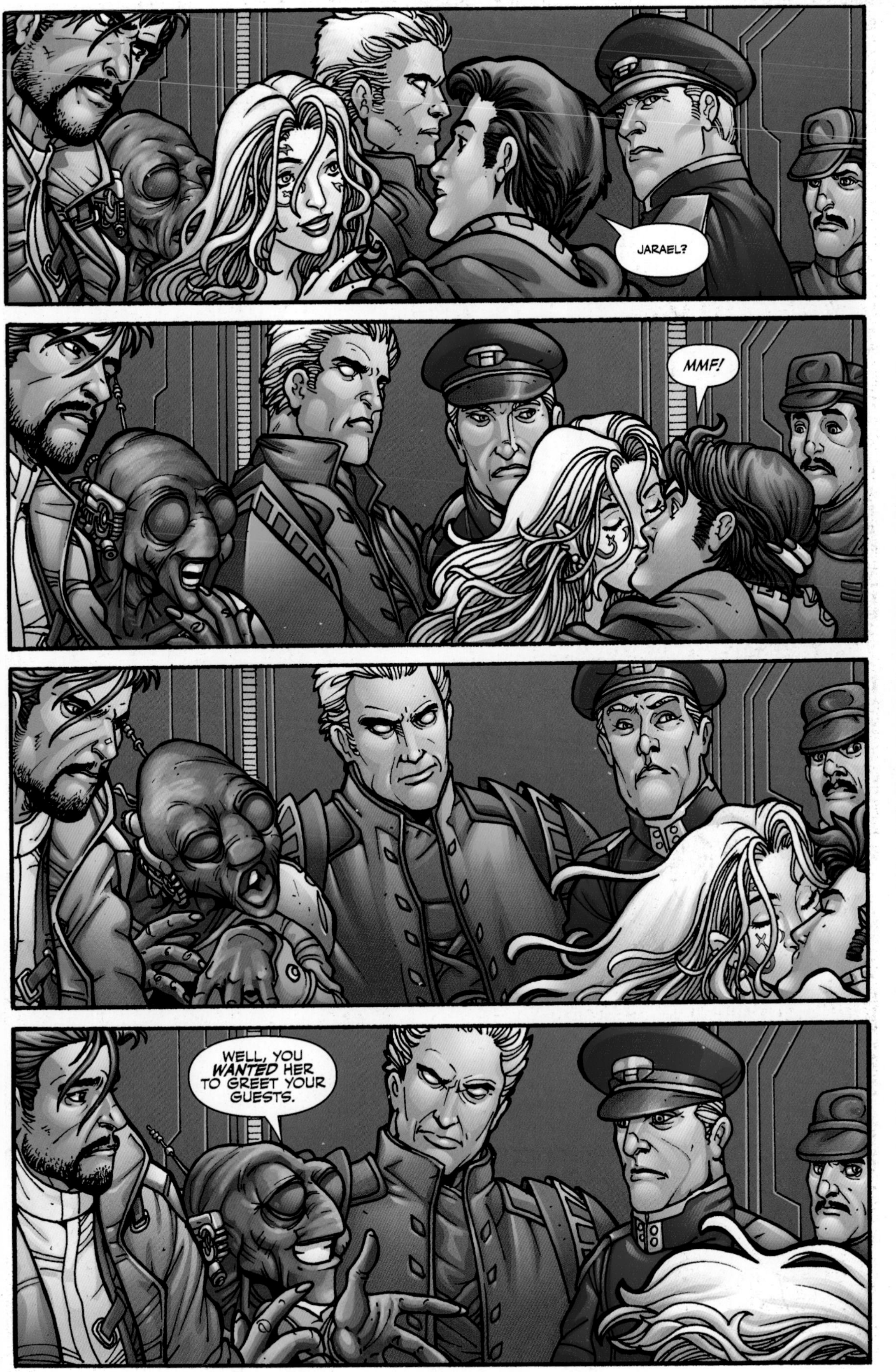
JARAEL?
MMF!
WELL, YOU WANTED HER TO GREET YOUR GUESTS.

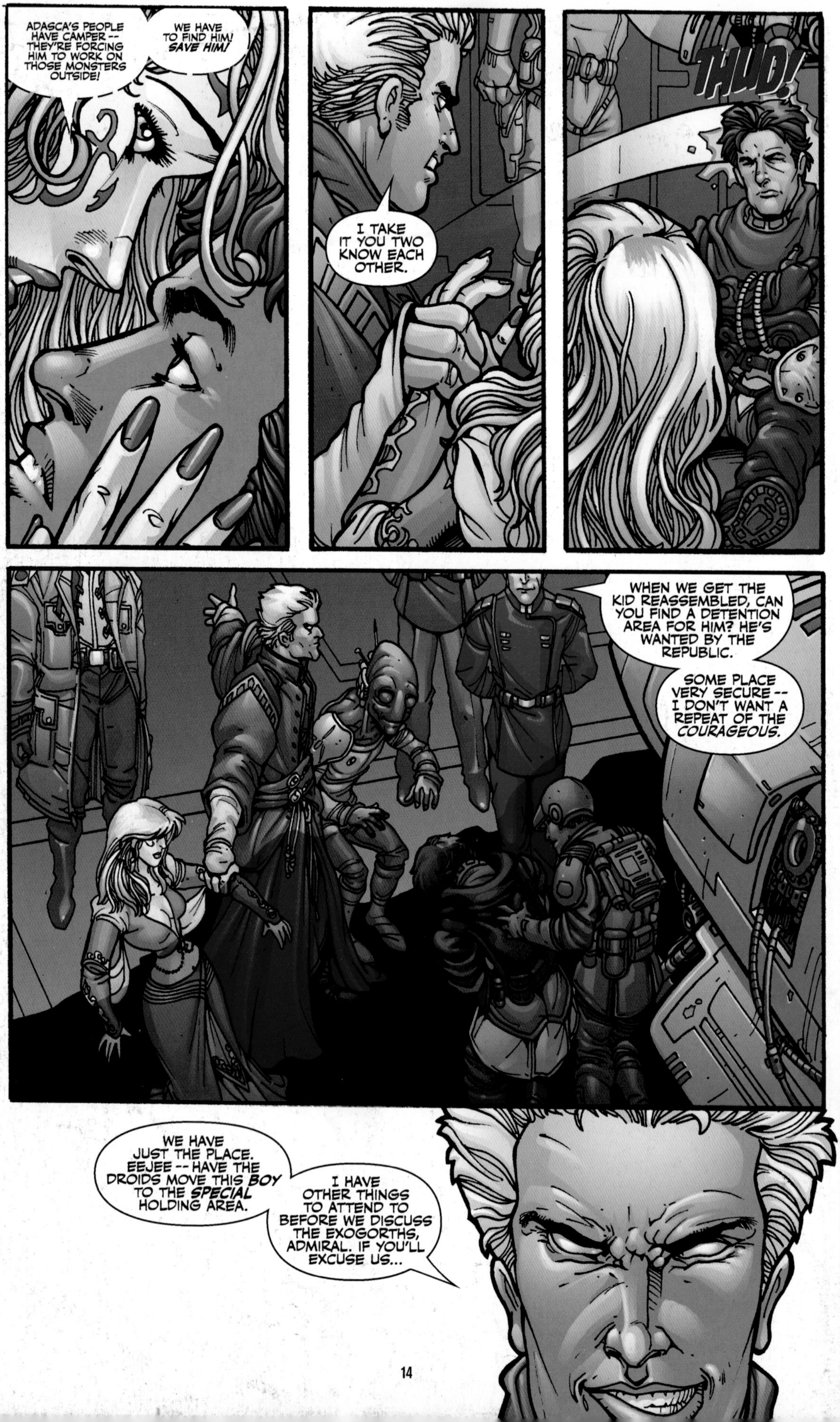
ADASCA'S PEOPLE HAVE CAMPER -- THEY'RE FORCING HIM TO WORK ON THOSE MONSTERS OUTSIDE!
WE HAVE TO FIND HIM! *SAVE HIM!*
I TAKE IT YOU TWO KNOW EACH OTHER.
THUD!
WHEN WE GET THE KID REASSEMBLED, CAN YOU FIND A DETENTION AREA FOR HIM? HE'S WANTED BY THE REPUBLIC.
SOME PLACE VERY SECURE -- I DON'T WANT A REPEAT OF THE *COURAGEOUS.*
WE HAVE JUST THE PLACE. EEJEE -- HAVE THE DROIDS MOVE THIS *BOY* TO THE *SPECIAL* HOLDING AREA.
I HAVE OTHER THINGS TO ATTEND TO BEFORE WE DISCUSS THE EXOGORTHS, ADMIRAL. IF YOU'LL EXCUSE US...

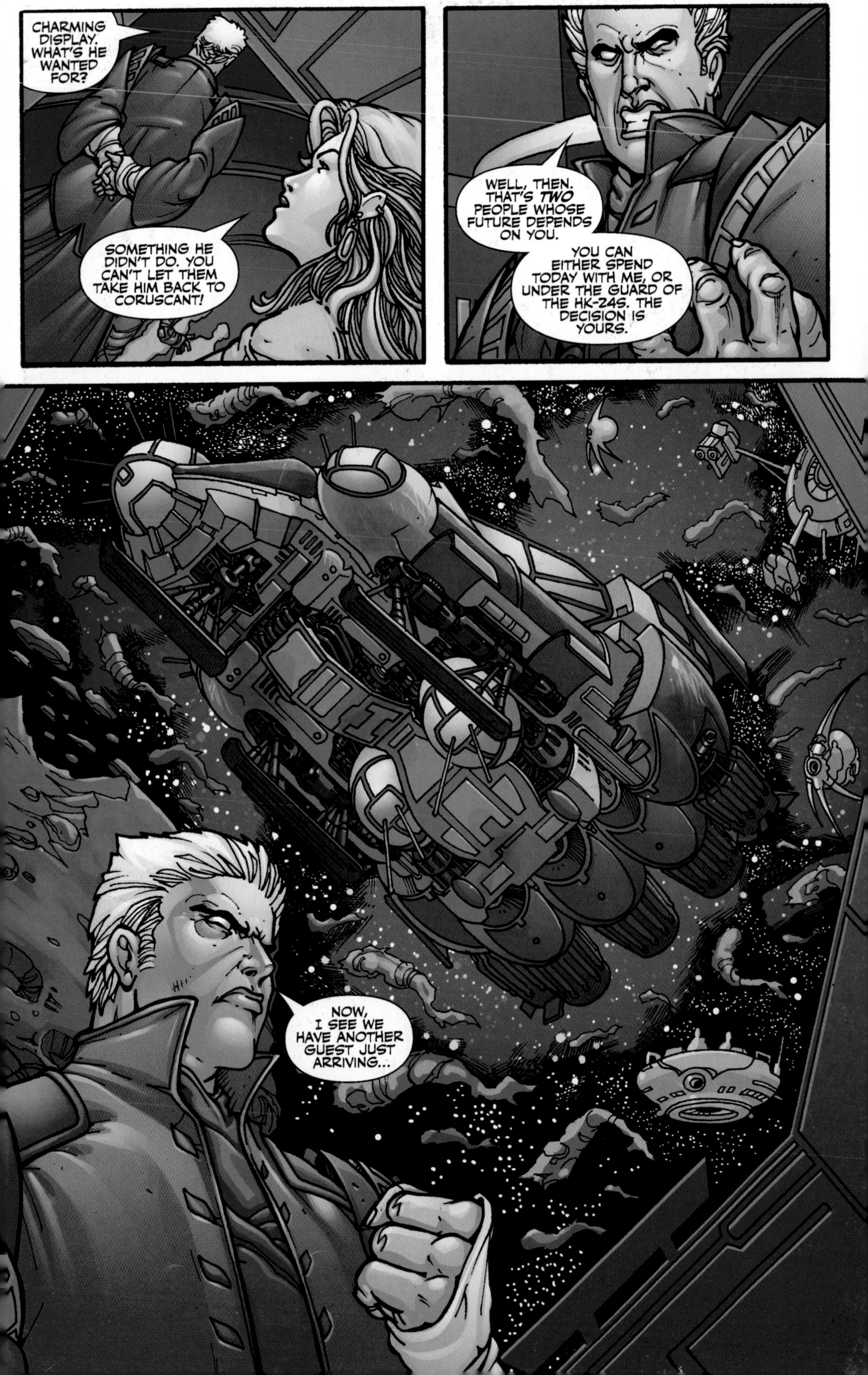
CHARMING DISPLAY. WHAT'S HE WANTED FOR?
SOMETHING HE DIDN'T DO. YOU CAN'T LET THEM TAKE HIM BACK TO CORUSCANT!
WELL, THEN. THAT'S *TWO* PEOPLE WHOSE FUTURE DEPENDS ON YOU.
YOU CAN EITHER SPEND TODAY WITH ME, OR UNDER THE GUARD OF THE HK-24S. THE DECISION IS YOURS.
NOW, I SEE WE HAVE ANOTHER GUEST JUST ARRIVING...

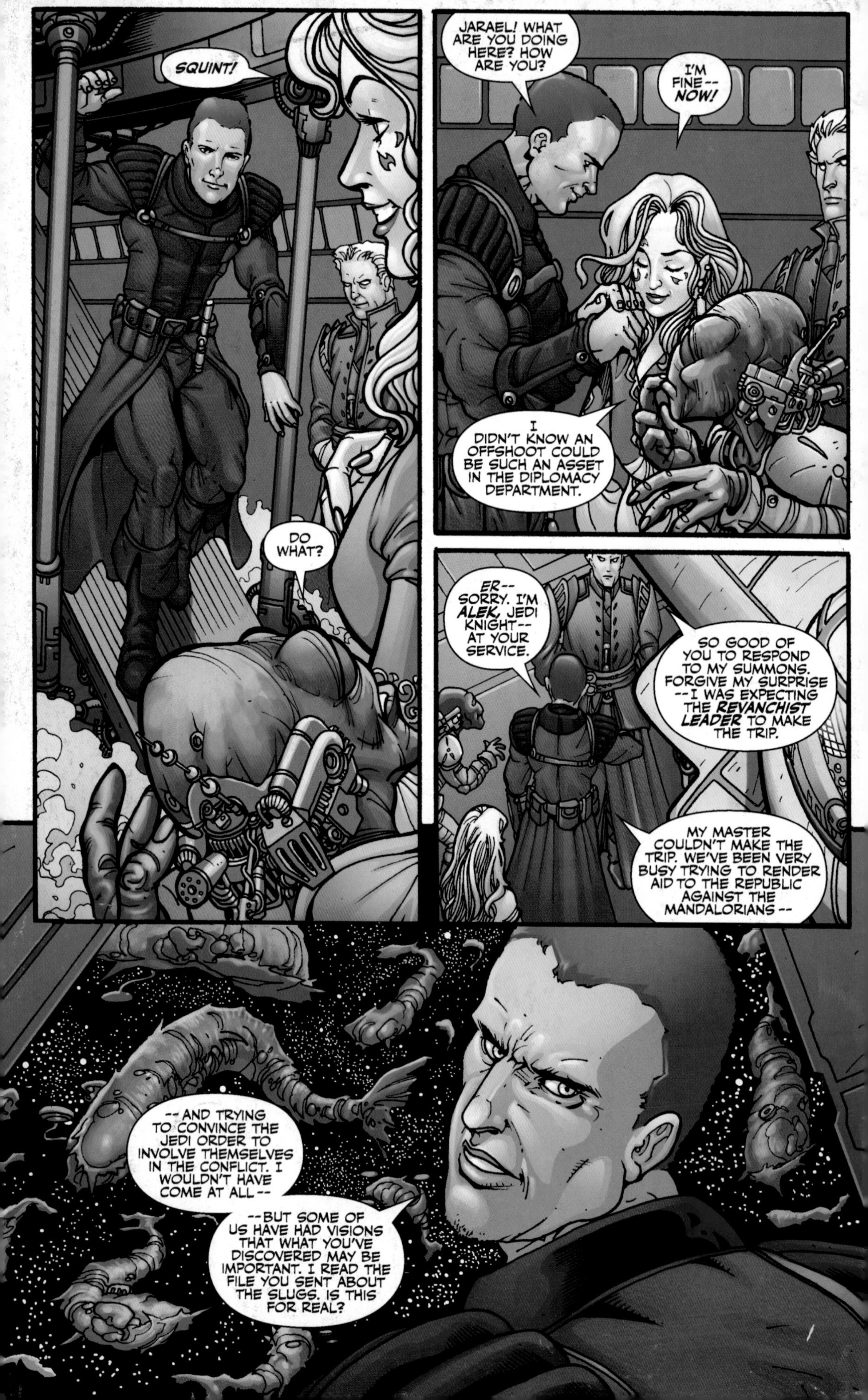
SQUINT!
DO WHAT?
JARAEL! WHAT ARE YOU DOING HERE? HOW ARE YOU?
I'M FINE-- NOW!
I DIDN'T KNOW AN OFFSHOOT COULD BE SUCH AN ASSET IN THE DIPLOMACY DEPARTMENT.
ER-- SORRY. I'M ALEK, JEDI KNIGHT-- AT YOUR SERVICE.
SO GOOD OF YOU TO RESPOND TO MY SUMMONS. FORGIVE MY SURPRISE --I WAS EXPECTING THE REVANCHIST LEADER TO MAKE THE TRIP.
MY MASTER COULDN'T MAKE THE TRIP. WE'VE BEEN VERY BUSY TRYING TO RENDER AID TO THE REPUBLIC AGAINST THE MANDALORIANS --
-- AND TRYING TO CONVINCE THE JEDI ORDER TO INVOLVE THEMSELVES IN THE CONFLICT. I WOULDN'T HAVE COME AT ALL --
--BUT SOME OF US HAVE HAD VISIONS THAT WHAT YOU'VE DISCOVERED MAY BE IMPORTANT. I READ THE FILE YOU SENT ABOUT THE SLUGS. IS THIS FOR REAL?

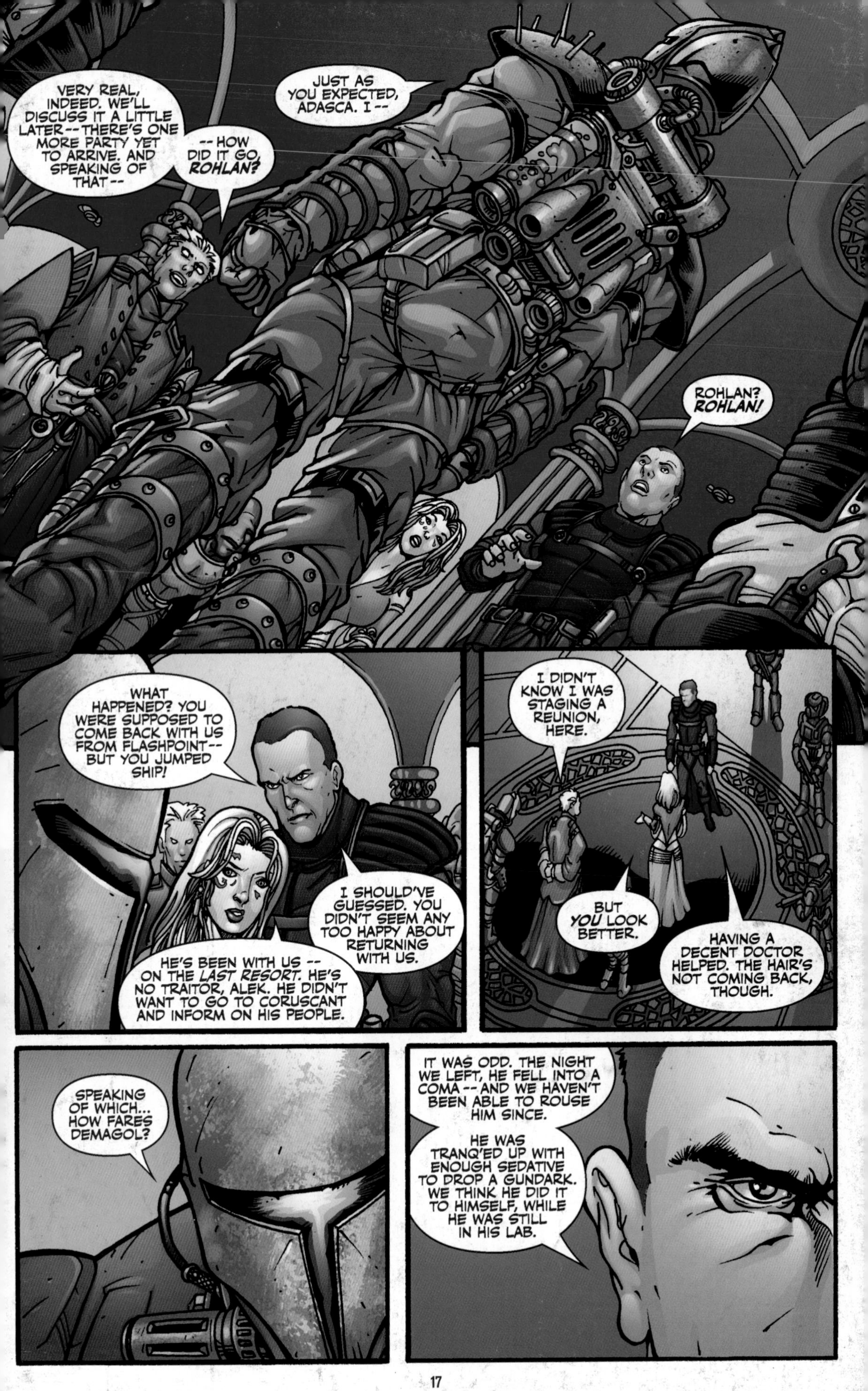

VERY REAL, INDEED. WE'LL DISCUSS IT A LITTLE LATER--THERE'S ONE MORE PARTY YET TO ARRIVE. AND SPEAKING OF THAT--
--HOW DID IT GO, ROHLAN?
JUST AS YOU EXPECTED, ADASCA. I--
ROHLAN? ROHLAN!
WHAT HAPPENED? YOU WERE SUPPOSED TO COME BACK WITH US FROM FLASHPOINT--BUT YOU JUMPED SHIP!
I SHOULD'VE GUESSED. YOU DIDN'T SEEM ANY TOO HAPPY ABOUT RETURNING WITH US.
HE'S BEEN WITH US--ON THE LAST RESORT. HE'S NO TRAITOR, ALEK. HE DIDN'T WANT TO GO TO CORUSCANT AND INFORM ON HIS PEOPLE.
I DIDN'T KNOW I WAS STAGING A REUNION, HERE.
BUT YOU LOOK BETTER.
HAVING A DECENT DOCTOR HELPED. THE HAIR'S NOT COMING BACK, THOUGH.
SPEAKING OF WHICH... HOW FARES DEMAGOL?
IT WAS ODD. THE NIGHT WE LEFT, HE FELL INTO A COMA--AND WE HAVEN'T BEEN ABLE TO ROUSE HIM SINCE.
HE WAS TRANQ'ED UP WITH ENOUGH SEDATIVE TO DROP A GUNDARK. WE THINK HE DID IT TO HIMSELF, WHILE HE WAS STILL IN HIS LAB.

HE COULD HAVE. HE WOULD NOT HAVE WANTED TO REVEAL ANYTHING. YOU REMEMBER THE TROUBLE HE HAD WALKING.

I WOULD NOT TRY TOO HARD TO PRESERVE HIS LIFE.

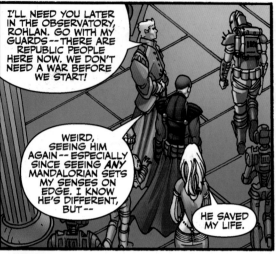

I'LL NEED YOU LATER IN THE OBSERVATORY, ROHLAN. GO WITH MY GUARDS--THERE ARE REPUBLIC PEOPLE HERE NOW. WE DON'T NEED A WAR BEFORE WE START!

WEIRD, SEEING HIM AGAIN--ESPECIALLY SINCE SEEING *ANY* MANDALORIAN SETS MY SENSES ON EDGE. I KNOW HE'S DIFFERENT, BUT--

HE SAVED MY LIFE.

THAT'S GOOD ENOUGH FOR ME, THEN. IT'S GREAT SEEING *YOU* AGAIN, WHOEVER YOU'RE WITH.

THAT REMINDS ME--I HEARD WHAT ZAYNE WAS ACCUSED OF WHEN I GOT BACK! I DIDN'T BELIEVE A WORD OF IT. IS HE HERE, TOO?

YES! HE'S TRAPPED IN THIS MAD GAME OF ADASCA'S, JUST LIKE US! YOU'VE GOT TO--

SHE WAS GOING TO SAY, YOU'VE SIMPLY *GOT* TO SEE THE VIEW FROM OUR OBSERVATORY.

MY SERVANTS WILL ACCOMPANY YOU. THE OTHERS ARE THERE--AND I AM TOLD THAT OUR FINAL GUEST HAS JUST ARRIVED.

MILORD! IT'S NOT OUR *SPECIAL* GUEST. IT'S *ANOTHER JEDI!*

PROBABLY *THE REVANCHIST*, THEN. LET'S DO THE MEETING IN MY LOUNGE.

I'D RATHER DEAL WITH THE *HEAD* CRUSADER THAN THIS YOUNG PUP THEY SENT, ANYWAY!

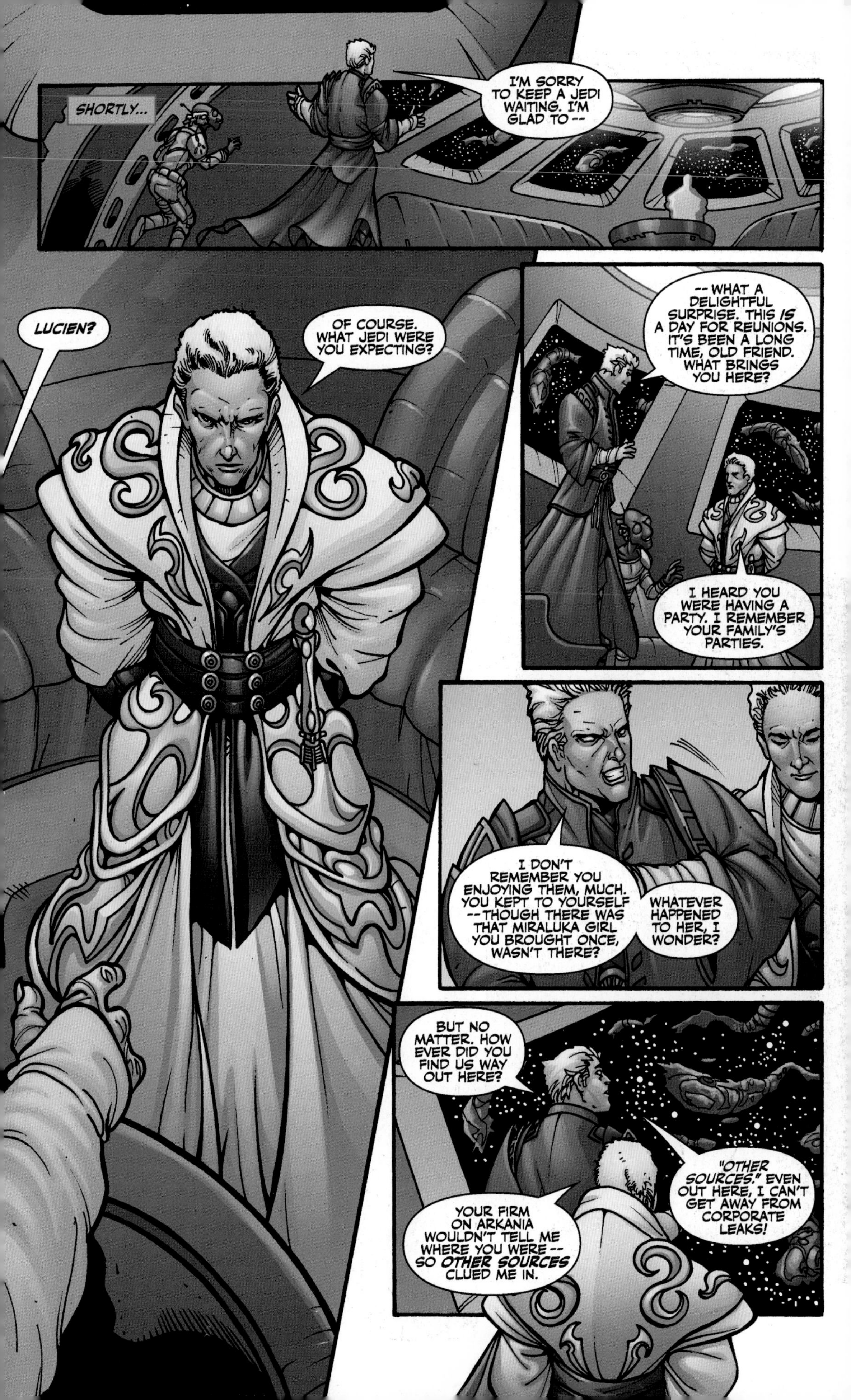
SHORTLY...
I'M SORRY TO KEEP A JEDI WAITING. I'M GLAD TO --
LUCIEN?
OF COURSE. WHAT JEDI WERE YOU EXPECTING?
-- WHAT A DELIGHTFUL SURPRISE. THIS *IS* A DAY FOR REUNIONS. IT'S BEEN A LONG TIME, OLD FRIEND. WHAT BRINGS YOU HERE?
I HEARD YOU WERE HAVING A PARTY. I REMEMBER YOUR FAMILY'S PARTIES.
I DON'T REMEMBER YOU ENJOYING THEM, MUCH. YOU KEPT TO YOURSELF --THOUGH THERE WAS THAT MIRALUKA GIRL YOU BROUGHT ONCE, WASN'T THERE?
WHATEVER HAPPENED TO HER, I WONDER?
BUT NO MATTER. HOW EVER DID YOU FIND US WAY OUT HERE?
YOUR FIRM ON ARKANIA WOULDN'T TELL ME WHERE YOU WERE -- SO *OTHER SOURCES* CLUED ME IN.
"OTHER SOURCES." EVEN OUT HERE, I CAN'T GET AWAY FROM CORPORATE LEAKS!

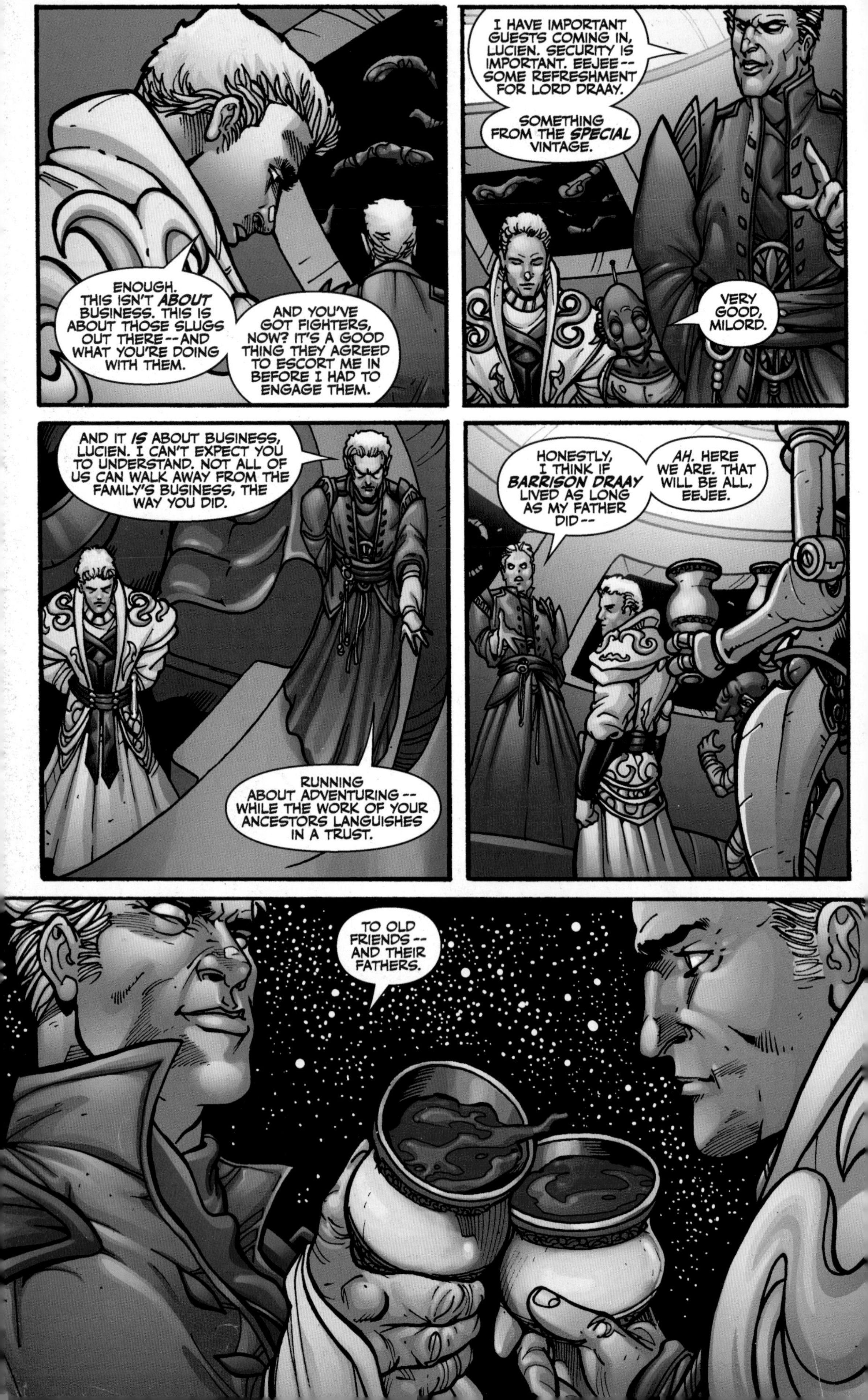

ENOUGH. THIS ISN'T *ABOUT* BUSINESS. THIS IS ABOUT THOSE SLUGS OUT THERE--AND WHAT YOU'RE DOING WITH THEM.
AND YOU'VE GOT FIGHTERS, NOW? IT'S A GOOD THING THEY AGREED TO ESCORT ME IN BEFORE I HAD TO ENGAGE THEM.
I HAVE IMPORTANT GUESTS COMING IN, LUCIEN. SECURITY IS IMPORTANT. EEJEE-- SOME REFRESHMENT FOR LORD DRAAY.
SOMETHING FROM THE *SPECIAL* VINTAGE.
VERY GOOD, MILORD.
AND IT *IS* ABOUT BUSINESS, LUCIEN. I CAN'T EXPECT YOU TO UNDERSTAND. NOT ALL OF US CAN WALK AWAY FROM THE FAMILY'S BUSINESS, THE WAY YOU DID.
RUNNING ABOUT ADVENTURING-- WHILE THE WORK OF YOUR ANCESTORS LANGUISHES IN A TRUST.
HONESTLY, I THINK IF *BARRISON DRAAY* LIVED AS LONG AS MY FATHER DID--
AH. HERE WE ARE. THAT WILL BE ALL, EEJEE.
TO OLD FRIENDS-- AND THEIR FATHERS.

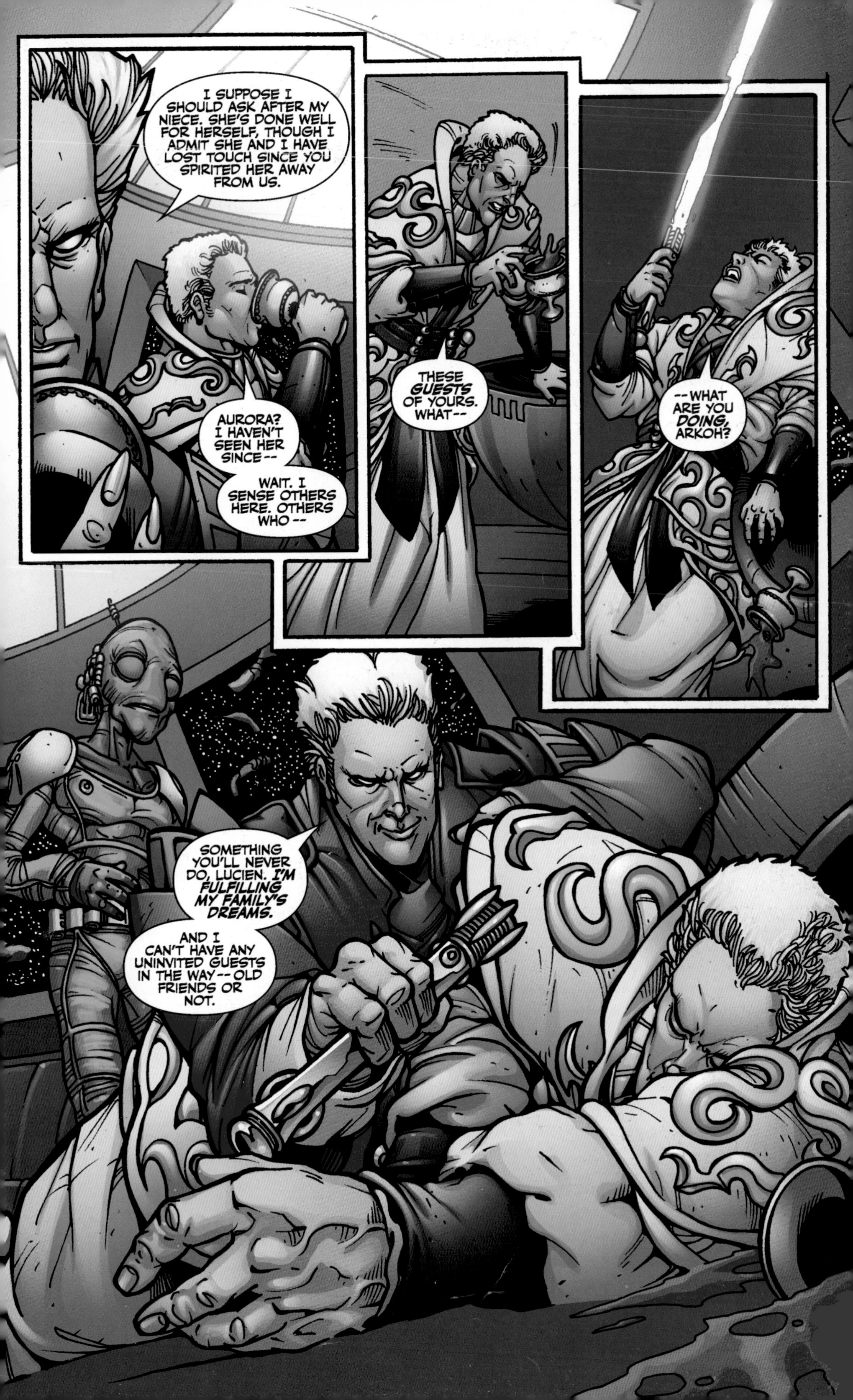
I SUPPOSE I SHOULD ASK AFTER MY NIECE. SHE'S DONE WELL FOR HERSELF, THOUGH I ADMIT SHE AND I HAVE LOST TOUCH SINCE YOU SPIRITED HER AWAY FROM US.
AURORA? I HAVEN'T SEEN HER SINCE--
WAIT. I SENSE OTHERS HERE. OTHERS WHO--
THESE *GUESTS* OF YOURS. WHAT--
--WHAT ARE YOU *DOING,* ARKOH?
SOMETHING YOU'LL NEVER DO, LUCIEN. *I'M FULFILLING MY FAMILY'S DREAMS.*
AND I CAN'T HAVE ANY UNINVITED GUESTS IN THE WAY--OLD FRIENDS OR NOT.

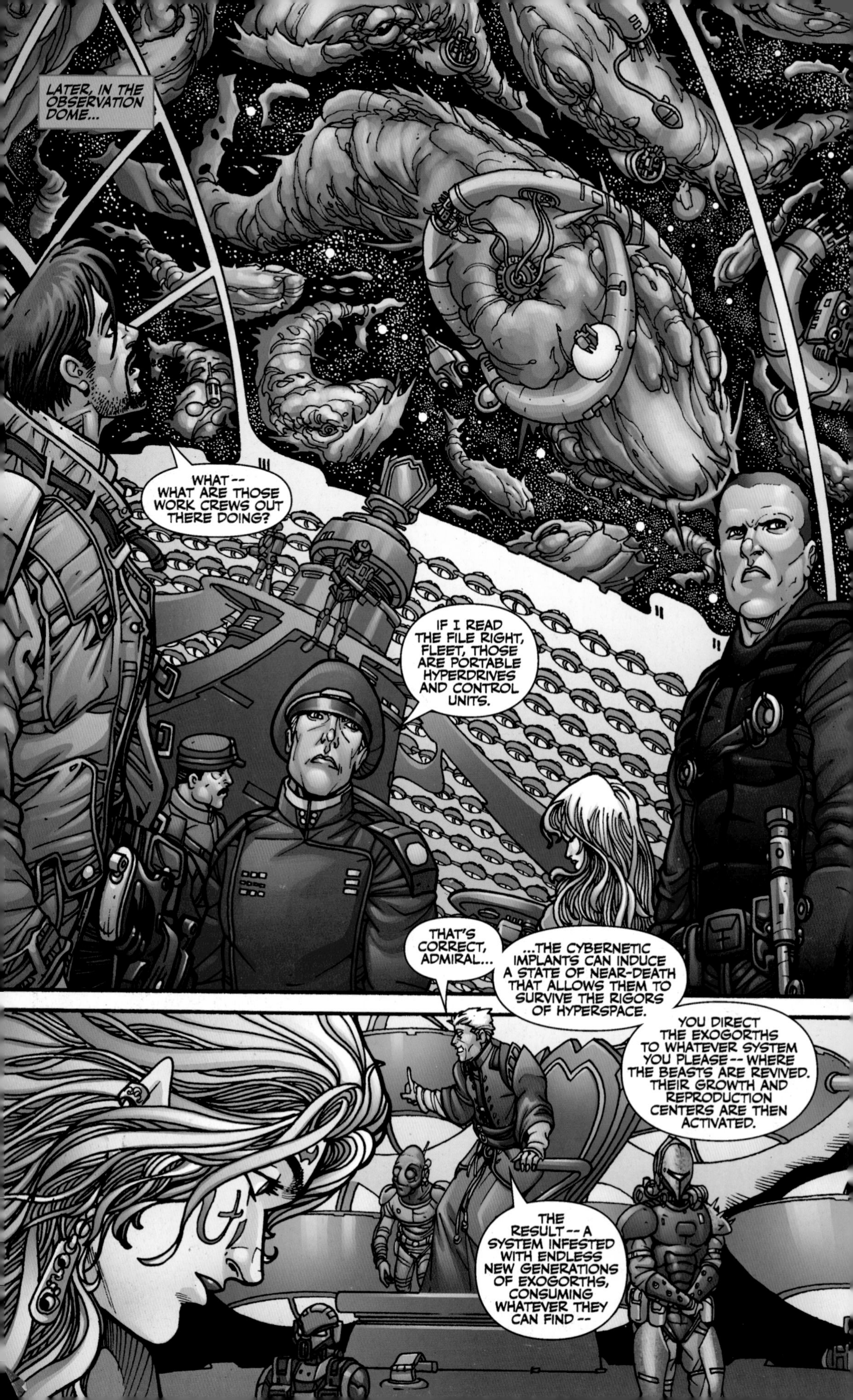
LATER, IN THE OBSERVATION DOME...
WHAT-- WHAT ARE THOSE WORK CREWS OUT THERE DOING?
IF I READ THE FILE RIGHT, FLEET, THOSE ARE PORTABLE HYPERDRIVES AND CONTROL UNITS.
THAT'S CORRECT, ADMIRAL...
...THE CYBERNETIC IMPLANTS CAN INDUCE A STATE OF NEAR-DEATH THAT ALLOWS THEM TO SURVIVE THE RIGORS OF HYPERSPACE.
YOU DIRECT THE EXOGORTHS TO WHATEVER SYSTEM YOU PLEASE-- WHERE THE BEASTS ARE REVIVED. THEIR GROWTH AND REPRODUCTION CENTERS ARE THEN ACTIVATED.
THE RESULT-- A SYSTEM INFESTED WITH ENDLESS NEW GENERATIONS OF EXOGORTHS, CONSUMING WHATEVER THEY CAN FIND--

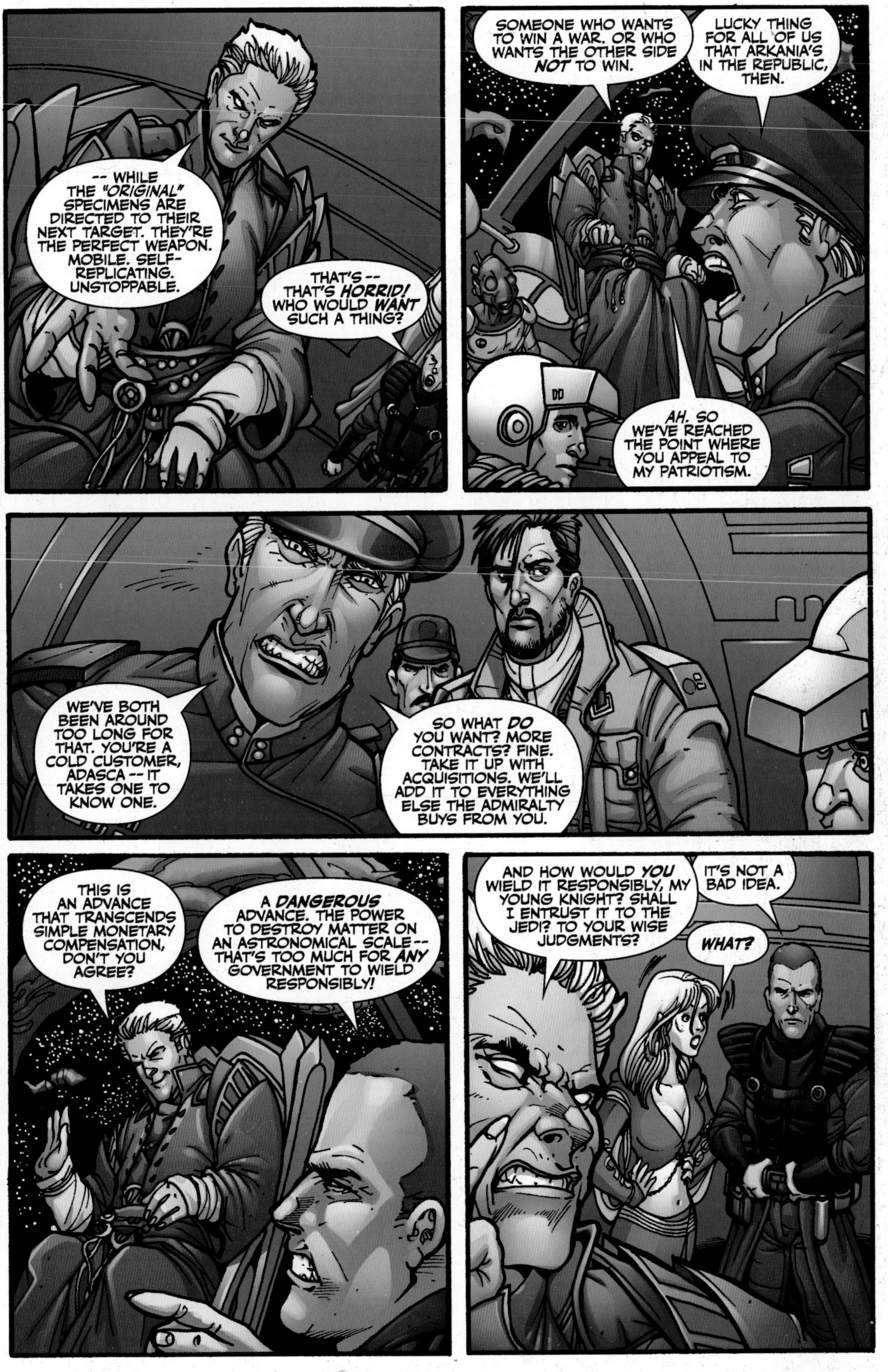

-- WHILE THE "ORIGINAL" SPECIMENS ARE DIRECTED TO THEIR NEXT TARGET. THEY'RE THE PERFECT WEAPON. MOBILE. SELF-REPLICATING. UNSTOPPABLE.
THAT'S -- THAT'S HORRID! WHO WOULD WANT SUCH A THING?
SOMEONE WHO WANTS TO WIN A WAR. OR WHO WANTS THE OTHER SIDE NOT TO WIN.
LUCKY THING FOR ALL OF US THAT ARKANIA'S IN THE REPUBLIC, THEN.
AH. SO WE'VE REACHED THE POINT WHERE YOU APPEAL TO MY PATRIOTISM.
WE'VE BOTH BEEN AROUND TOO LONG FOR THAT. YOU'RE A COLD CUSTOMER, ADASCA -- IT TAKES ONE TO KNOW ONE.
SO WHAT DO YOU WANT? MORE CONTRACTS? FINE. TAKE IT UP WITH ACQUISITIONS. WE'LL ADD IT TO EVERYTHING ELSE THE ADMIRALTY BUYS FROM YOU.
THIS IS AN ADVANCE THAT TRANSCENDS SIMPLE MONETARY COMPENSATION, DON'T YOU AGREE?
A DANGEROUS ADVANCE. THE POWER TO DESTROY MATTER ON AN ASTRONOMICAL SCALE -- THAT'S TOO MUCH FOR ANY GOVERNMENT TO WIELD RESPONSIBLY!
AND HOW WOULD YOU WIELD IT RESPONSIBLY, MY YOUNG KNIGHT? SHALL I ENTRUST IT TO THE JEDI? TO YOUR WISE JUDGMENTS?
IT'S NOT A BAD IDEA.
WHAT?

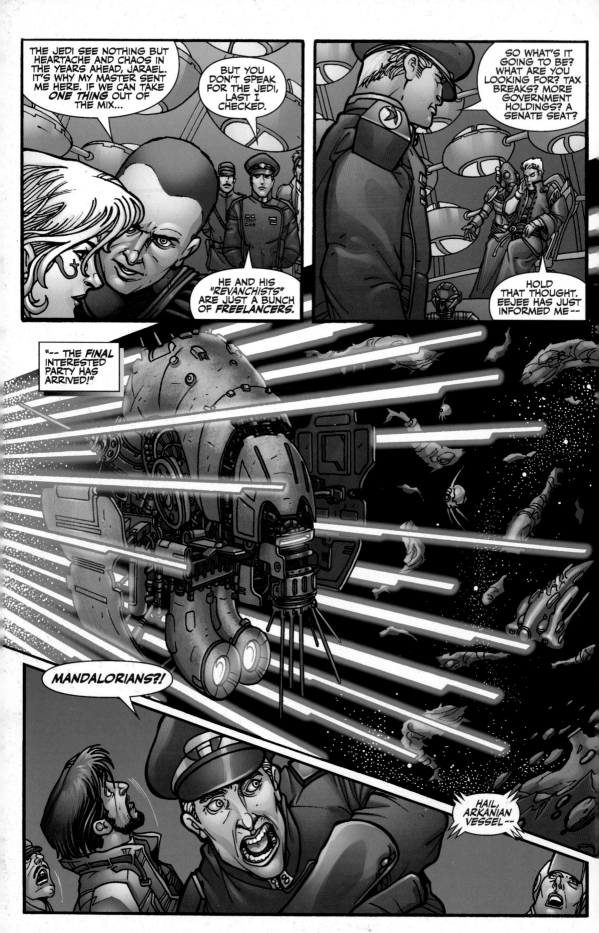

THE JEDI SEE NOTHING BUT HEARTACHE AND CHAOS IN THE YEARS AHEAD, JARAEL. IT'S WHY MY MASTER SENT ME HERE. IF WE CAN TAKE *ONE THING* OUT OF THE MIX...

BUT YOU DON'T SPEAK FOR THE JEDI, LAST I CHECKED.

HE AND HIS "*REVANCHISTS*" ARE JUST A BUNCH OF *FREELANCERS*.

SO WHAT'S IT GOING TO BE? WHAT ARE YOU LOOKING FOR? TAX BREAKS? MORE GOVERNMENT HOLDINGS? A SENATE SEAT?

HOLD THAT THOUGHT. EEJEE HAS JUST INFORMED ME--

"-- THE *FINAL* INTERESTED PARTY HAS ARRIVED!"

MANDALORIANS?!

HAIL, ARKANIAN VESSEL--

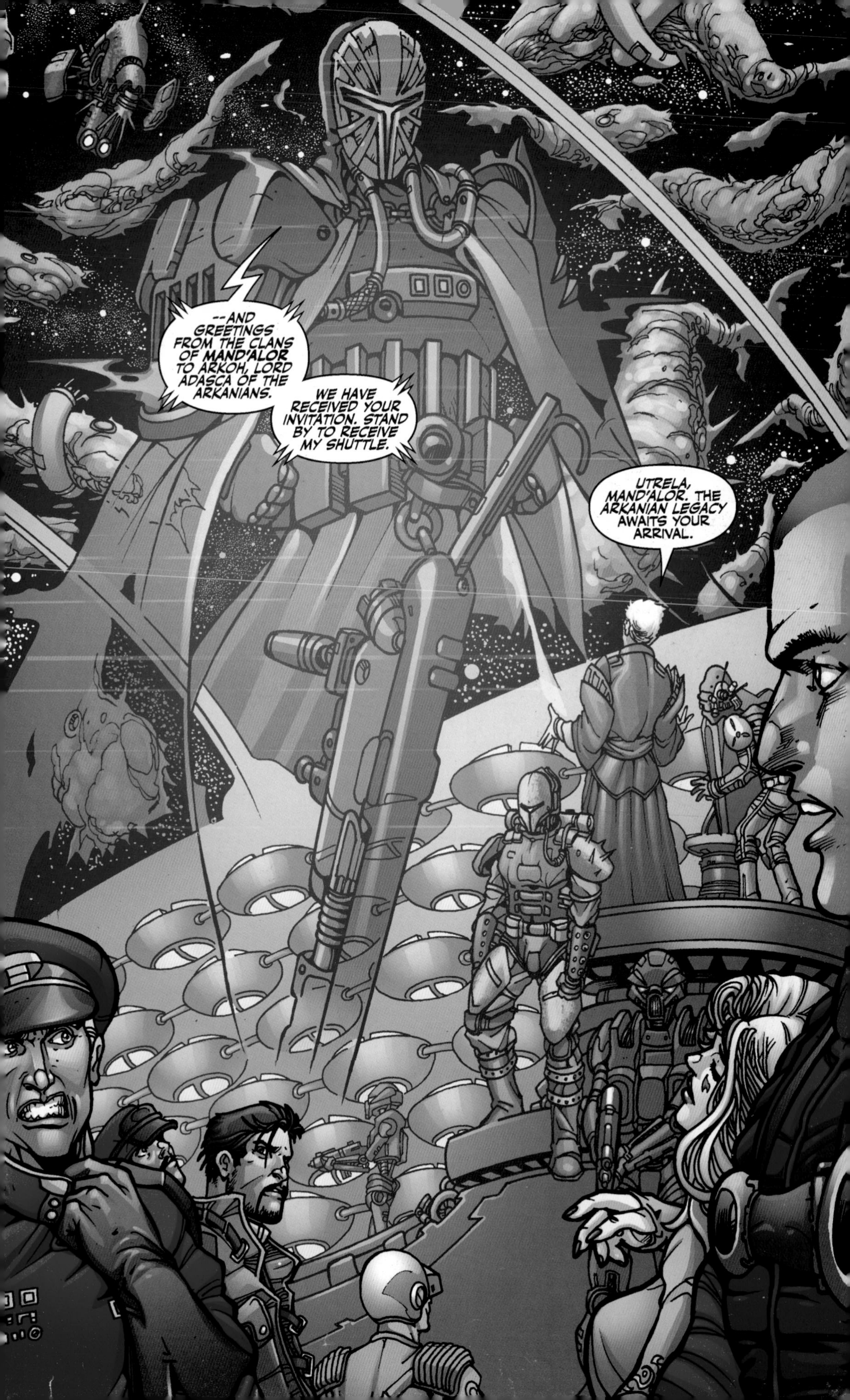
--AND GREETINGS FROM THE CLANS OF MAND'ALOR TO ARKOH, LORD ADASCA OF THE ARKANIANS.
WE HAVE RECEIVED YOUR INVITATION. STAND BY TO RECEIVE MY SHUTTLE.
UTRELA, MAND'ALOR. THE ARKANIAN LEGACY AWAITS YOUR ARRIVAL.

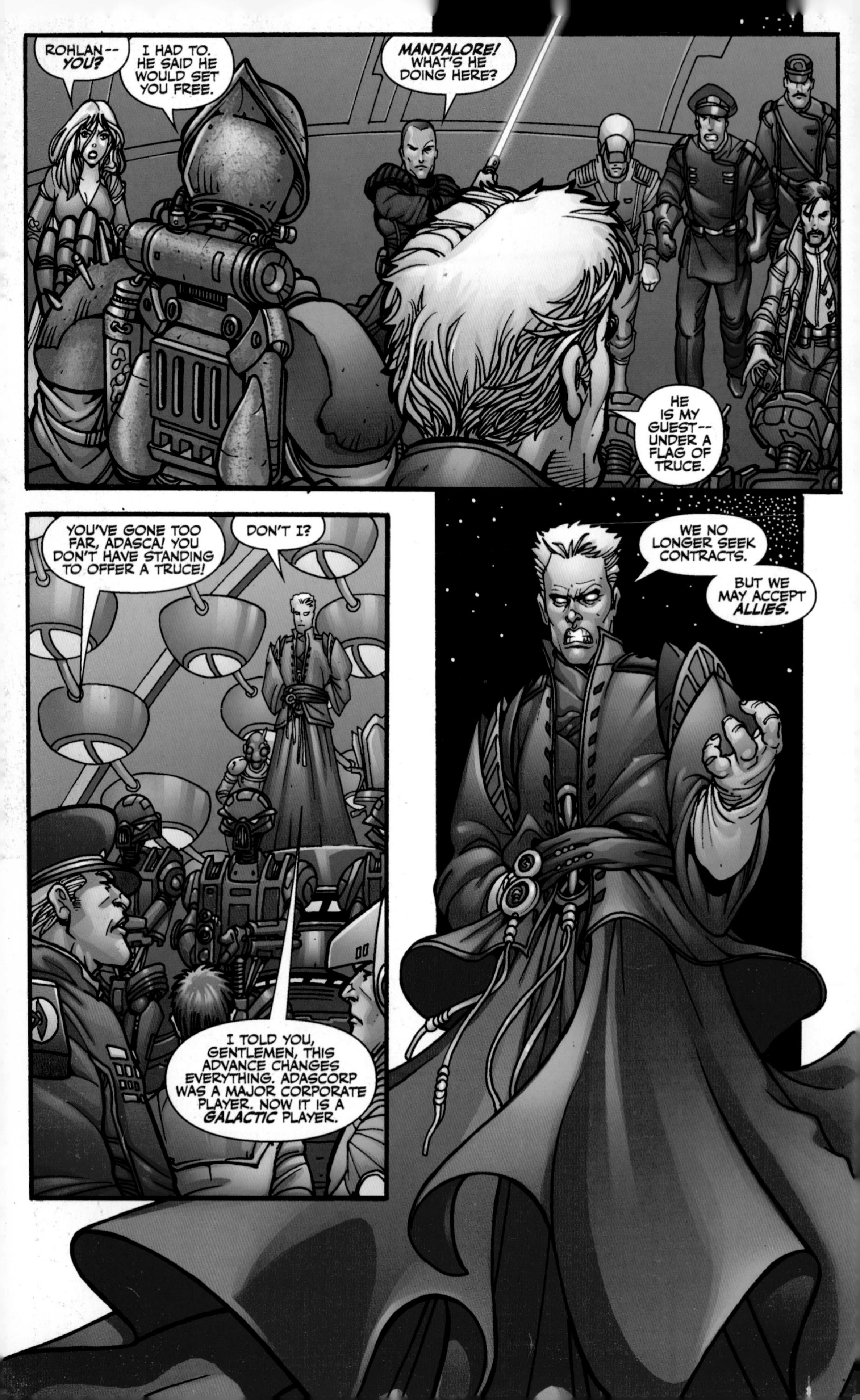
ROHLAN-- *YOU?*
I HAD TO. HE SAID HE WOULD SET YOU FREE.
MANDALORE! WHAT'S HE DOING HERE?
HE IS MY GUEST-- UNDER A FLAG OF TRUCE.
YOU'VE GONE TOO FAR, ADASCA! YOU DON'T HAVE STANDING TO OFFER A TRUCE!
DON'T I?
I TOLD YOU, GENTLEMEN, THIS ADVANCE CHANGES EVERYTHING. ADASCORP WAS A MAJOR CORPORATE PLAYER. NOW IT IS A *GALACTIC* PLAYER.
WE NO LONGER SEEK CONTRACTS.
BUT WE MAY ACCEPT *ALLIES.*

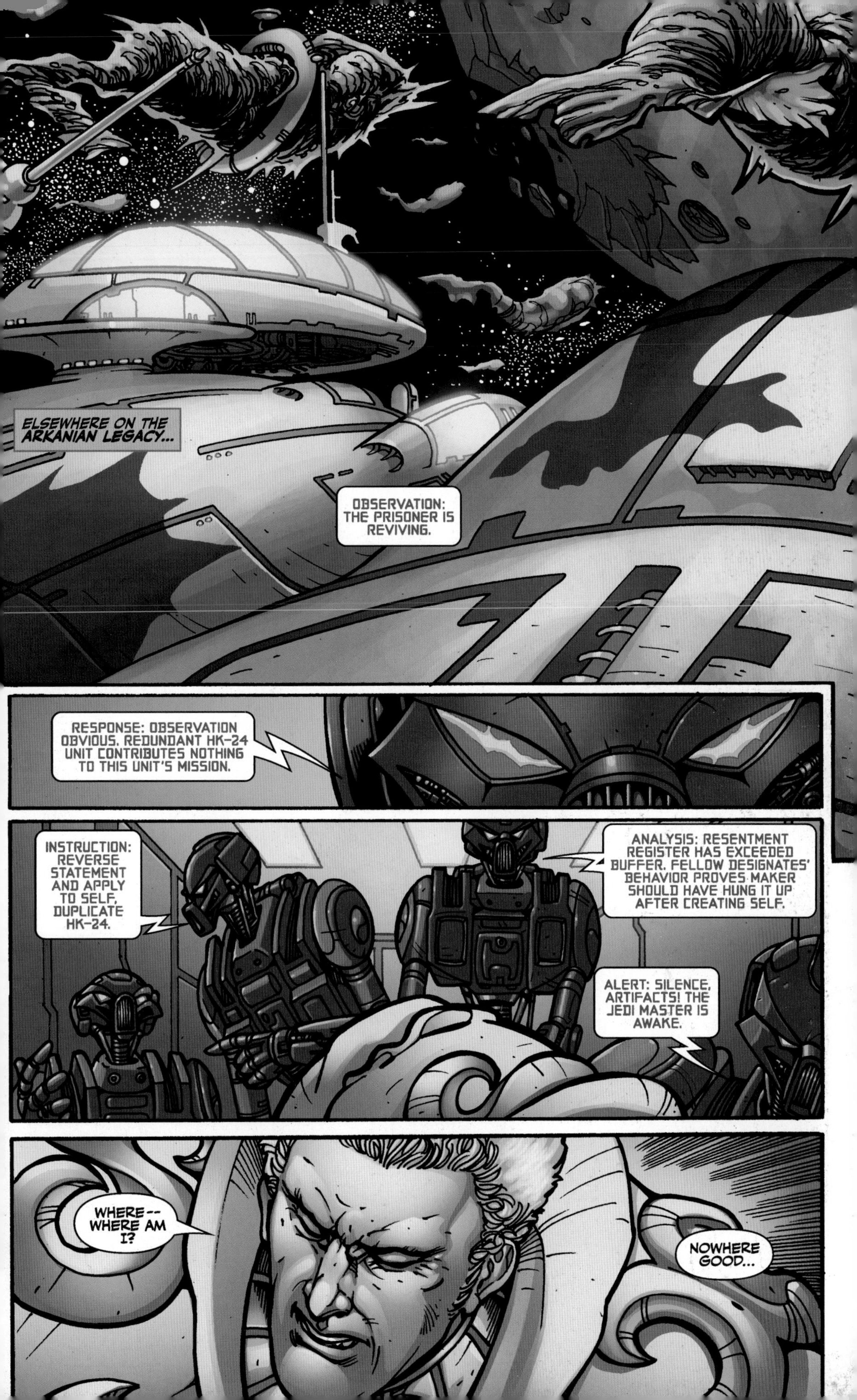
ELSEWHERE ON THE ARKANIAN LEGACY...
OBSERVATION: THE PRISONER IS REVIVING.
RESPONSE: OBSERVATION OBVIOUS. REDUNDANT HK-24 UNIT CONTRIBUTES NOTHING TO THIS UNIT'S MISSION.
INSTRUCTION: REVERSE STATEMENT AND APPLY TO SELF, DUPLICATE HK-24.
ANALYSIS: RESENTMENT REGISTER HAS EXCEEDED BUFFER. FELLOW DESIGNATES' BEHAVIOR PROVES MAKER SHOULD HAVE HUNG IT UP AFTER CREATING SELF.
ALERT: SILENCE, ARTIFACTS! THE JEDI MASTER IS AWAKE.
WHERE-- WHERE AM I?
NOWHERE GOOD...

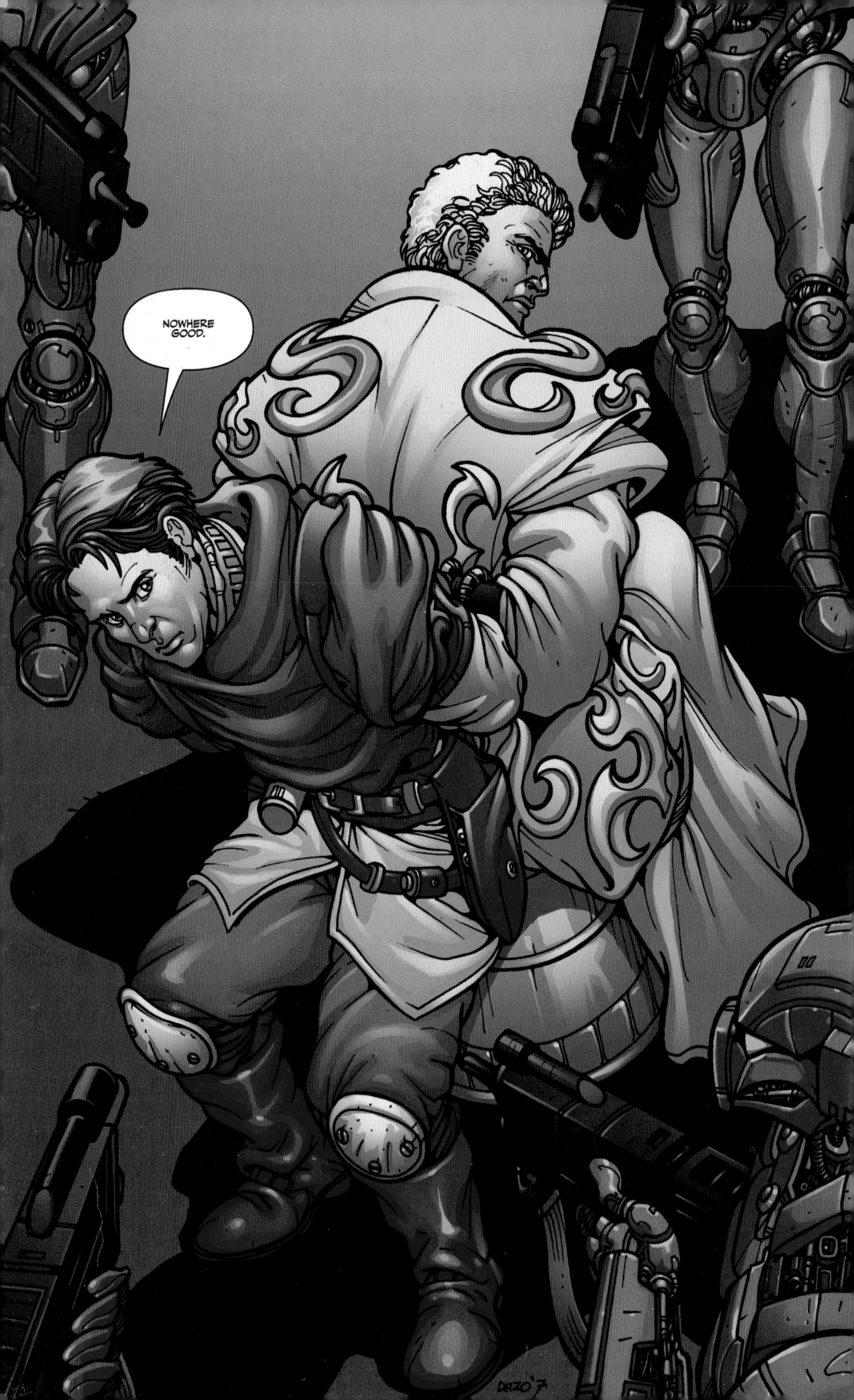
NOWHERE GOOD.

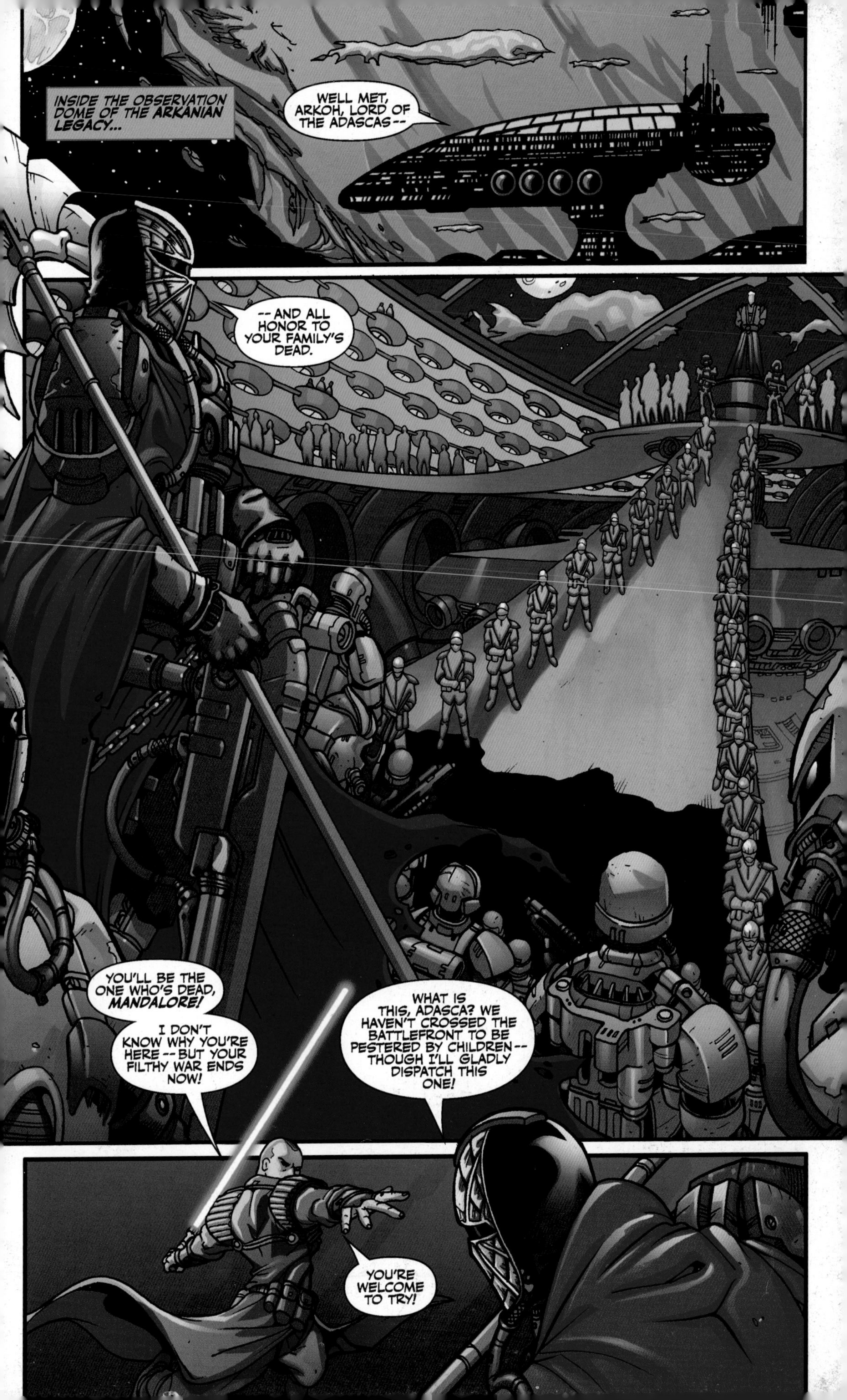
INSIDE THE OBSERVATION DOME OF THE ARKANIAN LEGACY...
WELL MET, ARKOH, LORD OF THE ADASCAS--
--AND ALL HONOR TO YOUR FAMILY'S DEAD.
YOU'LL BE THE ONE WHO'S DEAD, MANDALORE!
I DON'T KNOW WHY YOU'RE HERE--BUT YOUR FILTHY WAR ENDS NOW!
WHAT IS THIS, ADASCA? WE HAVEN'T CROSSED THE BATTLEFRONT TO BE PESTERED BY CHILDREN--THOUGH I'LL GLADLY DISPATCH THIS ONE!
YOU'RE WELCOME TO TRY!

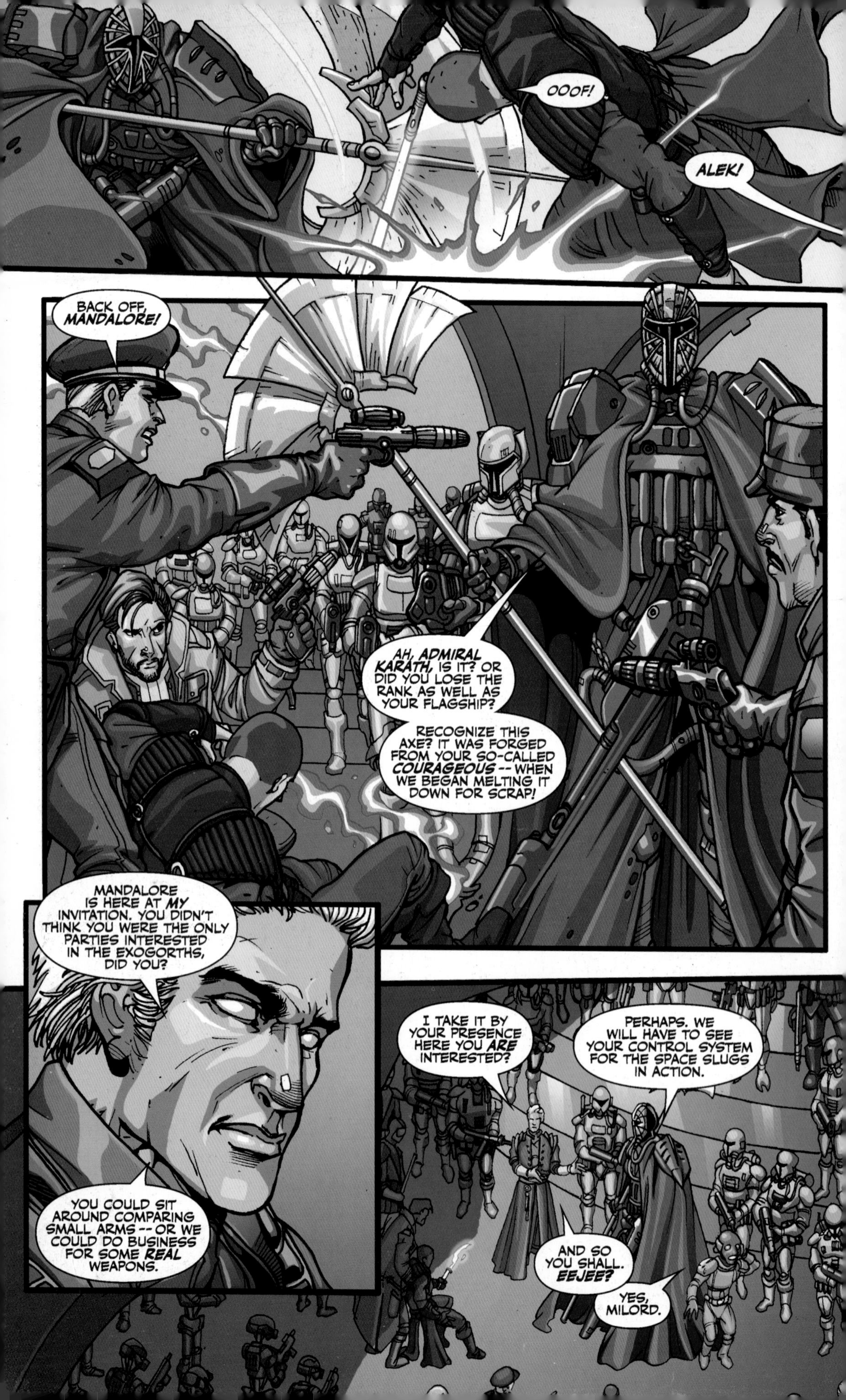
OOOF!
ALEK!
BACK OFF, MANDALORE!
AH, ADMIRAL KARATH, IS IT? OR DID YOU LOSE THE RANK AS WELL AS YOUR FLAGSHIP?
RECOGNIZE THIS AXE? IT WAS FORGED FROM YOUR SO-CALLED COURAGEOUS -- WHEN WE BEGAN MELTING IT DOWN FOR SCRAP!
MANDALORE IS HERE AT MY INVITATION. YOU DIDN'T THINK YOU WERE THE ONLY PARTIES INTERESTED IN THE EXOGORTHS, DID YOU?
YOU COULD SIT AROUND COMPARING SMALL ARMS -- OR WE COULD DO BUSINESS FOR SOME REAL WEAPONS.
I TAKE IT BY YOUR PRESENCE HERE YOU ARE INTERESTED?
PERHAPS. WE WILL HAVE TO SEE YOUR CONTROL SYSTEM FOR THE SPACE SLUGS IN ACTION.
AND SO YOU SHALL. EEJEE?
YES, MILORD.

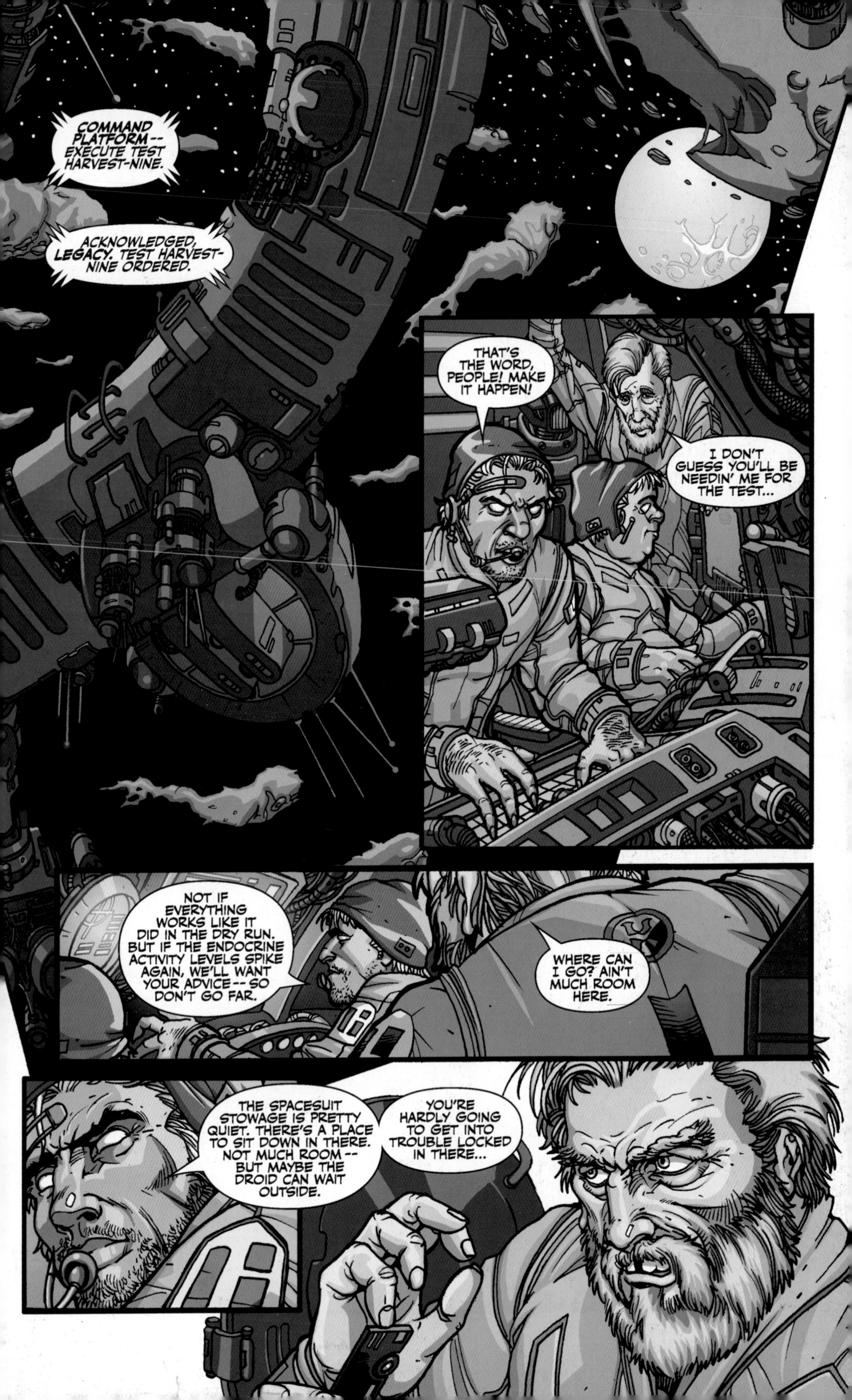
COMMAND PLATFORM -- EXECUTE TEST HARVEST-NINE.
ACKNOWLEDGED, LEGACY. TEST HARVEST-NINE ORDERED.
THAT'S THE WORD, PEOPLE! MAKE IT HAPPEN!
I DON'T GUESS YOU'LL BE NEEDIN' ME FOR THE TEST...
NOT IF EVERYTHING WORKS LIKE IT DID IN THE DRY RUN. BUT IF THE ENDOCRINE ACTIVITY LEVELS SPIKE AGAIN, WE'LL WANT YOUR ADVICE -- SO DON'T GO FAR.
WHERE CAN I GO? AIN'T MUCH ROOM HERE.
THE SPACESUIT STOWAGE IS PRETTY QUIET. THERE'S A PLACE TO SIT DOWN IN THERE. NOT MUCH ROOM -- BUT MAYBE THE DROID CAN WAIT OUTSIDE.
YOU'RE HARDLY GOING TO GET INTO TROUBLE LOCKED IN THERE...

THE TEST WILL BEGIN SHORTLY, MAND'ALOR.

THEN I WOULD LIKE TO SPEAK WITH MY-- FELLOW WARRIOR.

I REQUIRE MY AMBASSADOR AGAIN, ROHLAN. GREET HIM, WON'T YOU?

GO ON. IT'S PART OF OUR ARRANGEMENT. AND RELAX. THEY'LL BE TAKING NO DESERTERS BACK TODAY, I PROMISE.

SU'CUY, MAND'ALOR.

WELL MET, INDEED. IT ISN'T OFTEN I HEAR FROM A DEAD MAN -- MUCH LESS ONE WITH SUCH AN INTERESTING PROPOSITION!

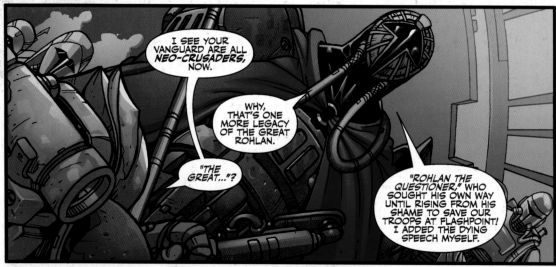

I SEE YOUR VANGUARD ARE ALL NEO-CRUSADERS, NOW.

WHY, THAT'S ONE MORE LEGACY OF THE GREAT ROHLAN.

"THE GREAT..."?

"ROHLAN THE QUESTIONER," WHO SOUGHT HIS OWN WAY UNTIL RISING FROM HIS SHAME TO SAVE OUR TROOPS AT FLASHPOINT! I ADDED THE DYING SPEECH MYSELF.

DYING SPEECH?

WHERE HE ADMITS THAT ONLY IN STRICTLY OBEYING COMMANDS CAN VICTORY BE ACHIEVED. "THE QUESTIONER" ACCEPTS THAT THERE IS ONLY ONE ANSWER--

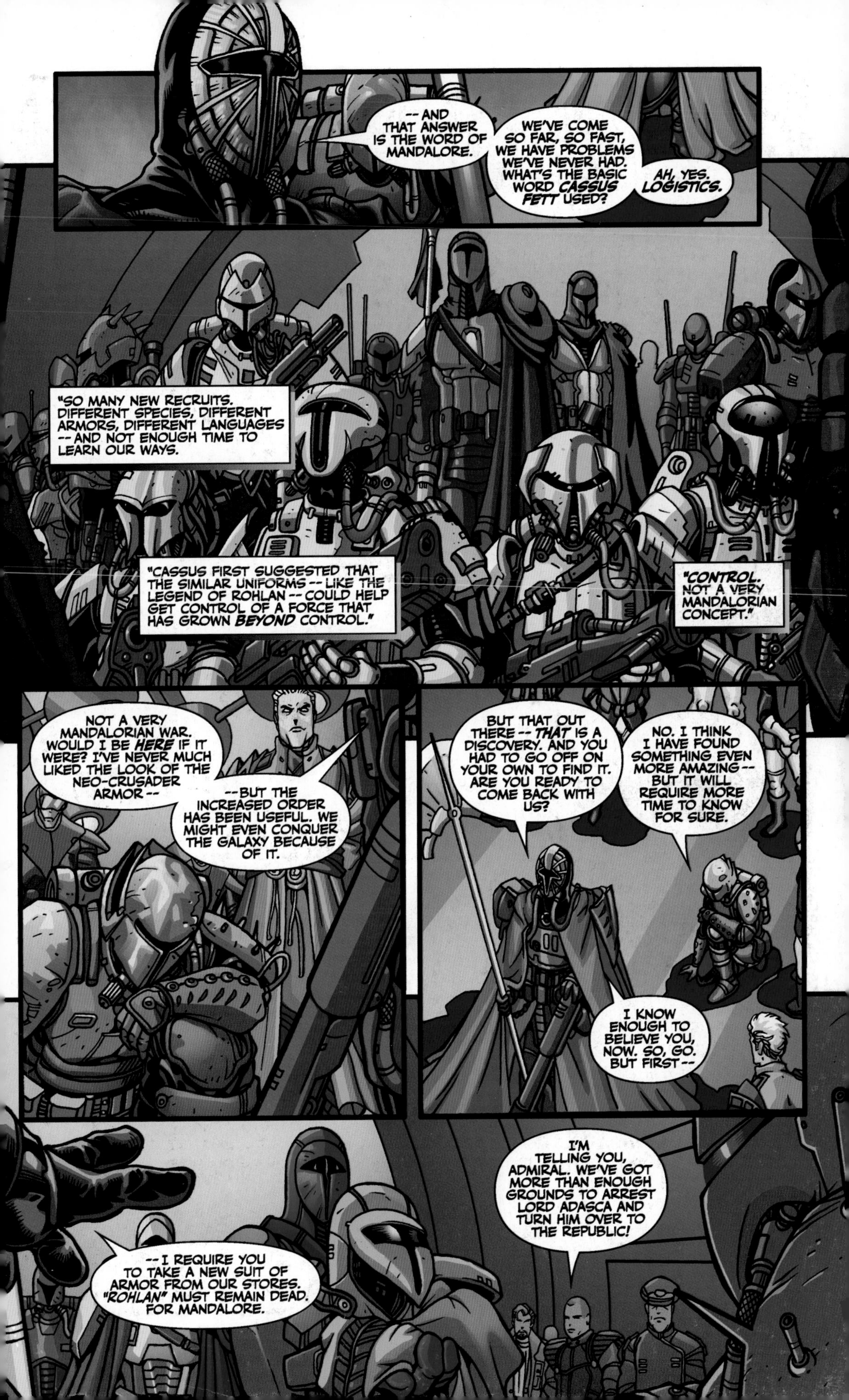
-- AND THAT ANSWER IS THE WORD OF MANDALORE.
WE'VE COME SO FAR, SO FAST, WE HAVE PROBLEMS WE'VE NEVER HAD. WHAT'S THE BASIC WORD CASSUS FETT USED?
AH, YES. LOGISTICS.
"SO MANY NEW RECRUITS. DIFFERENT SPECIES, DIFFERENT ARMORS, DIFFERENT LANGUAGES -- AND NOT ENOUGH TIME TO LEARN OUR WAYS.
"CASSUS FIRST SUGGESTED THAT THE SIMILAR UNIFORMS -- LIKE THE LEGEND OF ROHLAN -- COULD HELP GET CONTROL OF A FORCE THAT HAS GROWN BEYOND CONTROL."
"CONTROL. NOT A VERY MANDALORIAN CONCEPT."
NOT A VERY MANDALORIAN WAR. WOULD I BE HERE IF IT WERE? I'VE NEVER MUCH LIKED THE LOOK OF THE NEO-CRUSADER ARMOR --
-- BUT THE INCREASED ORDER HAS BEEN USEFUL. WE MIGHT EVEN CONQUER THE GALAXY BECAUSE OF IT.
BUT THAT OUT THERE -- THAT IS A DISCOVERY. AND YOU HAD TO GO OFF ON YOUR OWN TO FIND IT. ARE YOU READY TO COME BACK WITH US?
NO. I THINK I HAVE FOUND SOMETHING EVEN MORE AMAZING -- BUT IT WILL REQUIRE MORE TIME TO KNOW FOR SURE.
I KNOW ENOUGH TO BELIEVE YOU, NOW. SO, GO. BUT FIRST --
-- I REQUIRE YOU TO TAKE A NEW SUIT OF ARMOR FROM OUR STORES. "ROHLAN" MUST REMAIN DEAD. FOR MANDALORE.
I'M TELLING YOU, ADMIRAL. WE'VE GOT MORE THAN ENOUGH GROUNDS TO ARREST LORD ADASCA AND TURN HIM OVER TO THE REPUBLIC!

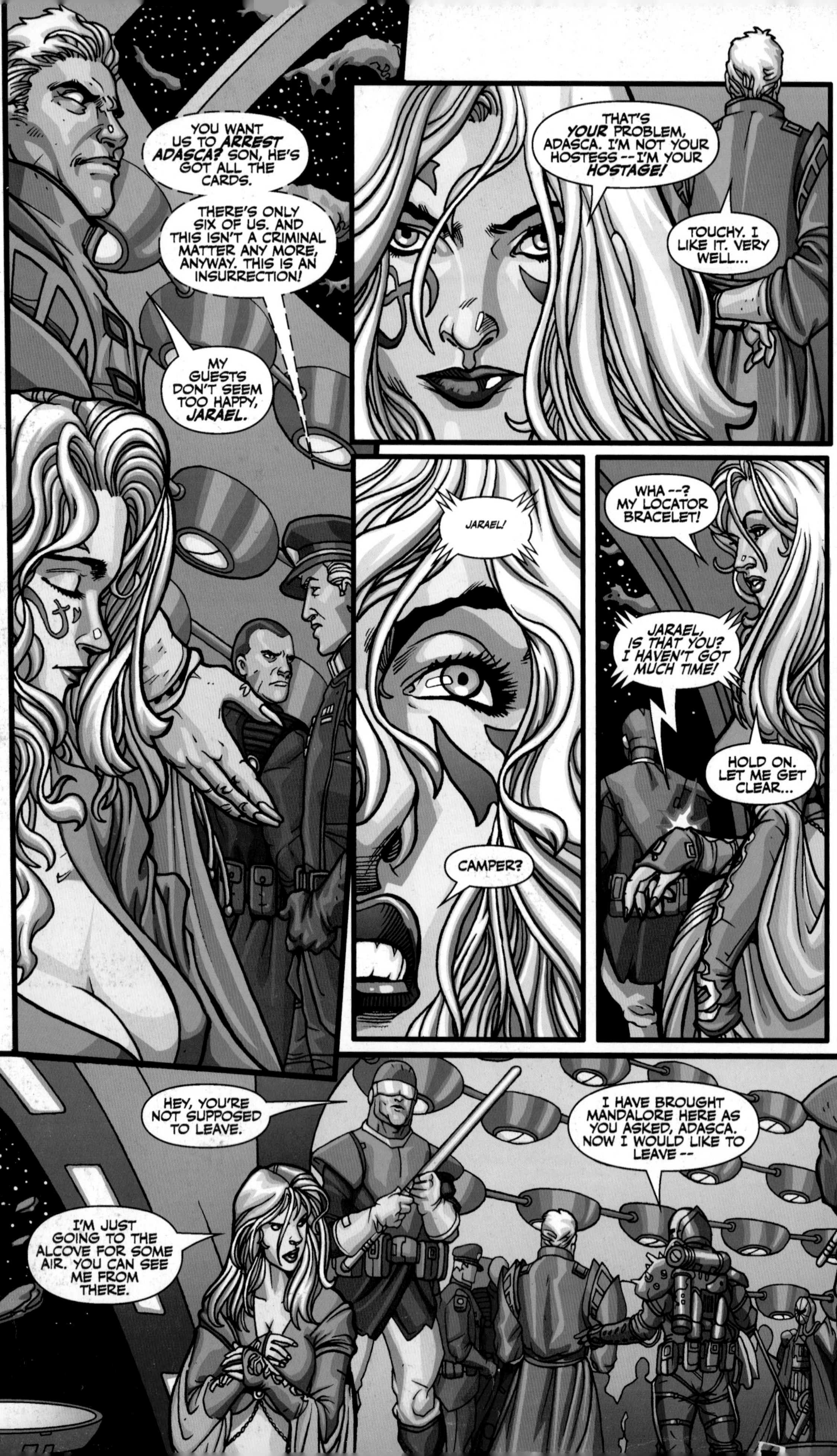
YOU WANT US TO ARREST ADASCA? SON, HE'S GOT ALL THE CARDS.
THERE'S ONLY SIX OF US. AND THIS ISN'T A CRIMINAL MATTER ANY MORE, ANYWAY. THIS IS AN INSURRECTION!
MY GUESTS DON'T SEEM TOO HAPPY, JARAEL.
THAT'S YOUR PROBLEM, ADASCA. I'M NOT YOUR HOSTESS--I'M YOUR HOSTAGE!
TOUCHY. I LIKE IT. VERY WELL...
JARAEL!
CAMPER?
WHA--? MY LOCATOR BRACELET!
JARAEL, IS THAT YOU? I HAVEN'T GOT MUCH TIME!
HOLD ON. LET ME GET CLEAR...
HEY, YOU'RE NOT SUPPOSED TO LEAVE.
I'M JUST GOING TO THE ALCOVE FOR SOME AIR. YOU CAN SEE ME FROM THERE.
I HAVE BROUGHT MANDALORE HERE AS YOU ASKED, ADASCA. NOW I WOULD LIKE TO LEAVE--

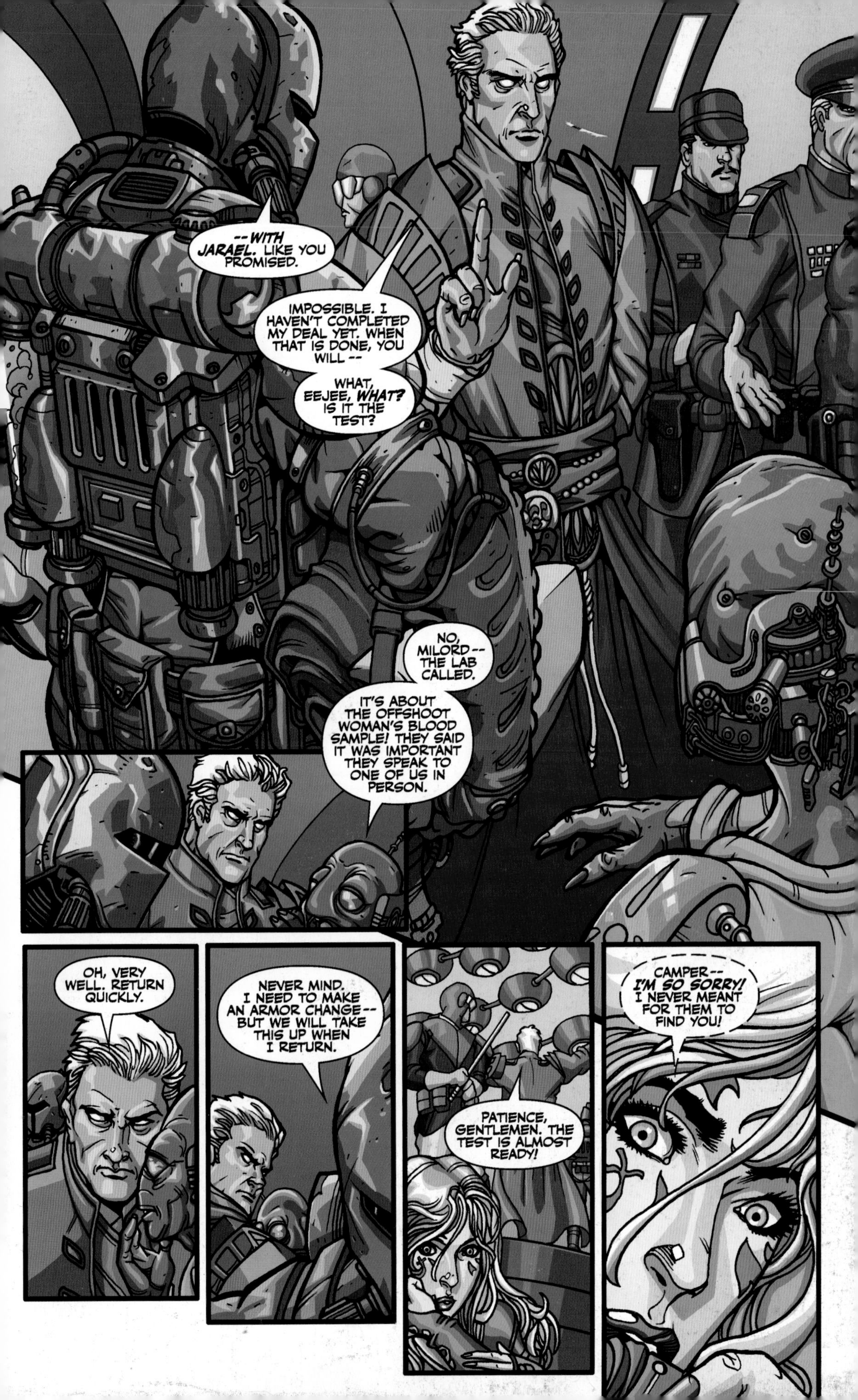
--WITH JARAEL. LIKE YOU PROMISED.
IMPOSSIBLE. I HAVEN'T COMPLETED MY DEAL YET. WHEN THAT IS DONE, YOU WILL --
WHAT, EEJEE, WHAT? IS IT THE TEST?
NO, MILORD-- THE LAB CALLED.
IT'S ABOUT THE OFFSHOOT WOMAN'S BLOOD SAMPLE! THEY SAID IT WAS IMPORTANT THEY SPEAK TO ONE OF US IN PERSON.
OH, VERY WELL. RETURN QUICKLY.
NEVER MIND. I NEED TO MAKE AN ARMOR CHANGE-- BUT WE WILL TAKE THIS UP WHEN I RETURN.
PATIENCE, GENTLEMEN. THE TEST IS ALMOST READY!
CAMPER-- I'M SO SORRY! I NEVER MEANT FOR THEM TO FIND YOU!

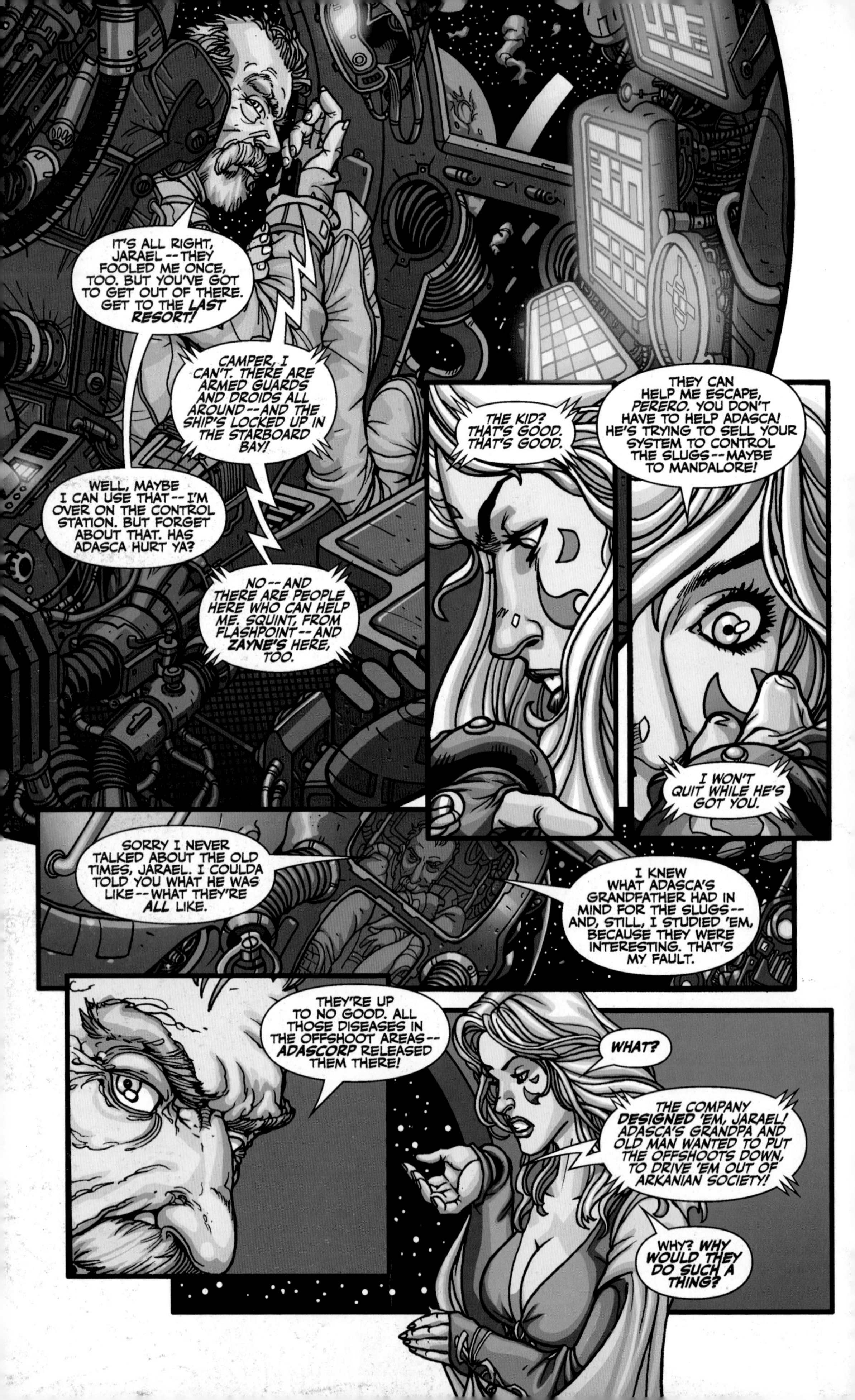
IT'S ALL RIGHT, JARAEL -- THEY FOOLED ME ONCE, TOO. BUT YOU'VE GOT TO GET OUT OF THERE. GET TO THE LAST RESORT!
CAMPER, I CAN'T. THERE ARE ARMED GUARDS AND DROIDS ALL AROUND -- AND THE SHIP'S LOCKED UP IN THE STARBOARD BAY!
WELL, MAYBE I CAN USE THAT -- I'M OVER ON THE CONTROL STATION. BUT FORGET ABOUT THAT. HAS ADASCA HURT YA?
NO -- AND THERE ARE PEOPLE HERE WHO CAN HELP ME. SQUINT, FROM FLASHPOINT -- AND ZAYNE'S HERE, TOO.
THE KID? THAT'S GOOD. THAT'S GOOD.
THEY CAN HELP ME ESCAPE, PERERO. YOU DON'T HAVE TO HELP ADASCA! HE'S TRYING TO SELL YOUR SYSTEM TO CONTROL THE SLUGS -- MAYBE TO MANDALORE!
I WON'T QUIT WHILE HE'S GOT YOU.
SORRY I NEVER TALKED ABOUT THE OLD TIMES, JARAEL. I COULDA TOLD YOU WHAT HE WAS LIKE -- WHAT THEY'RE ALL LIKE.
I KNEW WHAT ADASCA'S GRANDFATHER HAD IN MIND FOR THE SLUGS -- AND, STILL, I STUDIED 'EM, BECAUSE THEY WERE INTERESTING. THAT'S MY FAULT.
THEY'RE UP TO NO GOOD. ALL THOSE DISEASES IN THE OFFSHOOT AREAS -- ADASCORP RELEASED THEM THERE!
WHAT?
THE COMPANY DESIGNED 'EM, JARAEL! ADASCA'S GRANDPA AND OLD MAN WANTED TO PUT THE OFFSHOOTS DOWN, TO DRIVE 'EM OUT OF ARKANIAN SOCIETY!
WHY? WHY WOULD THEY DO SUCH A THING?

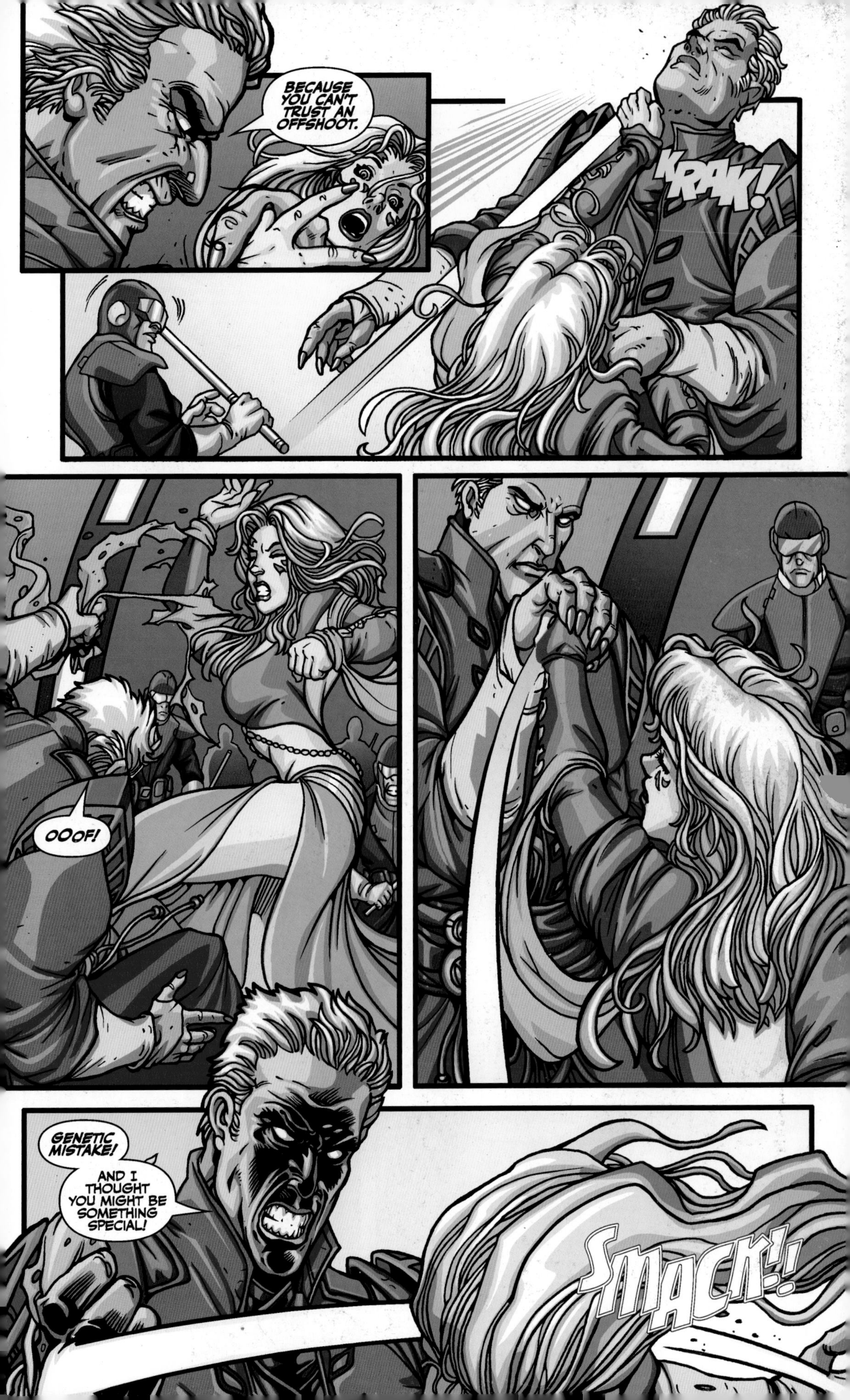
BECAUSE YOU CAN'T TRUST AN OFFSHOOT.
KRAK!
OOOF!
GENETIC MISTAKE!
AND I THOUGHT YOU MIGHT BE SOMETHING SPECIAL!
SMACK!!

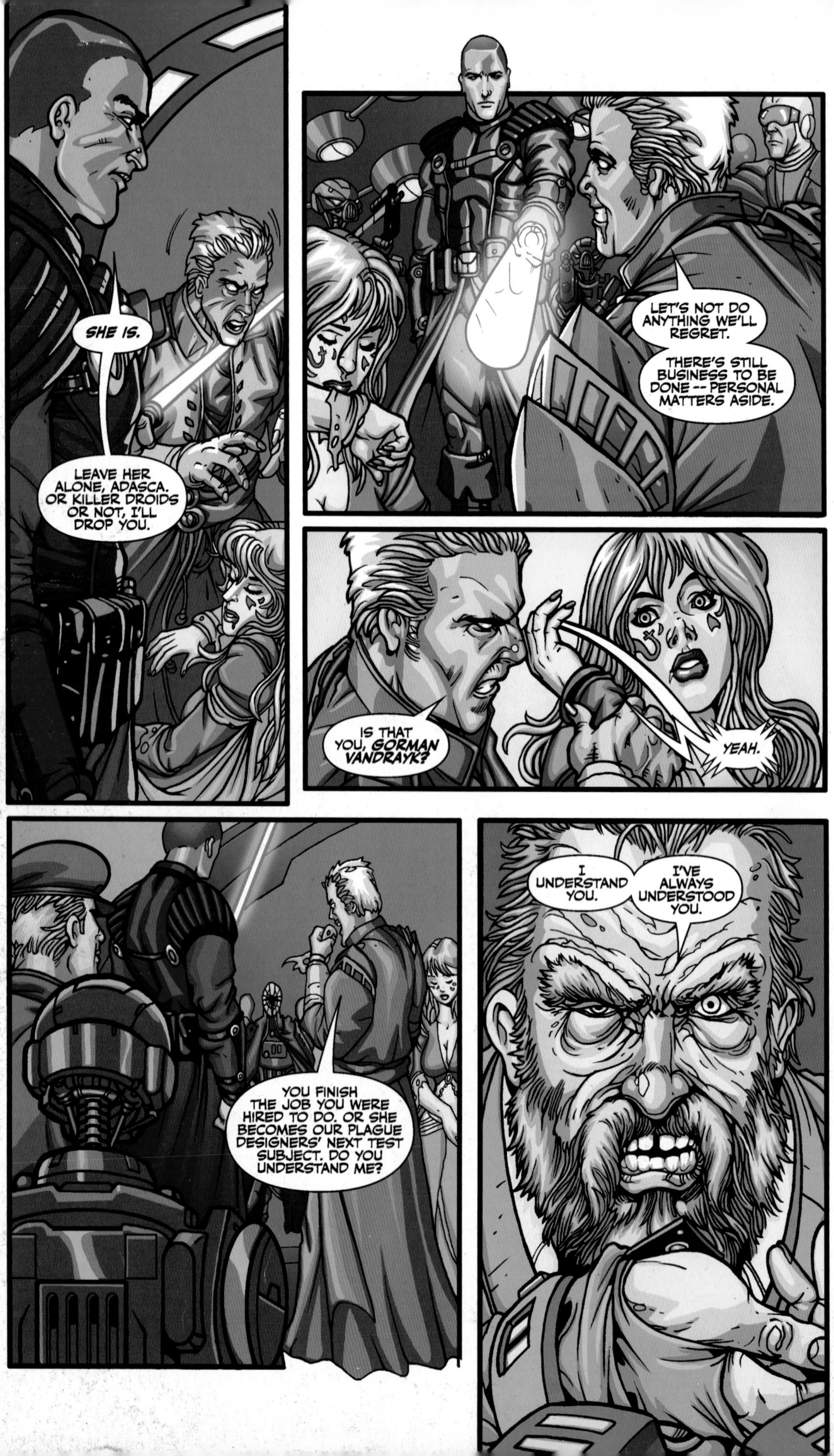
SHE IS.
LEAVE HER ALONE, ADASCA. OR KILLER DROIDS OR NOT, I'LL DROP YOU.
LET'S NOT DO ANYTHING WE'LL REGRET.
THERE'S STILL BUSINESS TO BE DONE -- PERSONAL MATTERS ASIDE.
IS THAT YOU, GORMAN VANDRAYK?
YEAH.
YOU FINISH THE JOB YOU WERE HIRED TO DO. OR SHE BECOMES OUR PLAGUE DESIGNERS' NEXT TEST SUBJECT. DO YOU UNDERSTAND ME?
I UNDERSTAND YOU.
I'VE ALWAYS UNDERSTOOD YOU.

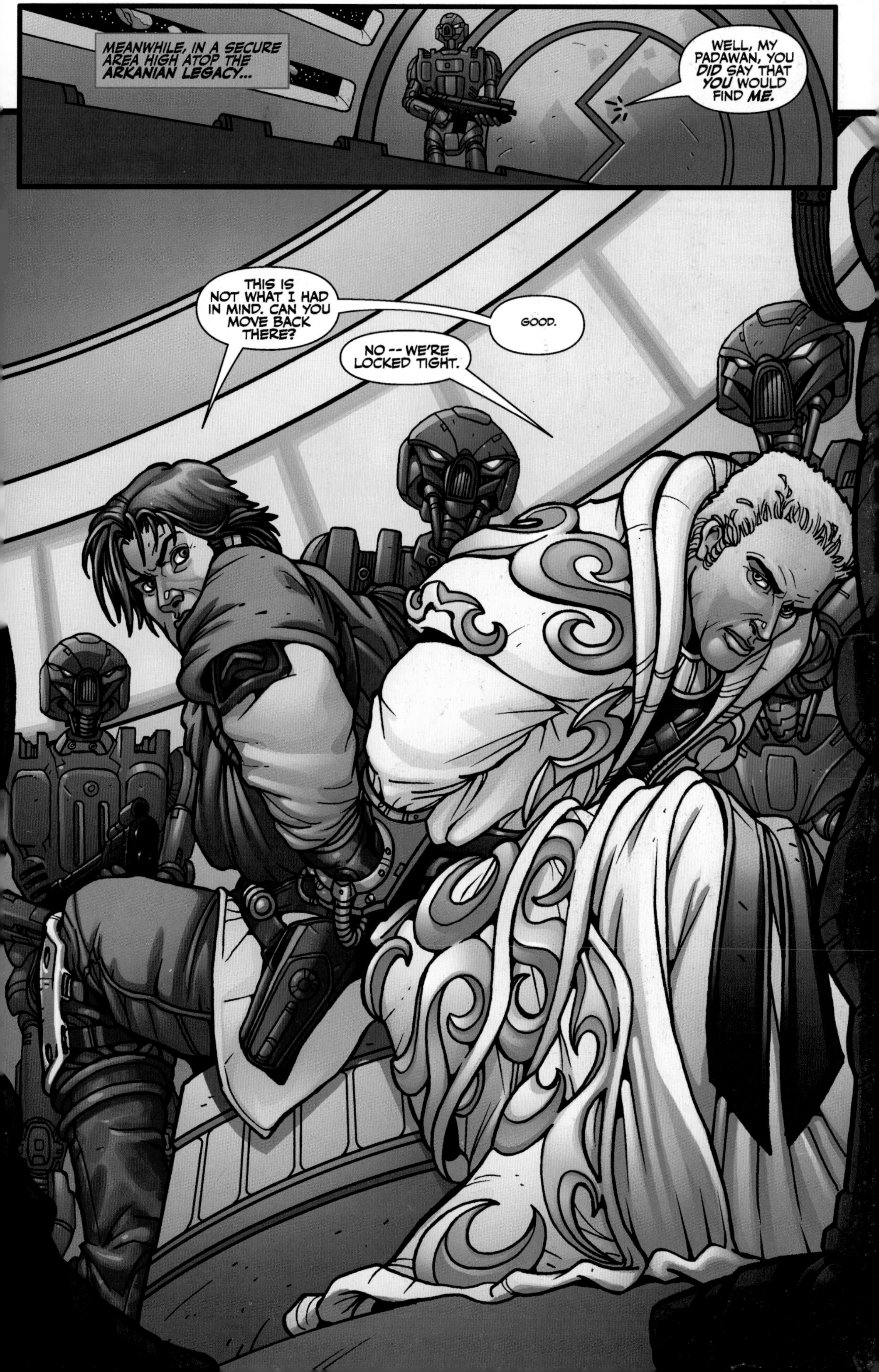

MEANWHILE, IN A SECURE AREA HIGH ATOP THE ARKANIAN LEGACY...
WELL, MY PADAWAN, YOU DID SAY THAT YOU WOULD FIND ME.
THIS IS NOT WHAT I HAD IN MIND. CAN YOU MOVE BACK THERE?
NO -- WE'RE LOCKED TIGHT.
GOOD.

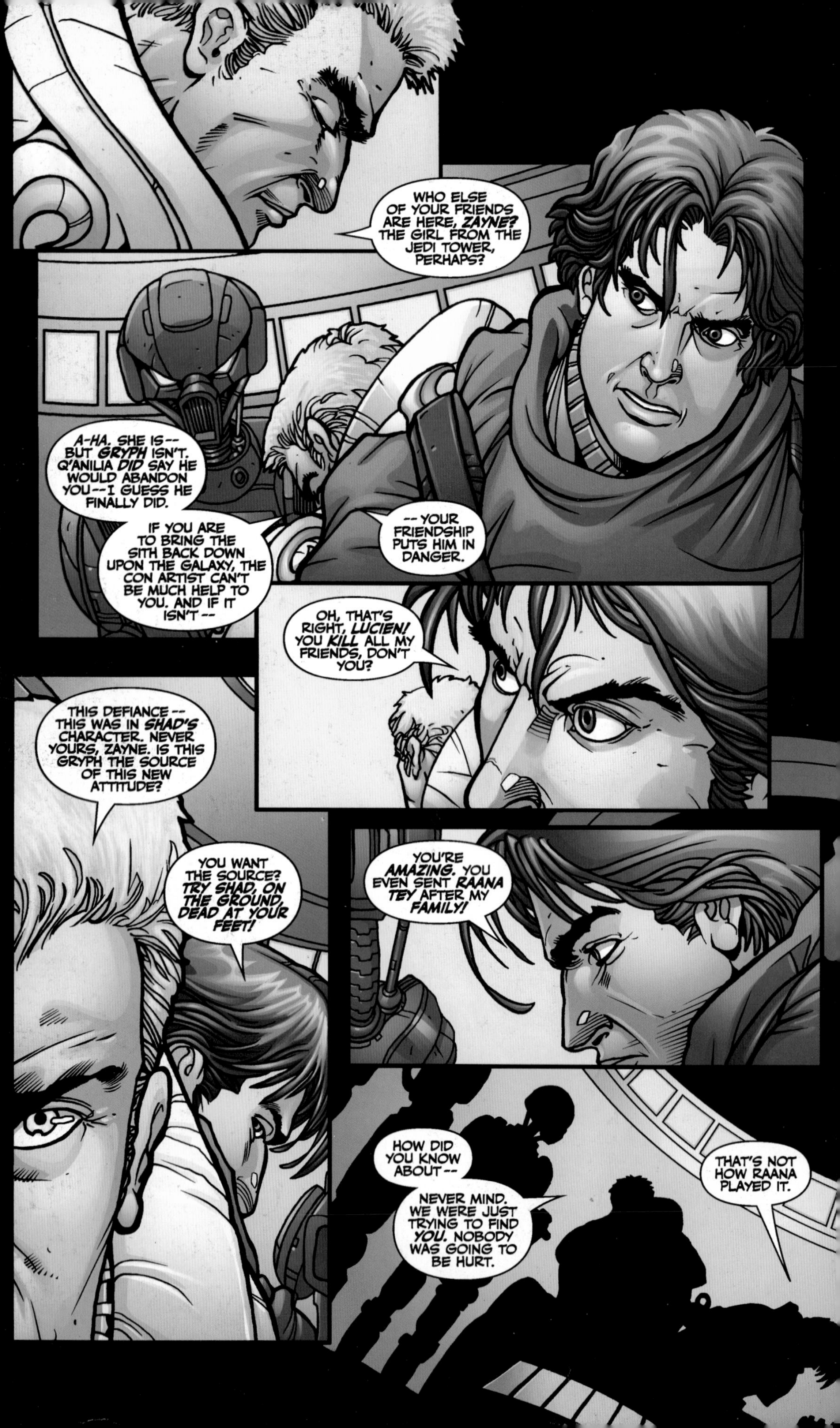
WHO ELSE OF YOUR FRIENDS ARE HERE, ZAYNE? THE GIRL FROM THE JEDI TOWER, PERHAPS?
A-HA. SHE IS-- BUT GRYPH ISN'T. Q'ANILIA DID SAY HE WOULD ABANDON YOU--I GUESS HE FINALLY DID.
IF YOU ARE TO BRING THE SITH BACK DOWN UPON THE GALAXY, THE CON ARTIST CAN'T BE MUCH HELP TO YOU. AND IF IT ISN'T--
--YOUR FRIENDSHIP PUTS HIM IN DANGER.
OH, THAT'S RIGHT, LUCIEN! YOU KILL ALL MY FRIENDS, DON'T YOU?
THIS DEFIANCE-- THIS WAS IN SHAD'S CHARACTER. NEVER YOURS, ZAYNE. IS THIS GRYPH THE SOURCE OF THIS NEW ATTITUDE?
YOU WANT THE SOURCE? TRY SHAD, ON THE GROUND, DEAD AT YOUR FEET!
YOU'RE AMAZING. YOU EVEN SENT RAANA TEY AFTER MY FAMILY!
HOW DID YOU KNOW ABOUT--
NEVER MIND. WE WERE JUST TRYING TO FIND YOU. NOBODY WAS GOING TO BE HURT.
THAT'S NOT HOW RAANA PLAYED IT.

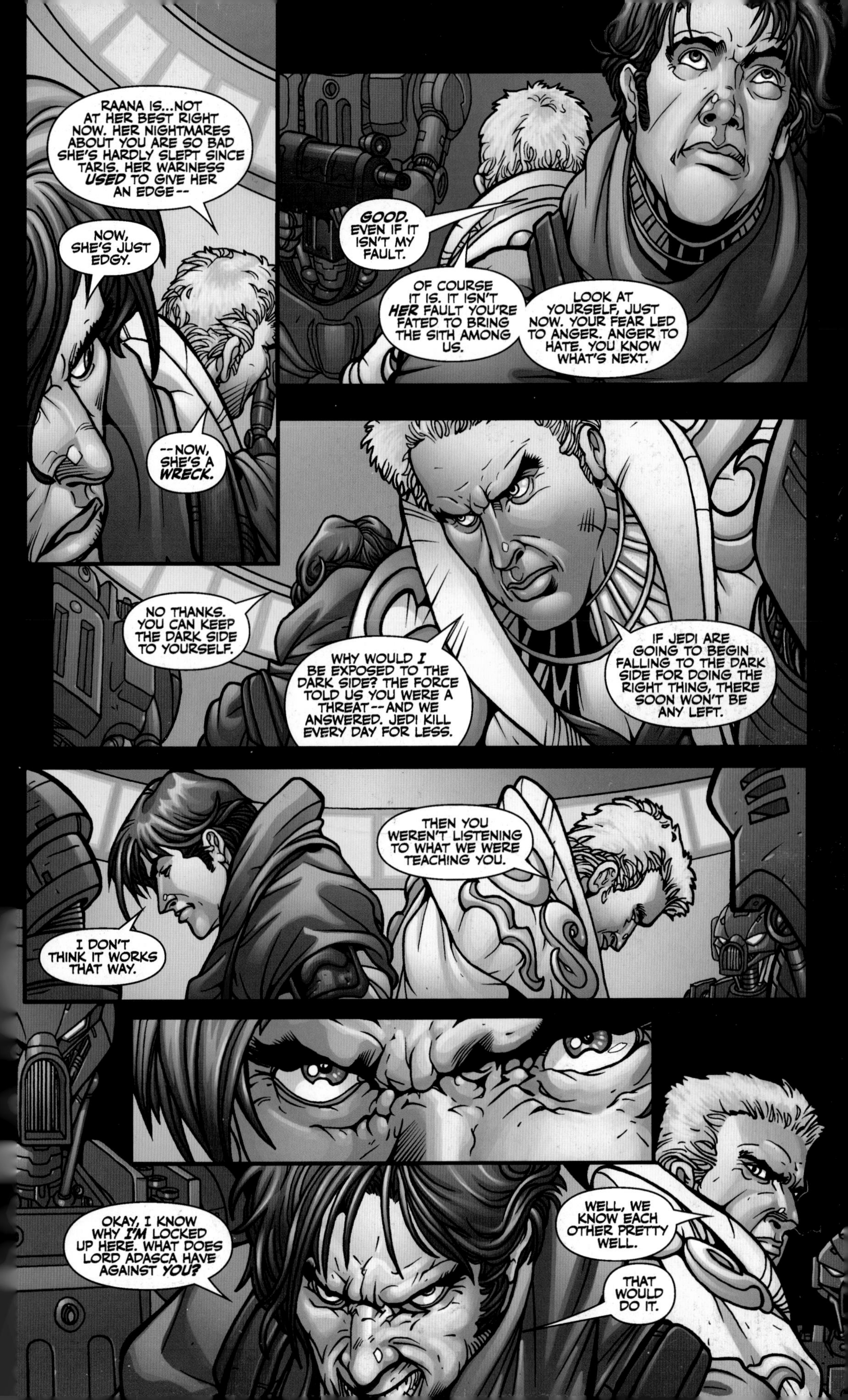
RAANA IS...NOT AT HER BEST RIGHT NOW. HER NIGHTMARES ABOUT YOU ARE SO BAD SHE'S HARDLY SLEPT SINCE TARIS. HER WARINESS USED TO GIVE HER AN EDGE--
NOW, SHE'S JUST EDGY.
--NOW, SHE'S A WRECK.
GOOD. EVEN IF IT ISN'T MY FAULT.
OF COURSE IT IS. IT ISN'T HER FAULT YOU'RE FATED TO BRING THE SITH AMONG US.
LOOK AT YOURSELF, JUST NOW. YOUR FEAR LED TO ANGER. ANGER TO HATE. YOU KNOW WHAT'S NEXT.
NO THANKS. YOU CAN KEEP THE DARK SIDE TO YOURSELF.
WHY WOULD I BE EXPOSED TO THE DARK SIDE? THE FORCE TOLD US YOU WERE A THREAT--AND WE ANSWERED. JEDI KILL EVERY DAY FOR LESS.
IF JEDI ARE GOING TO BEGIN FALLING TO THE DARK SIDE FOR DOING THE RIGHT THING, THERE SOON WON'T BE ANY LEFT.
THEN YOU WEREN'T LISTENING TO WHAT WE WERE TEACHING YOU.
I DON'T THINK IT WORKS THAT WAY.
OKAY, I KNOW WHY I'M LOCKED UP HERE. WHAT DOES LORD ADASCA HAVE AGAINST YOU?
WELL, WE KNOW EACH OTHER PRETTY WELL.
THAT WOULD DO IT.

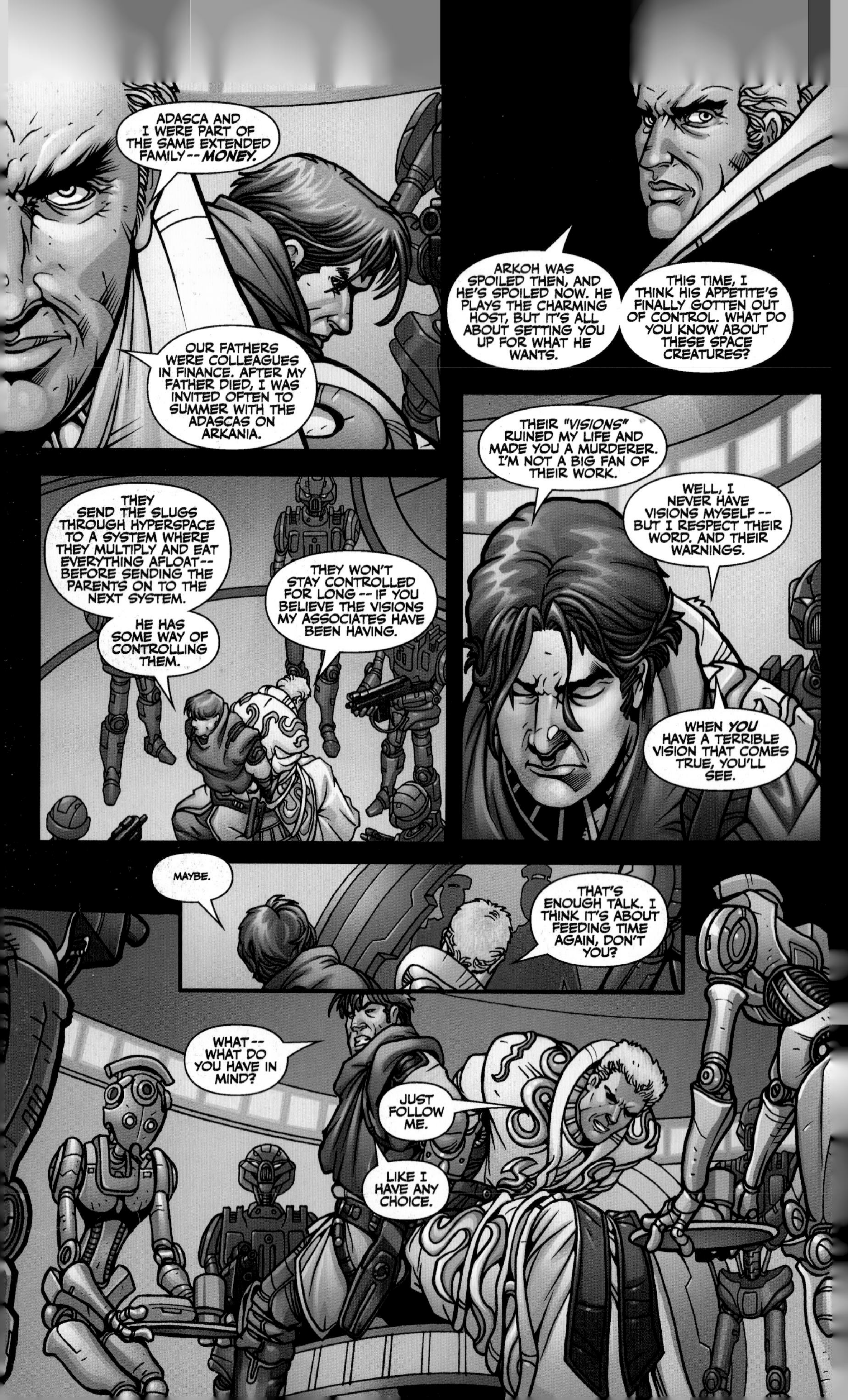
ADASCA AND I WERE PART OF THE SAME EXTENDED FAMILY -- *MONEY.*
OUR FATHERS WERE COLLEAGUES IN FINANCE. AFTER MY FATHER DIED, I WAS INVITED OFTEN TO SUMMER WITH THE ADASCAS ON ARKANIA.
ARKOH WAS SPOILED THEN, AND HE'S SPOILED NOW. HE PLAYS THE CHARMING HOST, BUT IT'S ALL ABOUT SETTING YOU UP FOR WHAT HE WANTS.
THIS TIME, I THINK HIS APPETITE'S FINALLY GOTTEN OUT OF CONTROL. WHAT DO YOU KNOW ABOUT THESE SPACE CREATURES?
THEY SEND THE SLUGS THROUGH HYPERSPACE TO A SYSTEM WHERE THEY MULTIPLY AND EAT EVERYTHING AFLOAT -- BEFORE SENDING THE PARENTS ON TO THE NEXT SYSTEM.
HE HAS SOME WAY OF CONTROLLING THEM.
THEY WON'T STAY CONTROLLED FOR LONG -- IF YOU BELIEVE THE VISIONS MY ASSOCIATES HAVE BEEN HAVING.
THEIR *"VISIONS"* RUINED MY LIFE AND MADE YOU A MURDERER. I'M NOT A BIG FAN OF THEIR WORK.
WELL, I NEVER HAVE VISIONS MYSELF -- BUT I RESPECT THEIR WORD. AND THEIR WARNINGS.
WHEN *YOU* HAVE A TERRIBLE VISION THAT COMES TRUE, YOU'LL SEE.
MAYBE.
THAT'S ENOUGH TALK. I THINK IT'S ABOUT FEEDING TIME AGAIN, DON'T YOU?
WHAT -- WHAT DO YOU HAVE IN MIND?
JUST FOLLOW ME.
LIKE I HAVE ANY CHOICE.

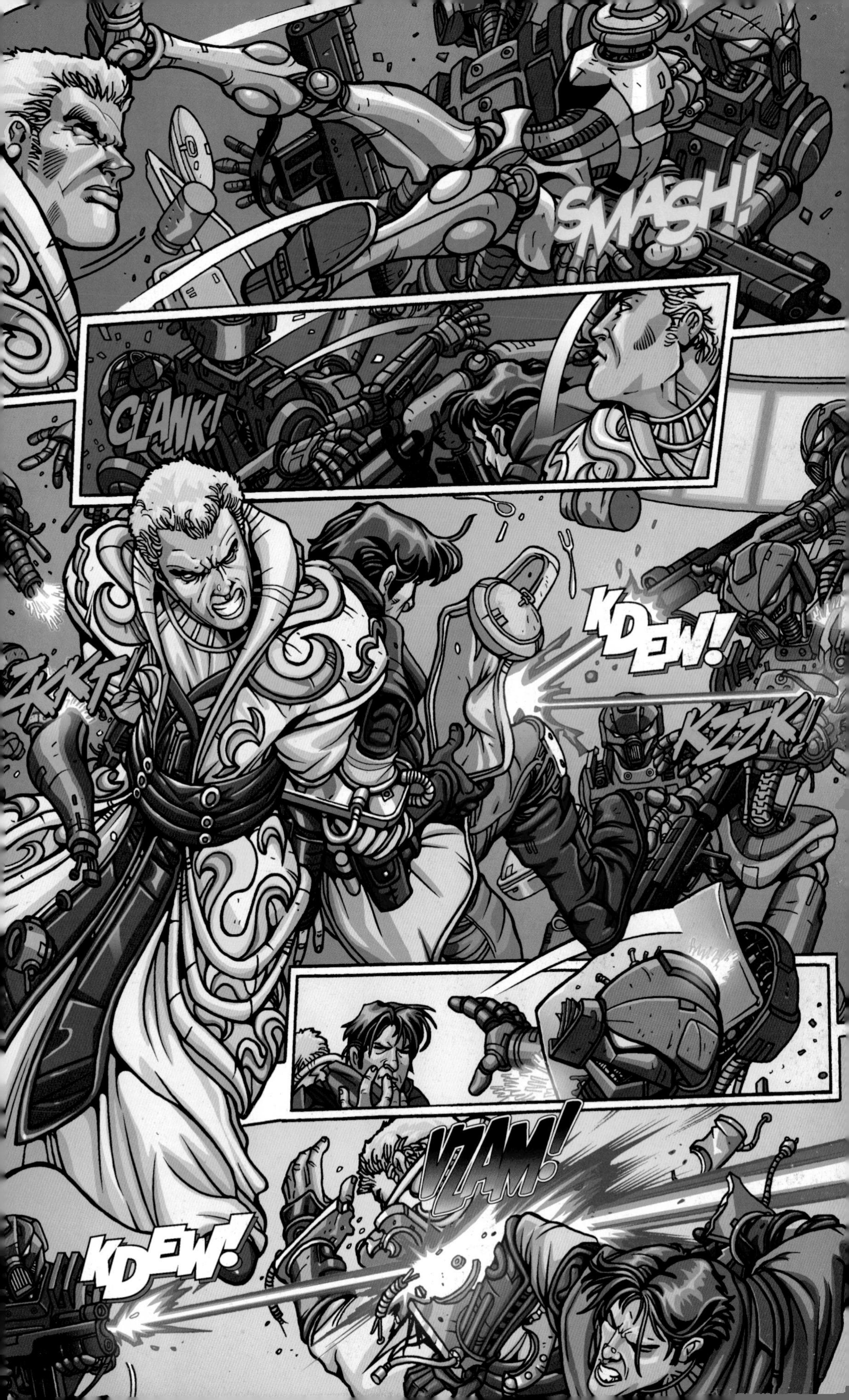
SMASH!
CLANK!
KDEW!
ZKKT!
KZZK!
VZAM!
KDEW!

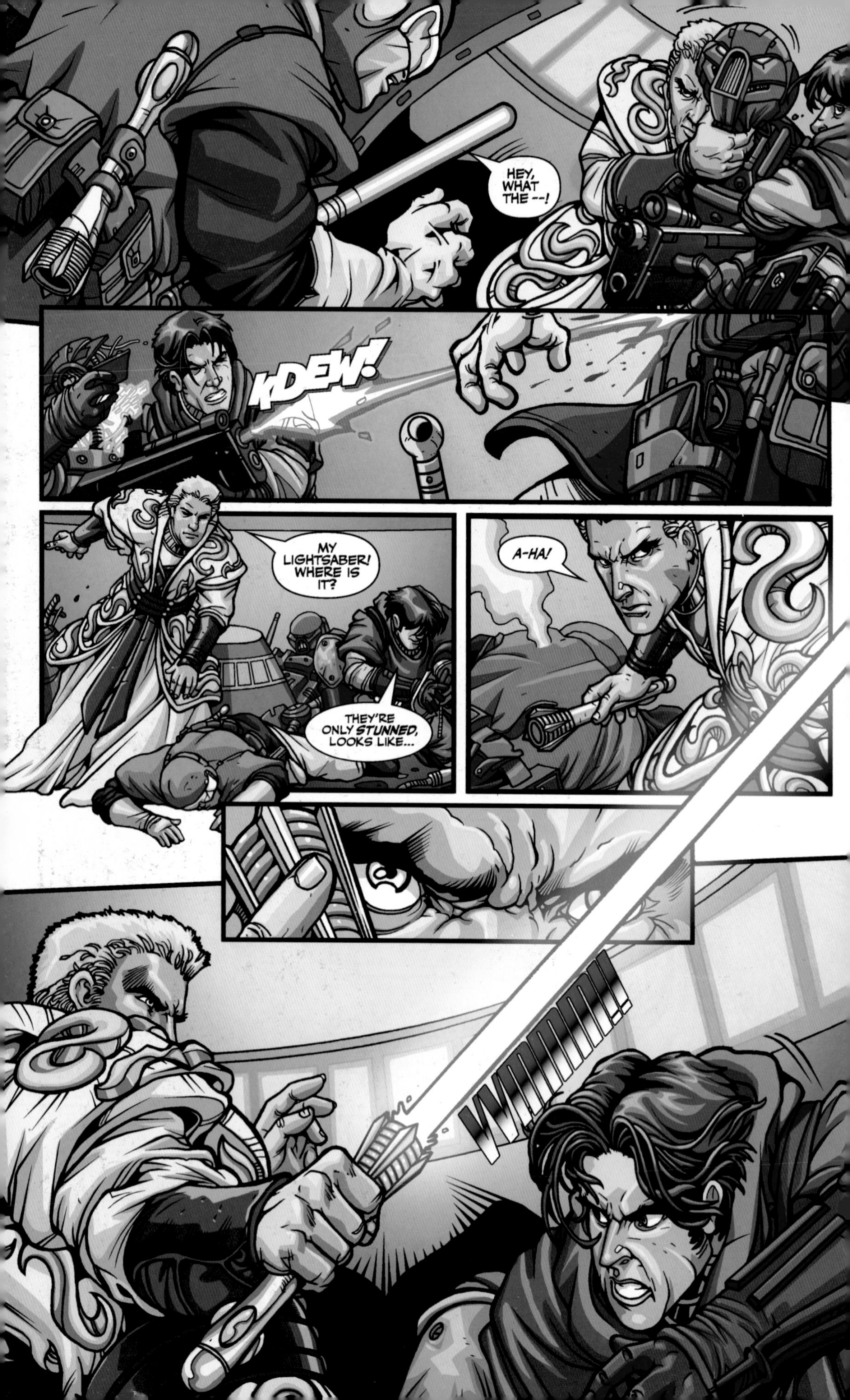
HEY, WHAT THE --!
KDEW!
MY LIGHTSABER! WHERE IS IT?
THEY'RE ONLY STUNNED, LOOKS LIKE...
A-HA!
VVMMM!!

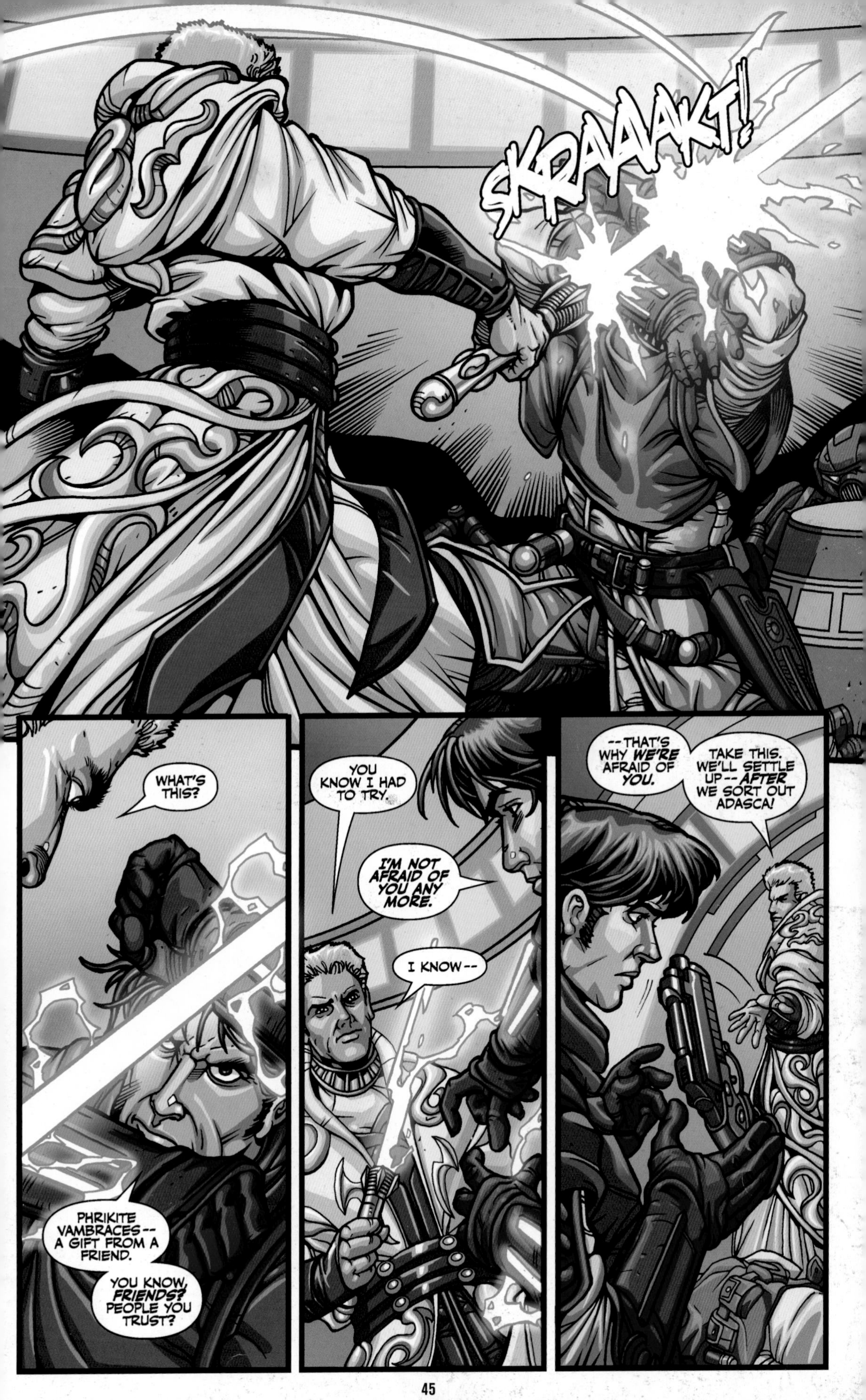
SKRAAAKT!
WHAT'S THIS?
PHRIKITE VAMBRACES-- A GIFT FROM A FRIEND.
YOU KNOW, FRIENDS? PEOPLE YOU TRUST?
YOU KNOW I HAD TO TRY.
I'M NOT AFRAID OF YOU ANY MORE.
I KNOW--
--THAT'S WHY WE'RE AFRAID OF YOU.
TAKE THIS. WE'LL SETTLE UP-- AFTER WE SORT OUT ADASCA!

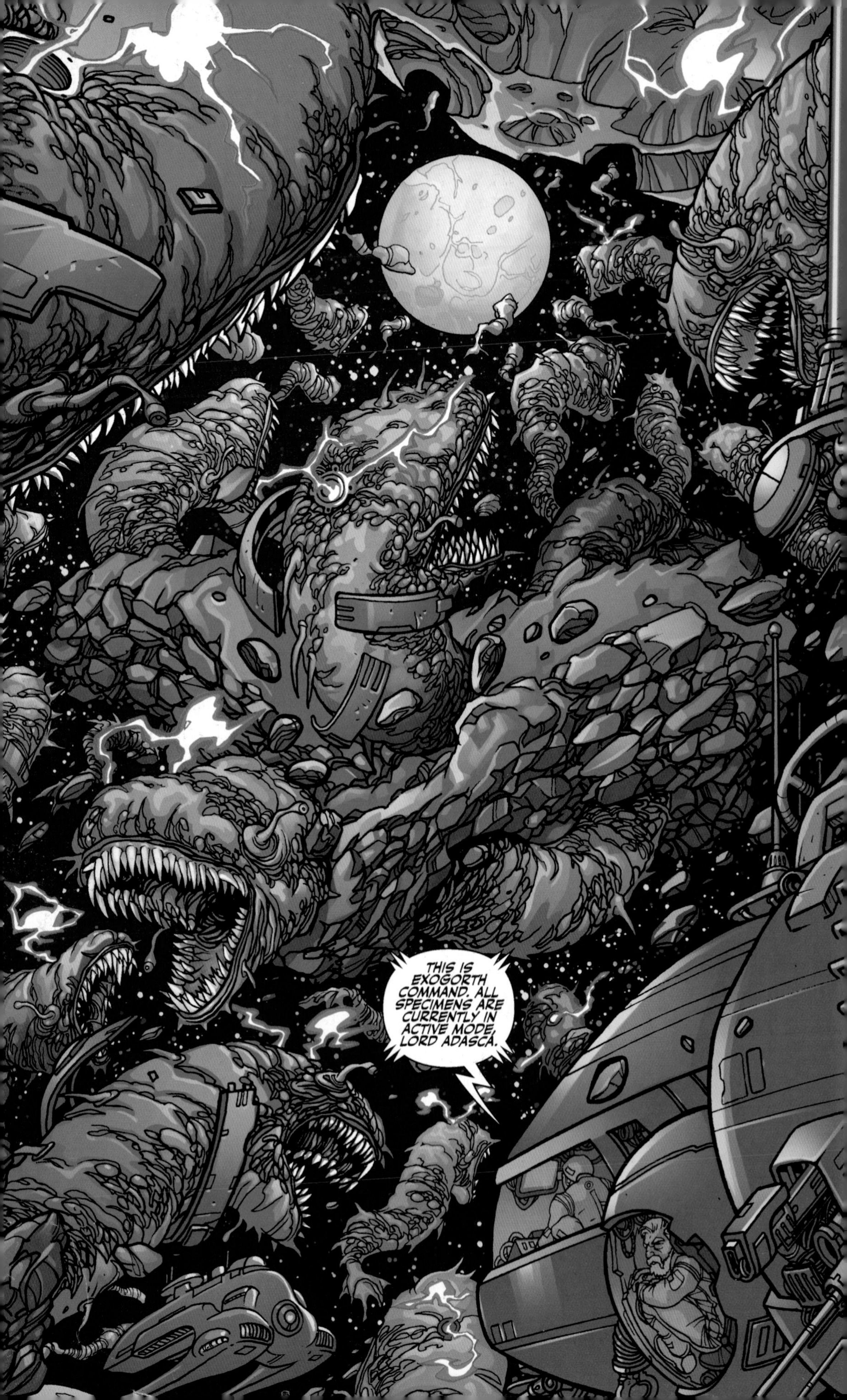
THIS IS EXOGORTH COMMAND. ALL SPECIMENS ARE CURRENTLY IN ACTIVE MODE, LORD ADASCA.

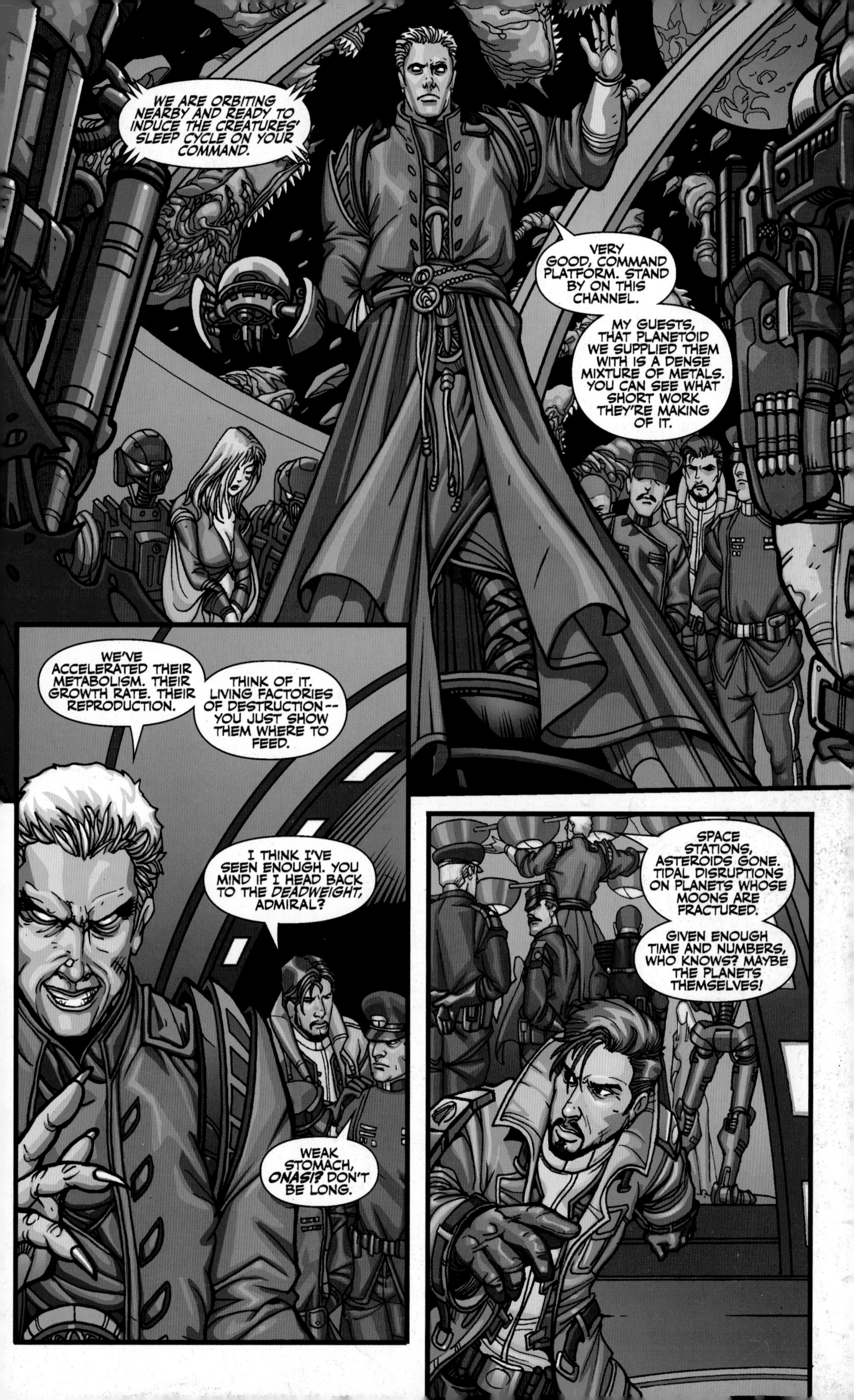
WE ARE ORBITING NEARBY AND READY TO INDUCE THE CREATURES' SLEEP CYCLE ON YOUR COMMAND.
VERY GOOD, COMMAND PLATFORM. STAND BY ON THIS CHANNEL.
MY GUESTS, THAT PLANETOID WE SUPPLIED THEM WITH IS A DENSE MIXTURE OF METALS. YOU CAN SEE WHAT SHORT WORK THEY'RE MAKING OF IT.
WE'VE ACCELERATED THEIR METABOLISM. THEIR GROWTH RATE. THEIR REPRODUCTION.
THINK OF IT. LIVING FACTORIES OF DESTRUCTION-- YOU JUST SHOW THEM WHERE TO FEED.
SPACE STATIONS, ASTEROIDS GONE. TIDAL DISRUPTIONS ON PLANETS WHOSE MOONS ARE FRACTURED.
GIVEN ENOUGH TIME AND NUMBERS, WHO KNOWS? MAYBE THE PLANETS THEMSELVES!
I THINK I'VE SEEN ENOUGH. YOU MIND IF I HEAD BACK TO THE *DEADWEIGHT*, ADMIRAL?
WEAK STOMACH, **ONASI?** DON'T BE LONG.

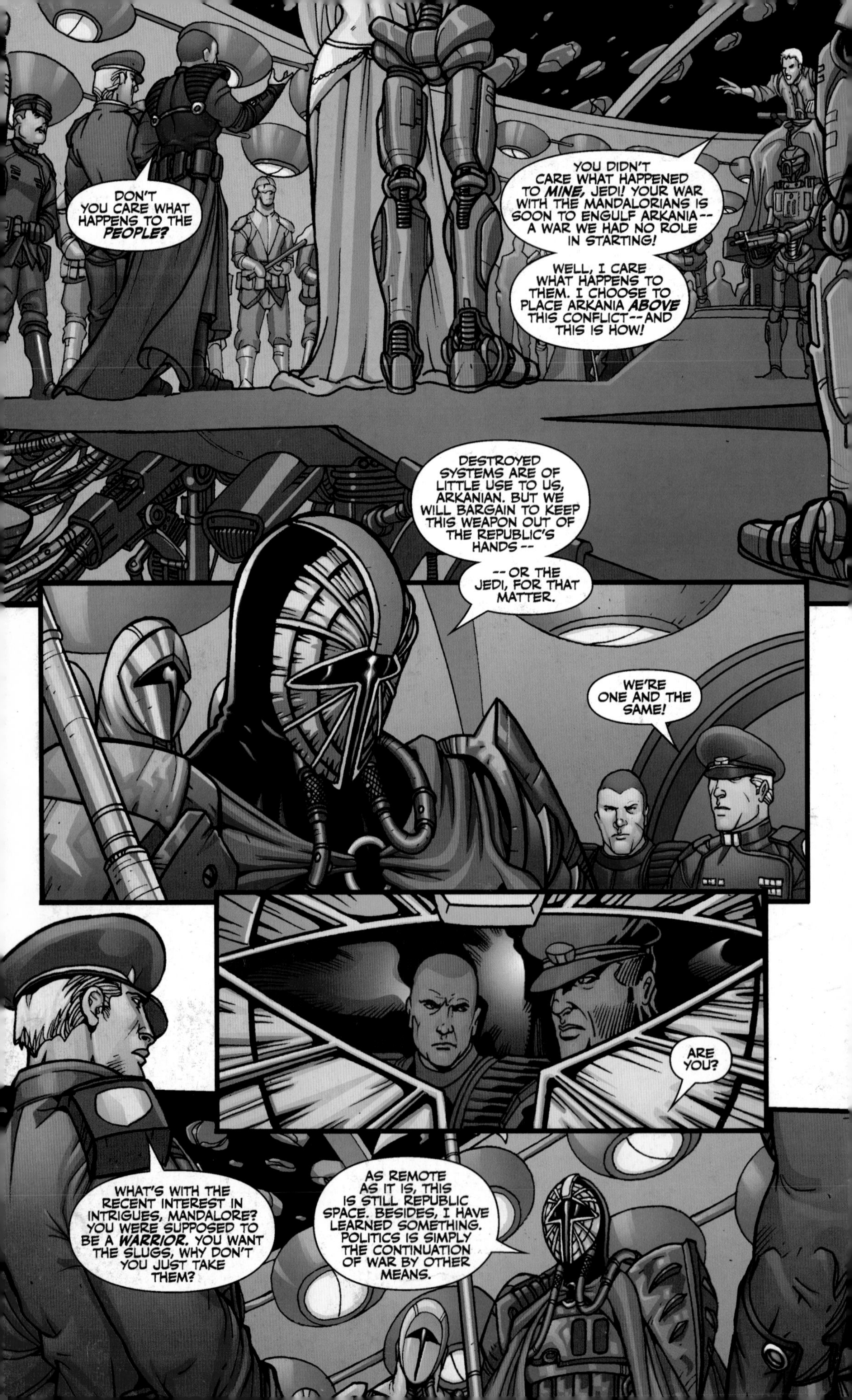
DON'T YOU CARE WHAT HAPPENS TO THE *PEOPLE?*
YOU DIDN'T CARE WHAT HAPPENED TO *MINE,* JEDI! YOUR WAR WITH THE MANDALORIANS IS SOON TO ENGULF ARKANIA-- A WAR WE HAD NO ROLE IN STARTING!
WELL, I CARE WHAT HAPPENS TO THEM. I CHOOSE TO PLACE ARKANIA *ABOVE* THIS CONFLICT--AND THIS IS HOW!
DESTROYED SYSTEMS ARE OF LITTLE USE TO US, ARKANIAN. BUT WE WILL BARGAIN TO KEEP THIS WEAPON OUT OF THE REPUBLIC'S HANDS --
-- OR THE JEDI, FOR THAT MATTER.
WE'RE ONE AND THE SAME!
ARE YOU?
WHAT'S WITH THE RECENT INTEREST IN INTRIGUES, MANDALORE? YOU WERE SUPPOSED TO BE A *WARRIOR.* YOU WANT THE SLUGS, WHY DON'T YOU JUST TAKE THEM?
AS REMOTE AS IT IS, THIS IS STILL REPUBLIC SPACE. BESIDES, I HAVE LEARNED SOMETHING. POLITICS IS SIMPLY THE CONTINUATION OF WAR BY OTHER MEANS.

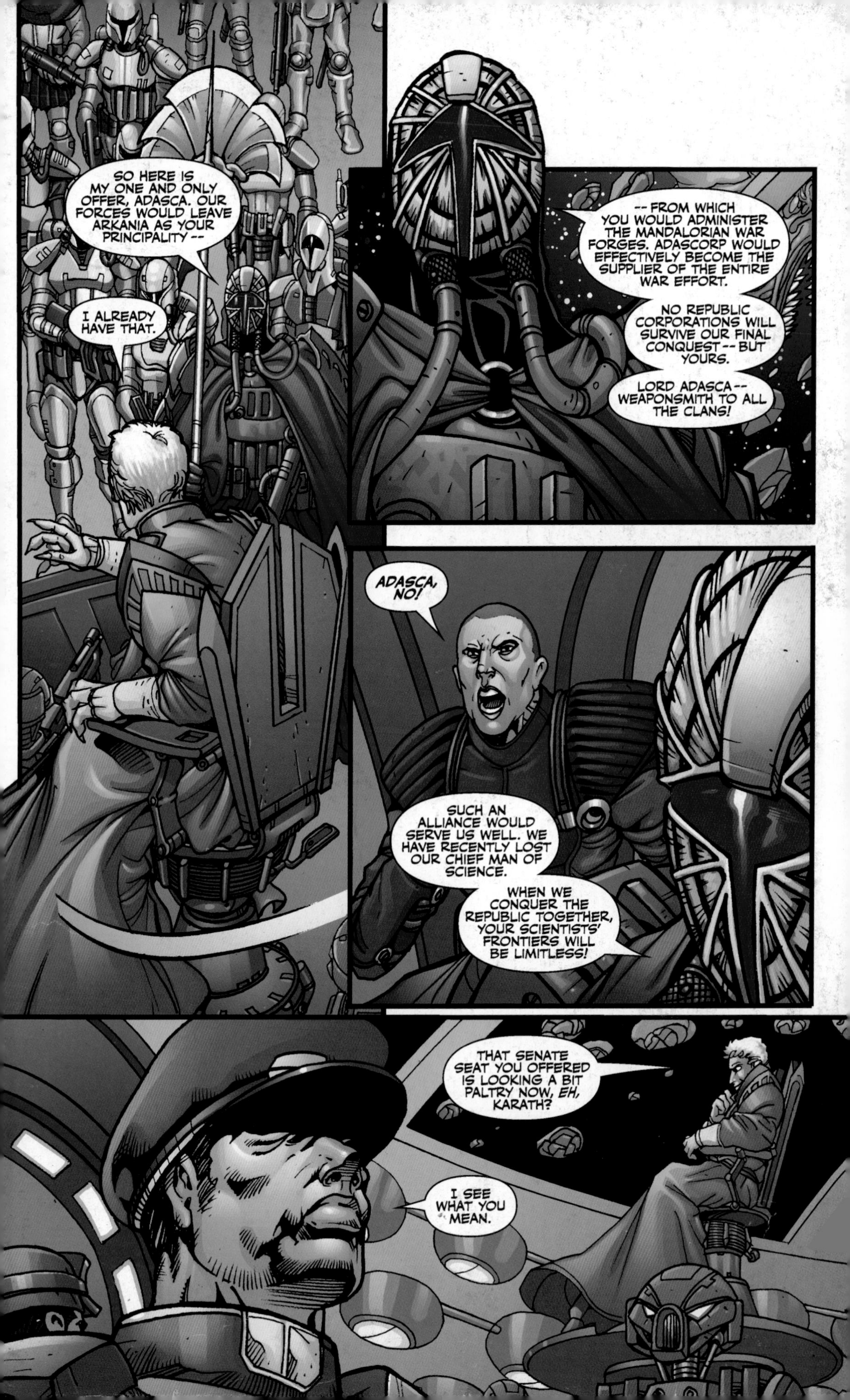
SO HERE IS MY ONE AND ONLY OFFER, ADASCA. OUR FORCES WOULD LEAVE ARKANIA AS YOUR PRINCIPALITY --
I ALREADY HAVE THAT.
-- FROM WHICH YOU WOULD ADMINISTER THE MANDALORIAN WAR FORGES. ADASCORP WOULD EFFECTIVELY BECOME THE SUPPLIER OF THE ENTIRE WAR EFFORT.
NO REPUBLIC CORPORATIONS WILL SURVIVE OUR FINAL CONQUEST -- BUT YOURS.
LORD ADASCA -- WEAPONSMITH TO ALL THE CLANS!
ADASCA, NO!
SUCH AN ALLIANCE WOULD SERVE US WELL. WE HAVE RECENTLY LOST OUR CHIEF MAN OF SCIENCE.
WHEN WE CONQUER THE REPUBLIC TOGETHER, YOUR SCIENTISTS' FRONTIERS WILL BE LIMITLESS!
THAT SENATE SEAT YOU OFFERED IS LOOKING A BIT PALTRY NOW, EH, KARATH?
I SEE WHAT YOU MEAN.

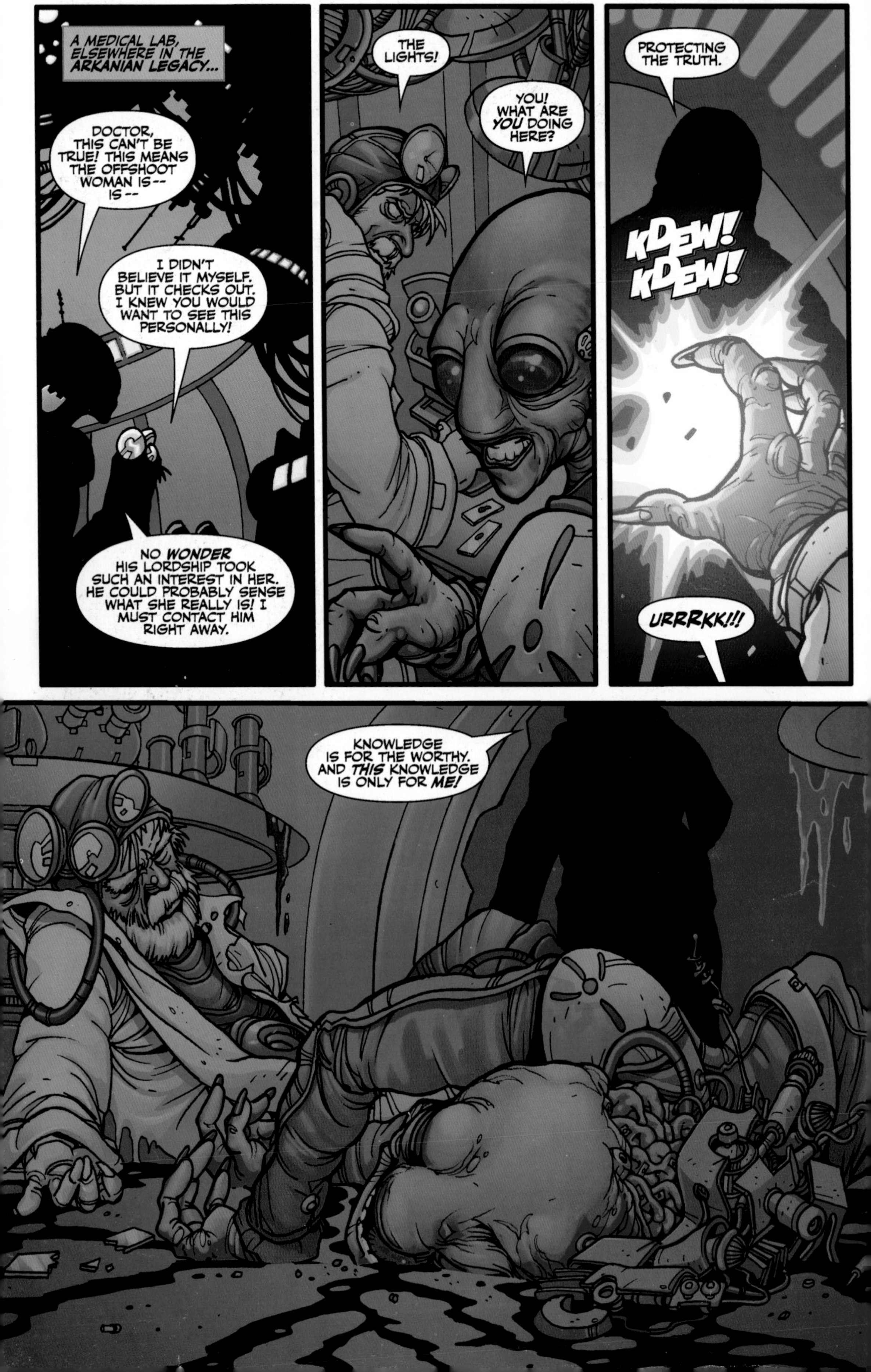
A MEDICAL LAB, ELSEWHERE IN THE ARKANIAN LEGACY...
DOCTOR, THIS CAN'T BE TRUE! THIS MEANS THE OFFSHOOT WOMAN IS-- IS--
I DIDN'T BELIEVE IT MYSELF. BUT IT CHECKS OUT. I KNEW YOU WOULD WANT TO SEE THIS PERSONALLY!
NO WONDER HIS LORDSHIP TOOK SUCH AN INTEREST IN HER. HE COULD PROBABLY SENSE WHAT SHE REALLY IS! I MUST CONTACT HIM RIGHT AWAY.
THE LIGHTS!
YOU! WHAT ARE YOU DOING HERE?
PROTECTING THE TRUTH.
KDEW! KDEW!
URRRKK!!!
KNOWLEDGE IS FOR THE WORTHY. AND THIS KNOWLEDGE IS ONLY FOR ME!

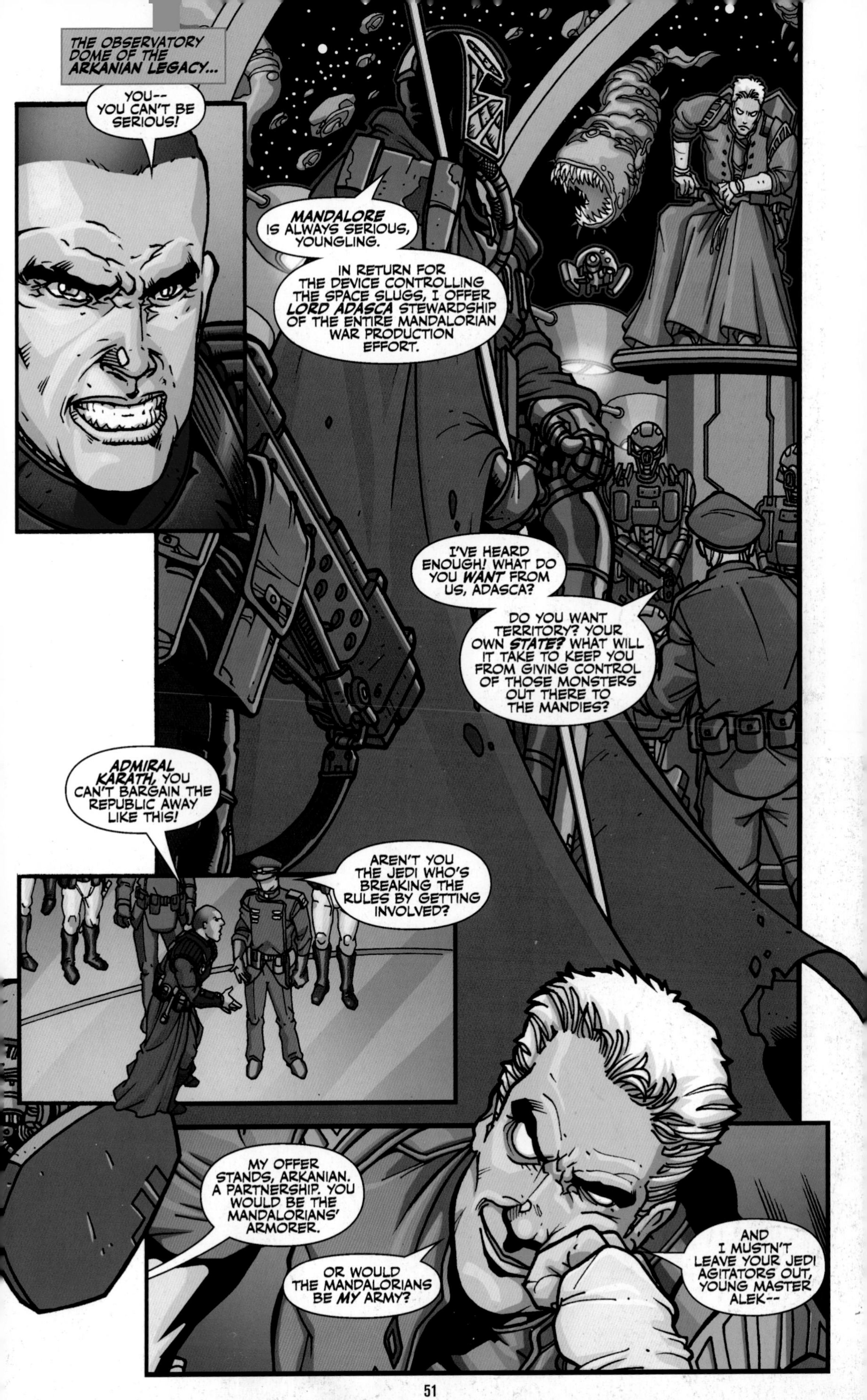
THE OBSERVATORY DOME OF THE ARKANIAN LEGACY...
YOU-- YOU CAN'T BE SERIOUS!
MANDALORE IS ALWAYS SERIOUS, YOUNGLING.
IN RETURN FOR THE DEVICE CONTROLLING THE SPACE SLUGS, I OFFER LORD ADASCA STEWARDSHIP OF THE ENTIRE MANDALORIAN WAR PRODUCTION EFFORT.
I'VE HEARD ENOUGH! WHAT DO YOU WANT FROM US, ADASCA?
DO YOU WANT TERRITORY? YOUR OWN STATE? WHAT WILL IT TAKE TO KEEP YOU FROM GIVING CONTROL OF THOSE MONSTERS OUT THERE TO THE MANDIES?
ADMIRAL KARATH, YOU CAN'T BARGAIN THE REPUBLIC AWAY LIKE THIS!
AREN'T YOU THE JEDI WHO'S BREAKING THE RULES BY GETTING INVOLVED?
MY OFFER STANDS, ARKANIAN. A PARTNERSHIP. YOU WOULD BE THE MANDALORIANS' ARMORER.
OR WOULD THE MANDALORIANS BE MY ARMY?
AND I MUSTN'T LEAVE YOUR JEDI AGITATORS OUT, YOUNG MASTER ALEK--

-- MAYBE I COULD USE MY OWN JEDI ORDER, TOO!

HE'S NOT HERE FOR THE JEDI ORDER. HE'S DEALING FOR HIS SO-CALLED MASTER -- FOR THE *REVANCHISTS*.

MANDALORIANS! ARKOH ADASCA, YOU *HAVE* GONE MAD!

WAIT A MINUTE. THAT'S *SQUINT* IN THERE! COULD THE *JEDI* HAVE BEEN INVITED TO THIS?

WHATEVER. THEY MUST BE IN THAT OBSERVATORY DOME. WHAT DO WE DO NOW?

I DON'T KNOW. I WASN'T EXPECTING TO GET THIS FAR. SOMETHING MUST HAVE HAPPENED TO ADASCA'S CYBERNETIC AIDE. I --

-- SOMEONE'S COMING!

ZAYNE! I WAS HOPING TO FIND YOU!

CARTH! MAN, I'M GLAD TO SEE YOU -- AND YOU BROUGHT MY *LIGHTSABER*!

I WAS ABLE TO GET YOUR STUFF OFF MY SHIP BEFORE SECURITY STARTED GOING CRAZY.

LIEUTENANT *CARTH ONASI*, BATTLE GROUP SERROCO -- OR WHAT'S LEFT OF IT.

MASTER *LUCIEN DRAAY*.

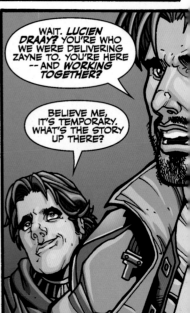

WAIT. *LUCIEN DRAAY?* YOU'RE WHO WE WERE DELIVERING ZAYNE TO. YOU'RE HERE -- AND *WORKING TOGETHER?*

BELIEVE ME, IT'S TEMPORARY. WHAT'S THE STORY UP THERE?

JUST ADASCA BARGAINING FOR HALF THE GALAXY. HE CAN INFEST SYSTEMS WITH THOSE SPACE SLUGS FASTER THAN WE CAN BUILD SHIPS TO TAKE THEM OUT!

IT'S FOR REAL, TOO--WE JUST SAW A TEST. HE'S GOT AN OPEN CHANNEL TO HIS PEOPLE AT SOME KIND OF CONTROL STATION OUTSIDE THE SHIP.

WAIT. THAT WOMAN! SHE'S THE ONE WHO-- ER, THAT'S THE WOMAN FROM TARIS.

JARAEL!

WHO?

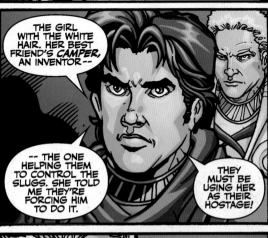

THE GIRL WITH THE WHITE HAIR. HER BEST FRIEND'S CAMPER, AN INVENTOR--

-- THE ONE HELPING THEM TO CONTROL THE SLUGS. SHE TOLD ME THEY'RE FORCING HIM TO DO IT.

THEY MUST BE USING HER AS THEIR HOSTAGE!

I DON'T SEE CAMPER ANYWHERE, THOUGH.

BEFORE ADASCA TOOK HER COMM, SHE WAS TALKING TO SOMEONE ON THE CONTROL PLATFORM, OFF-SHIP. BUT THAT'S OUT OF REACH.

AH. WE WOULDN'T HAVE TO SAVE HER, THEN.

WE'LL JUST KILL HER.

IF SHE DIES, ADASCA'S LEVERAGE IS GONE. IT'S THE SUREST WAY-- AND THE STAKES ARE TOO HIGH FOR ANYTHING ELSE. CAN YOU THINK OF A REASON IT WOULDN'T WORK?

WHAT?

JUST ONE...

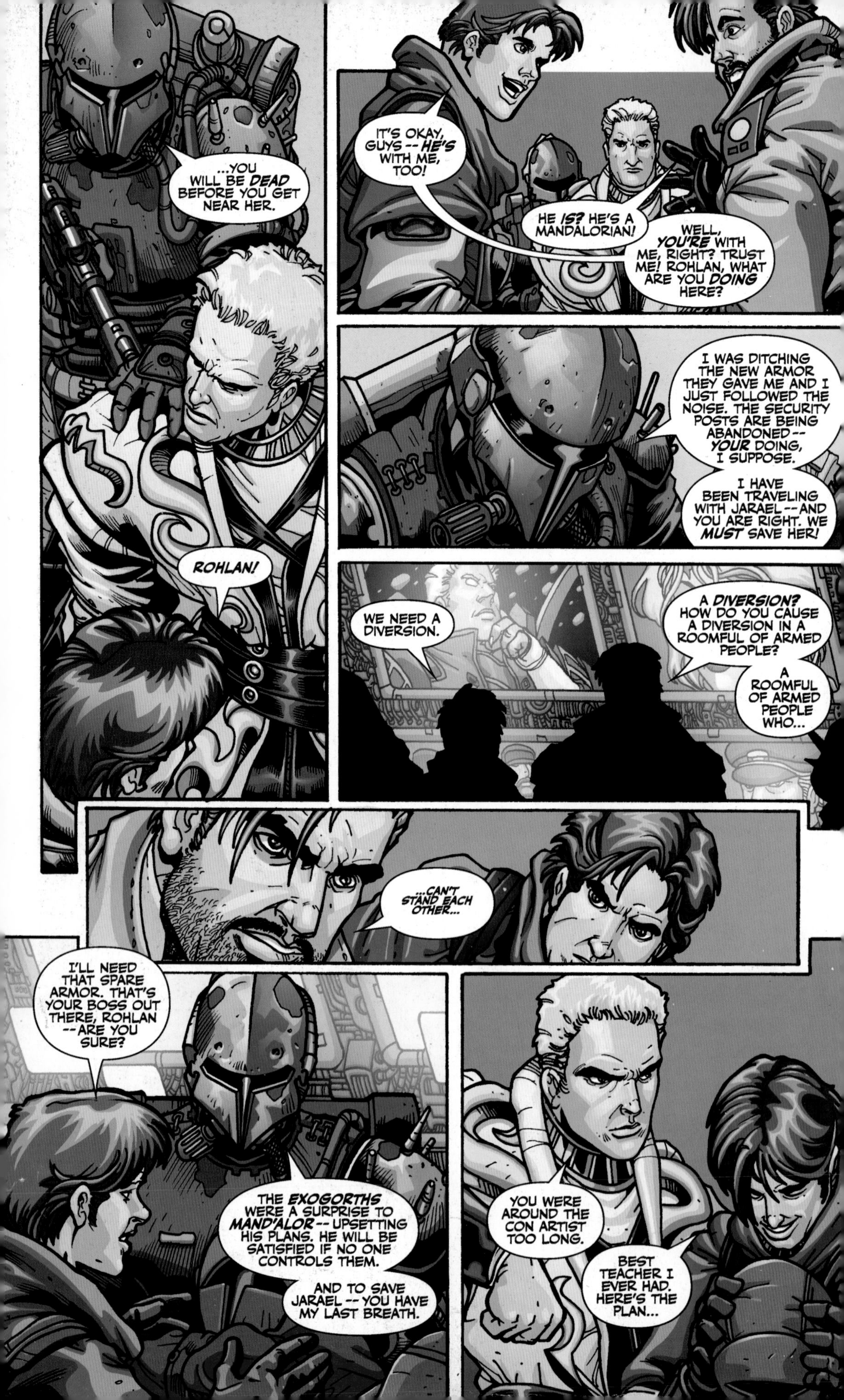

...YOU WILL BE DEAD BEFORE YOU GET NEAR HER.
ROHLAN!
IT'S OKAY, GUYS -- HE'S WITH ME, TOO!
HE IS? HE'S A MANDALORIAN!
WELL, YOU'RE WITH ME, RIGHT? TRUST ME! ROHLAN, WHAT ARE YOU DOING HERE?
I WAS DITCHING THE NEW ARMOR THEY GAVE ME AND I JUST FOLLOWED THE NOISE. THE SECURITY POSTS ARE BEING ABANDONED -- YOUR DOING, I SUPPOSE.
I HAVE BEEN TRAVELING WITH JARAEL -- AND YOU ARE RIGHT. WE MUST SAVE HER!
WE NEED A DIVERSION.
A DIVERSION? HOW DO YOU CAUSE A DIVERSION IN A ROOMFUL OF ARMED PEOPLE?
A ROOMFUL OF ARMED PEOPLE WHO...
...CAN'T STAND EACH OTHER...
I'LL NEED THAT SPARE ARMOR. THAT'S YOUR BOSS OUT THERE, ROHLAN -- ARE YOU SURE?
THE EXOGORTHS WERE A SURPRISE TO MAND'ALOR -- UPSETTING HIS PLANS. HE WILL BE SATISFIED IF NO ONE CONTROLS THEM.
AND TO SAVE JARAEL -- YOU HAVE MY LAST BREATH.
YOU WERE AROUND THE CON ARTIST TOO LONG.
BEST TEACHER I EVER HAD. HERE'S THE PLAN...

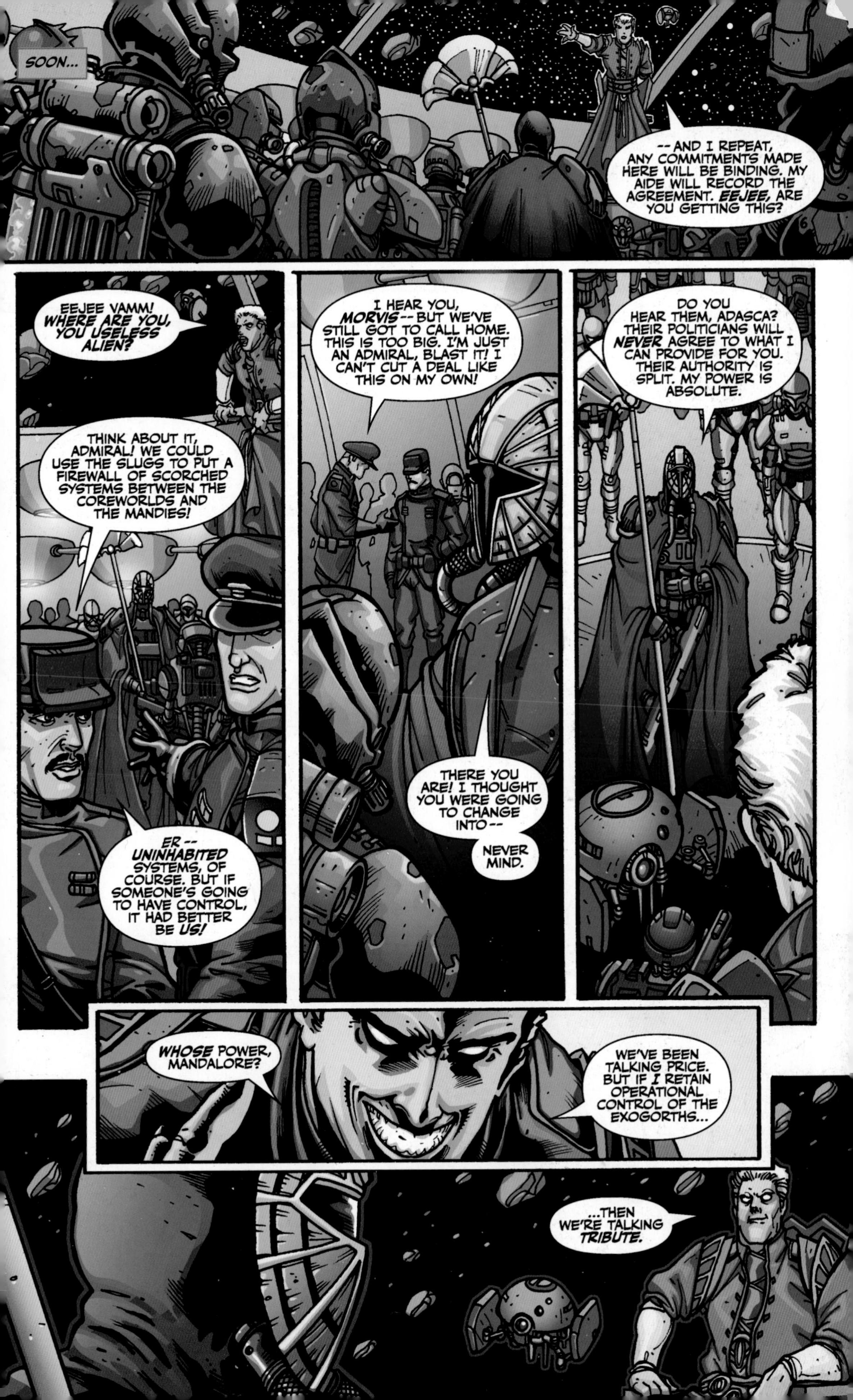
SOON...
--AND I REPEAT, ANY COMMITMENTS MADE HERE WILL BE BINDING. MY AIDE WILL RECORD THE AGREEMENT. EEJEE, ARE YOU GETTING THIS?
EEJEE VAMM! WHERE ARE YOU, YOU USELESS ALIEN?
THINK ABOUT IT, ADMIRAL! WE COULD USE THE SLUGS TO PUT A FIREWALL OF SCORCHED SYSTEMS BETWEEN THE COREWORLDS AND THE MANDIES!
ER -- UNINHABITED SYSTEMS, OF COURSE. BUT IF SOMEONE'S GOING TO HAVE CONTROL, IT HAD BETTER BE US!
I HEAR YOU, MORVIS-- BUT WE'VE STILL GOT TO CALL HOME. THIS IS TOO BIG. I'M JUST AN ADMIRAL, BLAST IT! I CAN'T CUT A DEAL LIKE THIS ON MY OWN!
THERE YOU ARE! I THOUGHT YOU WERE GOING TO CHANGE INTO--
NEVER MIND.
DO YOU HEAR THEM, ADASCA? THEIR POLITICIANS WILL NEVER AGREE TO WHAT I CAN PROVIDE FOR YOU. THEIR AUTHORITY IS SPLIT. MY POWER IS ABSOLUTE.
WHOSE POWER, MANDALORE?
WE'VE BEEN TALKING PRICE. BUT IF I RETAIN OPERATIONAL CONTROL OF THE EXOGORTHS...
...THEN WE'RE TALKING TRIBUTE.

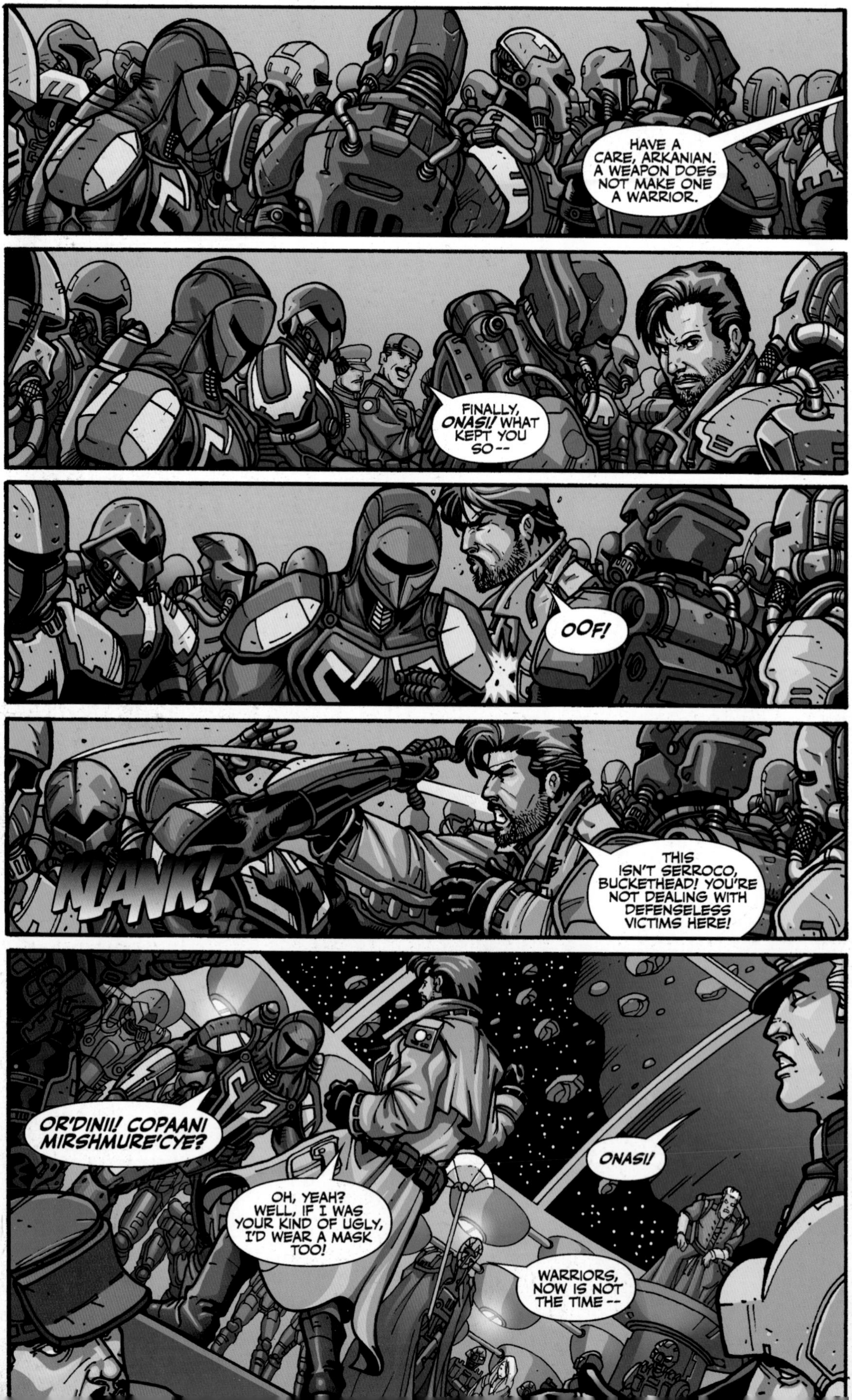
HAVE A CARE, ARKANIAN. A WEAPON DOES NOT MAKE ONE A WARRIOR.
FINALLY, ONASI! WHAT KEPT YOU SO--
OOF!
KLANK!
THIS ISN'T SERROCO, BUCKETHEAD! YOU'RE NOT DEALING WITH DEFENSELESS VICTIMS HERE!
OR'DINII! COPAANI MIRSHMURE'CYE?
OH, YEAH? WELL, IF I WAS YOUR KIND OF UGLY, I'D WEAR A MASK TOO!
ONASI!
WARRIORS, NOW IS NOT THE TIME --

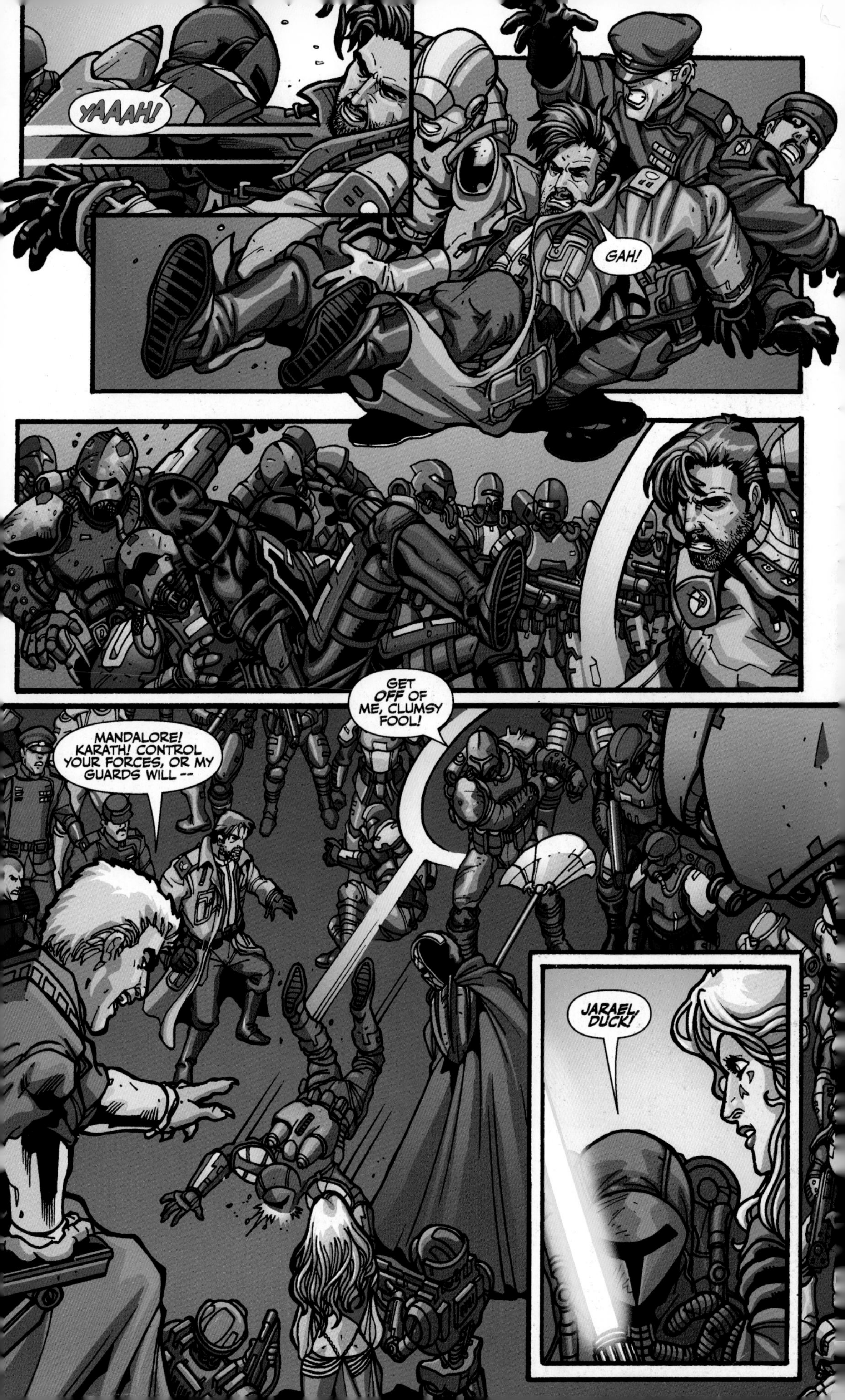
YAAAH!
GAH!
GET OFF OF ME, CLUMSY FOOL!
MANDALORE! KARATH! CONTROL YOUR FORCES, OR MY GUARDS WILL --
JARAEL, DUCK!

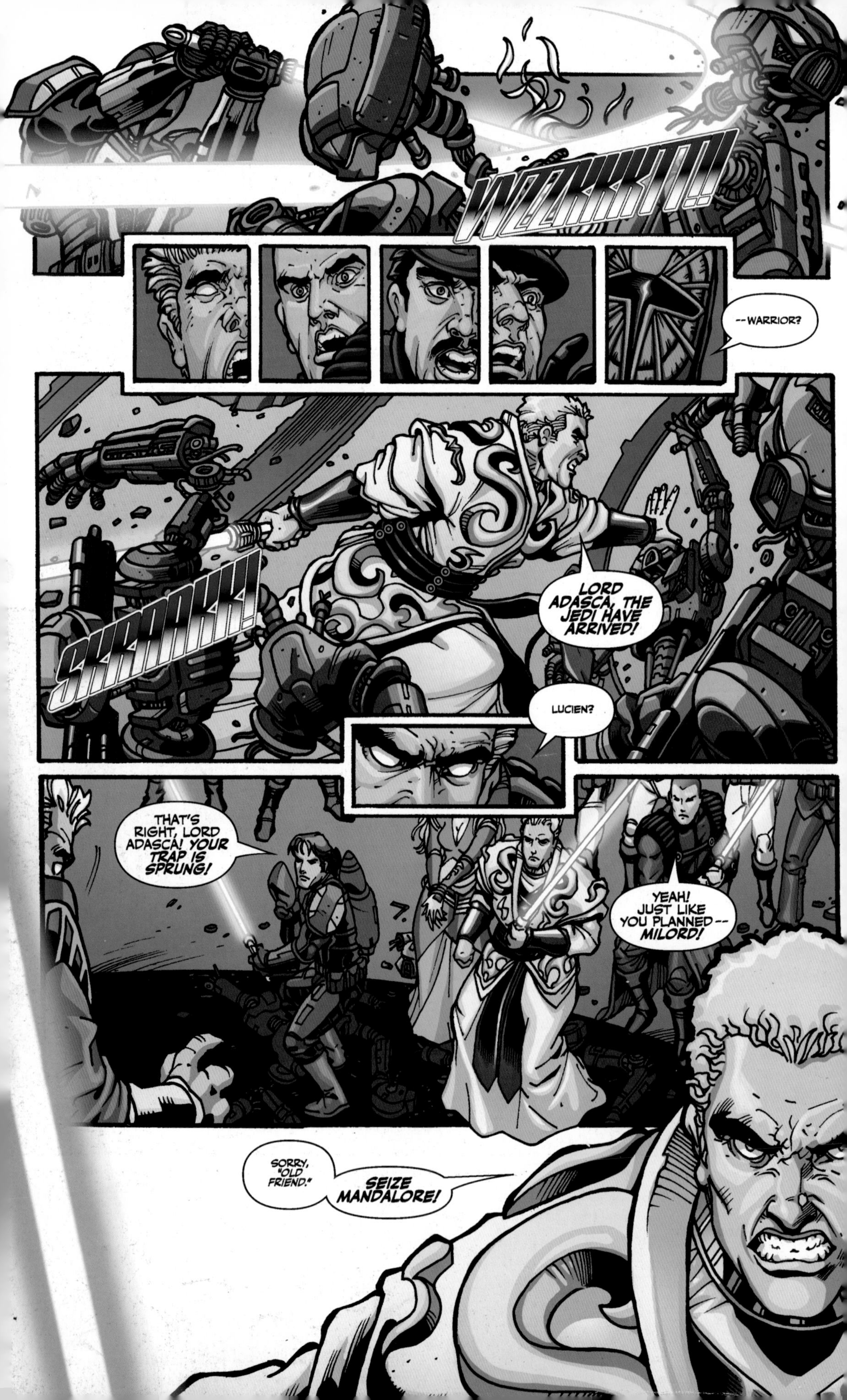
VVZZRKKKTT!!
--WARRIOR?
SKROAKK!
LORD ADASCA, THE JEDI HAVE ARRIVED!
LUCIEN?
THAT'S RIGHT, LORD ADASCA! YOUR TRAP IS SPRUNG!
YEAH! JUST LIKE YOU PLANNED-- MILORD!
SORRY, "OLD FRIEND."
SEIZE MANDALORE!

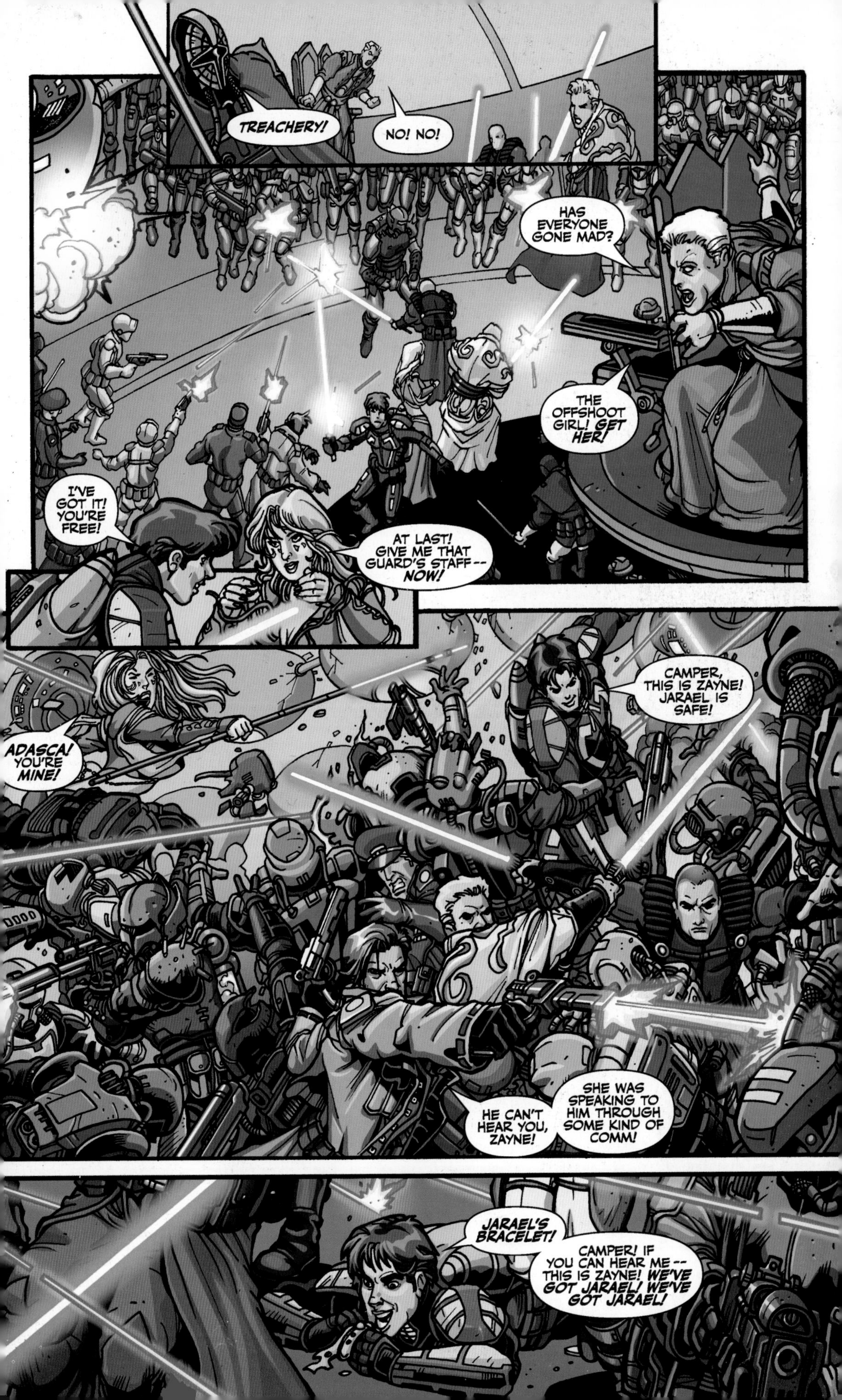

TREACHERY!
NO! NO!
HAS EVERYONE GONE MAD?
THE OFFSHOOT GIRL! GET HER!
I'VE GOT IT! YOU'RE FREE!
AT LAST! GIVE ME THAT GUARD'S STAFF-- NOW!
ADASCA! YOU'RE MINE!
CAMPER, THIS IS ZAYNE! JARAEL IS SAFE!
SHE WAS SPEAKING TO HIM THROUGH SOME KIND OF COMM!
HE CAN'T HEAR YOU, ZAYNE!
JARAEL'S BRACELET!
CAMPER! IF YOU CAN HEAR ME -- THIS IS ZAYNE! WE'VE GOT JARAEL! WE'VE GOT JARAEL!

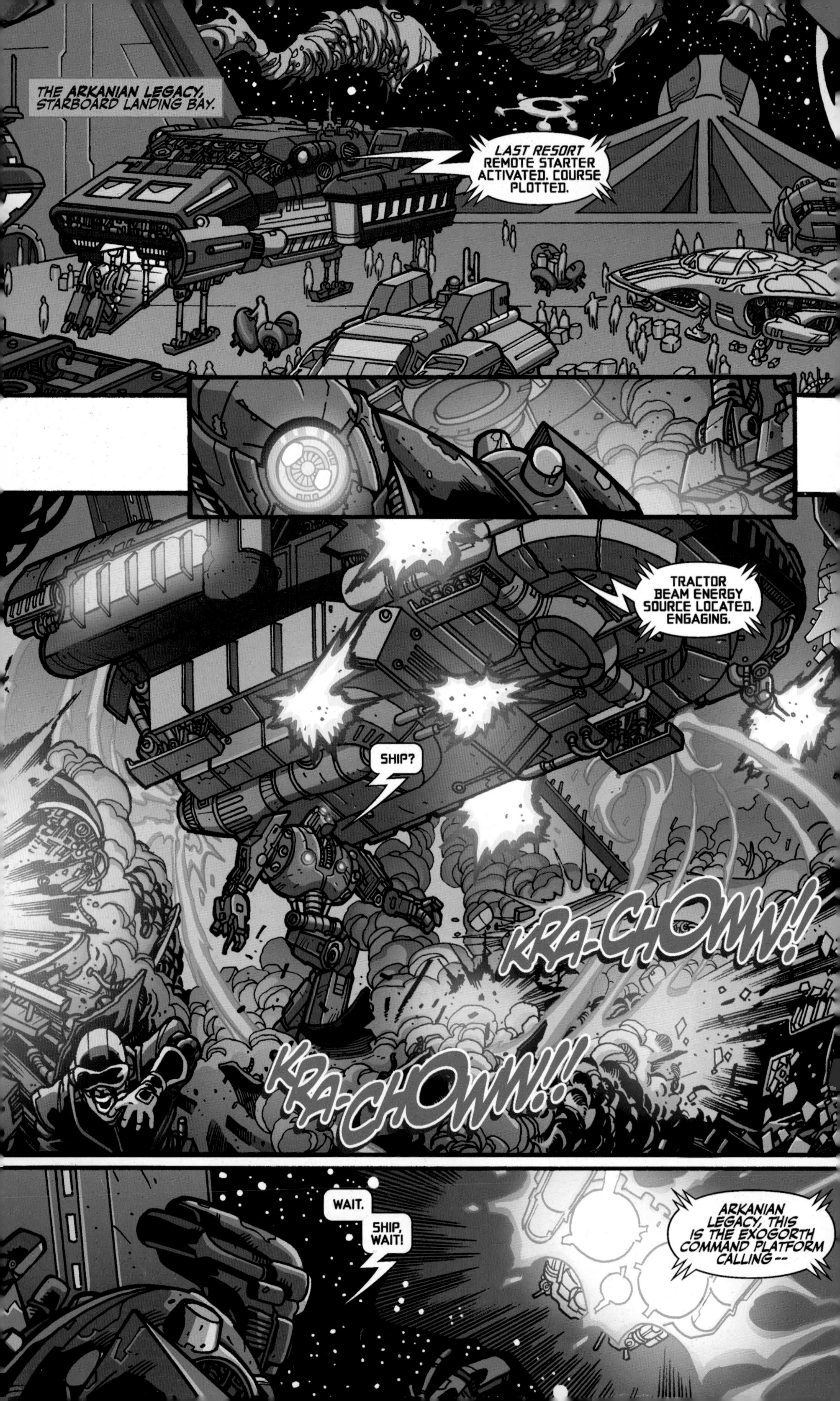
THE ARKANIAN LEGACY, STARBOARD LANDING BAY.
LAST RESORT REMOTE STARTER ACTIVATED. COURSE PLOTTED.
TRACTOR BEAM ENERGY SOURCE LOCATED. ENGAGING.
SHIP?
KRA-CHOWW!
KRA-CHOWW!!
WAIT.
SHIP, WAIT!
ARKANIAN LEGACY, THIS IS THE EXOGORTH COMMAND PLATFORM CALLING --

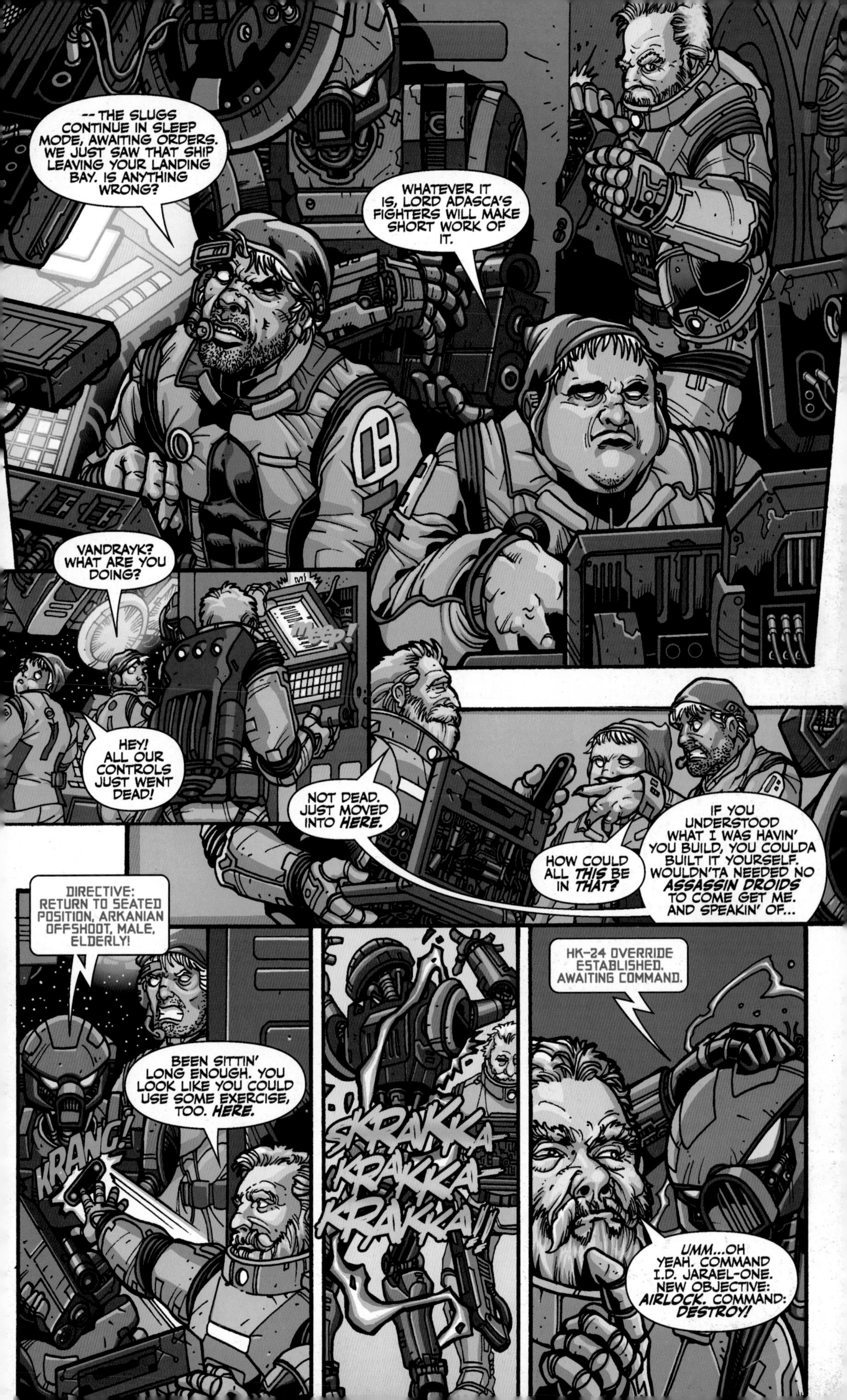
-- THE SLUGS CONTINUE IN SLEEP MODE, AWAITING ORDERS. WE JUST SAW THAT SHIP LEAVING YOUR LANDING BAY. IS ANYTHING WRONG?
WHATEVER IT IS, LORD ADASCA'S FIGHTERS WILL MAKE SHORT WORK OF IT.
VANDRAYK? WHAT ARE YOU DOING?
HEY! ALL OUR CONTROLS JUST WENT DEAD!
NOT DEAD. JUST MOVED INTO *HERE.*
HOW COULD ALL *THIS* BE IN *THAT?*
IF YOU UNDERSTOOD WHAT I WAS HAVIN' YOU BUILD, YOU COULDA BUILT IT YOURSELF. WOULDN'TA NEEDED NO *ASSASSIN DROIDS* TO COME GET ME. AND SPEAKIN' OF...
DIRECTIVE: RETURN TO SEATED POSITION, ARKANIAN OFFSHOOT, MALE, ELDERLY!
BEEN SITTIN' LONG ENOUGH. YOU LOOK LIKE YOU COULD USE SOME EXERCISE, TOO. *HERE.*
KRANG!
SKRAKKA KRAKKA KRAKKA!
HK-24 OVERRIDE ESTABLISHED. AWAITING COMMAND.
UMM...OH YEAH. COMMAND I.D. JARAEL-ONE. NEW OBJECTIVE: *AIRLOCK.* COMMAND: *DESTROY!*

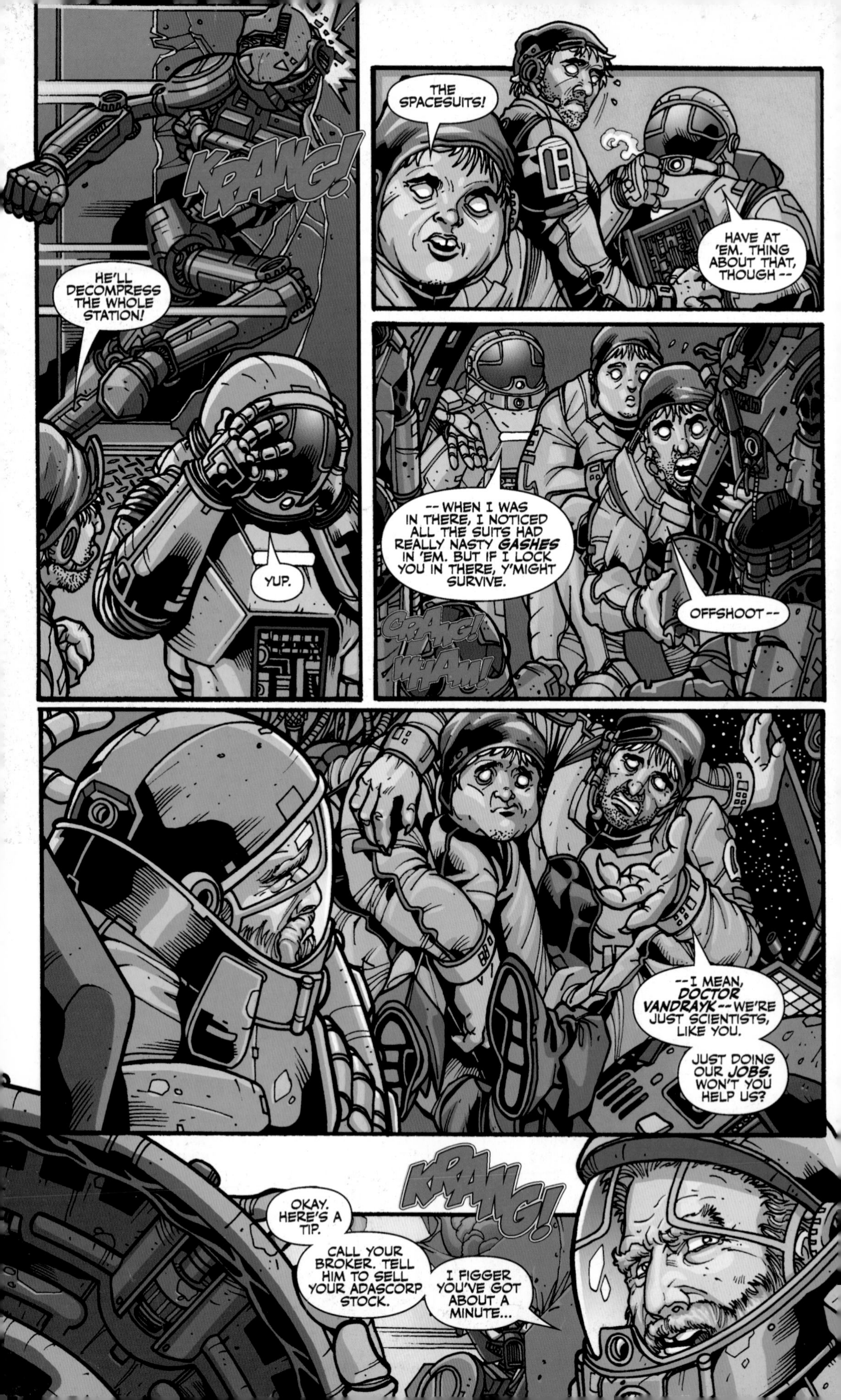
KRANG!
HE'LL DECOMPRESS THE WHOLE STATION!
YUP.
THE SPACESUITS!
HAVE AT 'EM. THING ABOUT THAT, THOUGH --
-- WHEN I WAS IN THERE, I NOTICED ALL THE SUITS HAD REALLY NASTY *GASHES* IN 'EM. BUT IF I LOCK YOU IN THERE, Y'MIGHT SURVIVE.
OFFSHOOT --
CRANG! WHAM!
-- I MEAN, ***DOCTOR VANDRAYK*** -- WE'RE JUST SCIENTISTS, LIKE YOU.
JUST DOING OUR *JOBS.* WON'T YOU HELP US?
KRANG!
OKAY. HERE'S A TIP.
CALL YOUR BROKER. TELL HIM TO SELL YOUR ADASCORP STOCK.
I FIGGER YOU'VE GOT ABOUT A MINUTE...

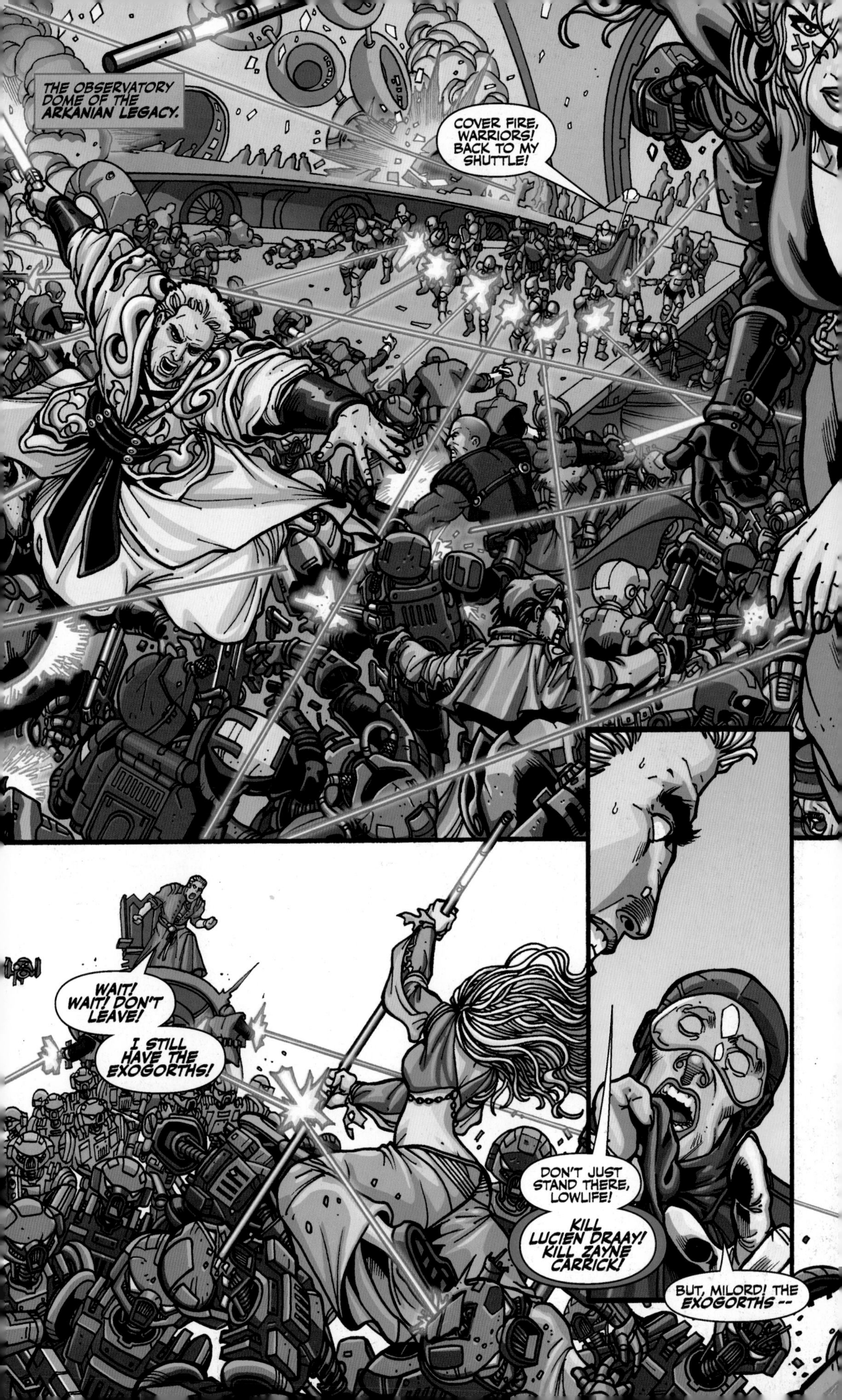
THE OBSERVATORY DOME OF THE ARKANIAN LEGACY.
COVER FIRE, WARRIORS! BACK TO MY SHUTTLE!
WAIT! WAIT! DON'T LEAVE!
I STILL HAVE THE EXOGORTHS!
DON'T JUST STAND THERE, LOWLIFE!
KILL LUCIEN DRAAY! KILL ZAYNE CARRICK!
BUT, MILORD! THE EXOGORTHS --

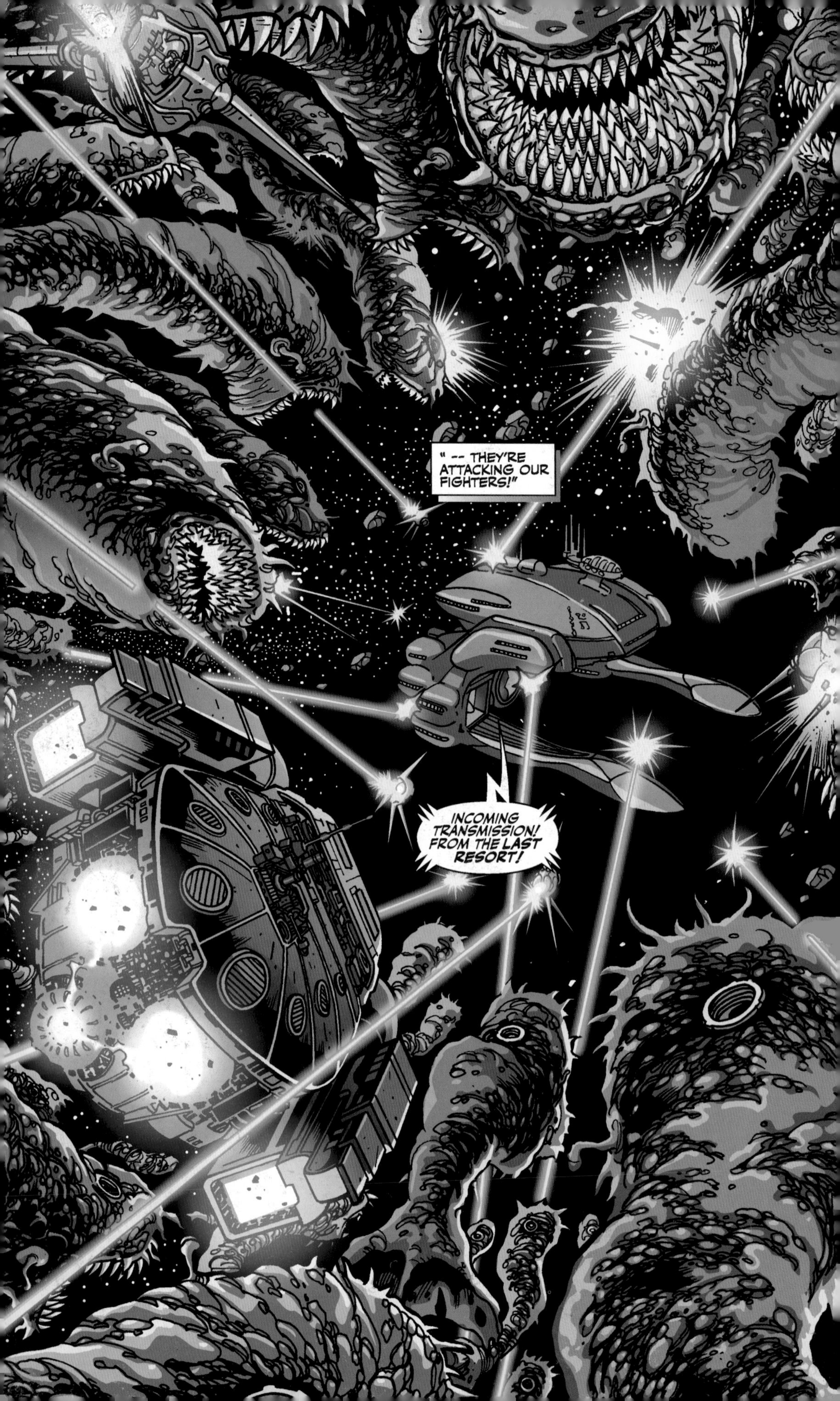
" -- THEY'RE ATTACKING OUR FIGHTERS!"
INCOMING TRANSMISSION! FROM THE LAST RESORT!

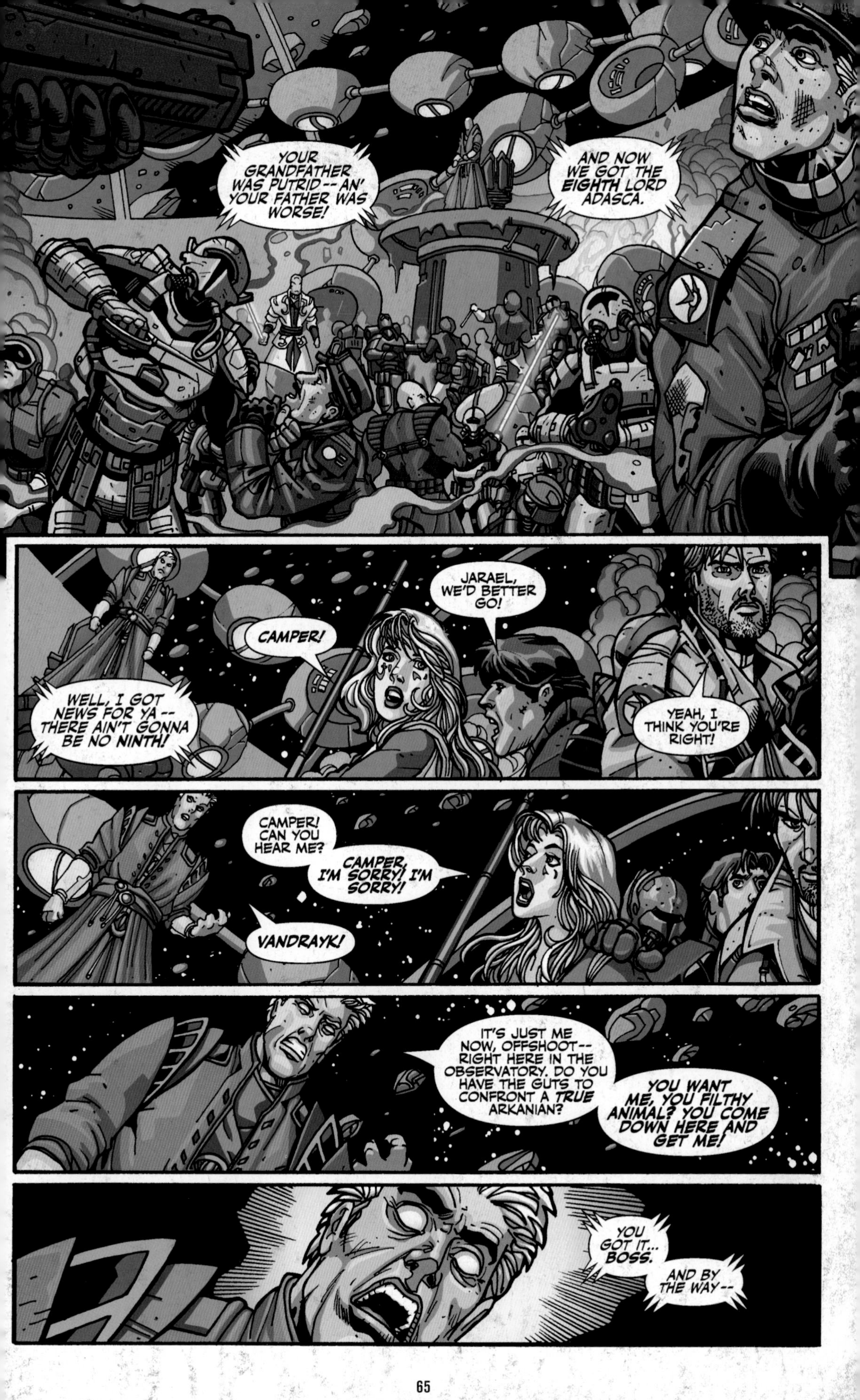
YOUR GRANDFATHER WAS PUTRID-- AN' YOUR FATHER WAS WORSE!
AND NOW WE GOT THE EIGHTH LORD ADASCA.
WELL, I GOT NEWS FOR YA-- THERE AIN'T GONNA BE NO NINTH!
CAMPER!
JARAEL, WE'D BETTER GO!
YEAH, I THINK YOU'RE RIGHT!
CAMPER! CAN YOU HEAR ME?
CAMPER, I'M SORRY! I'M SORRY!
VANDRAYK!
IT'S JUST ME NOW, OFFSHOOT-- RIGHT HERE IN THE OBSERVATORY. DO YOU HAVE THE GUTS TO CONFRONT A TRUE ARKANIAN?
YOU WANT ME, YOU FILTHY ANIMAL? YOU COME DOWN HERE AND GET ME!
YOU GOT IT... BOSS.
AND BY THE WAY--

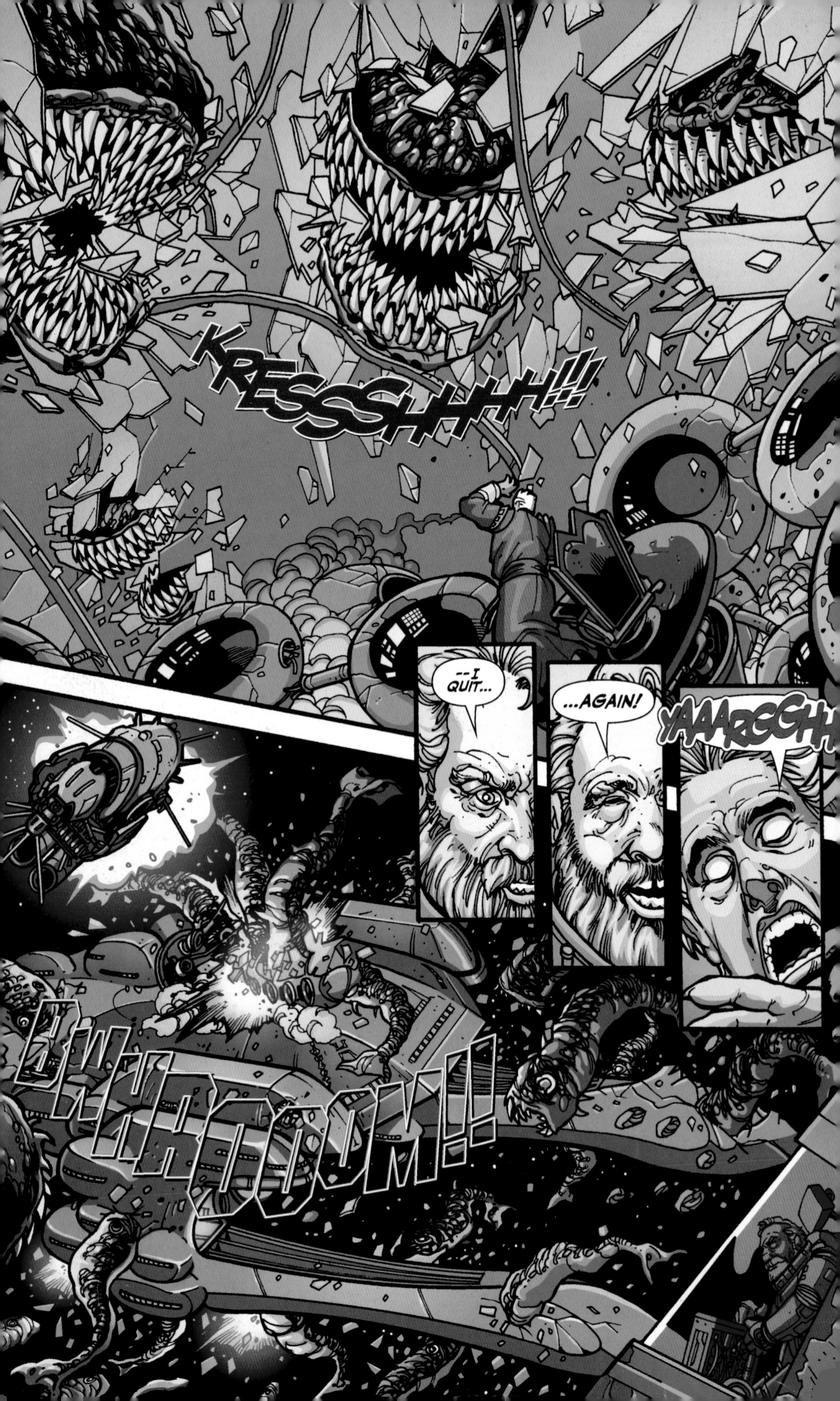
KRESSSHHHH!!!
--I QUIT...
...AGAIN!
YAAARGGHH
BWHOOOOM!!

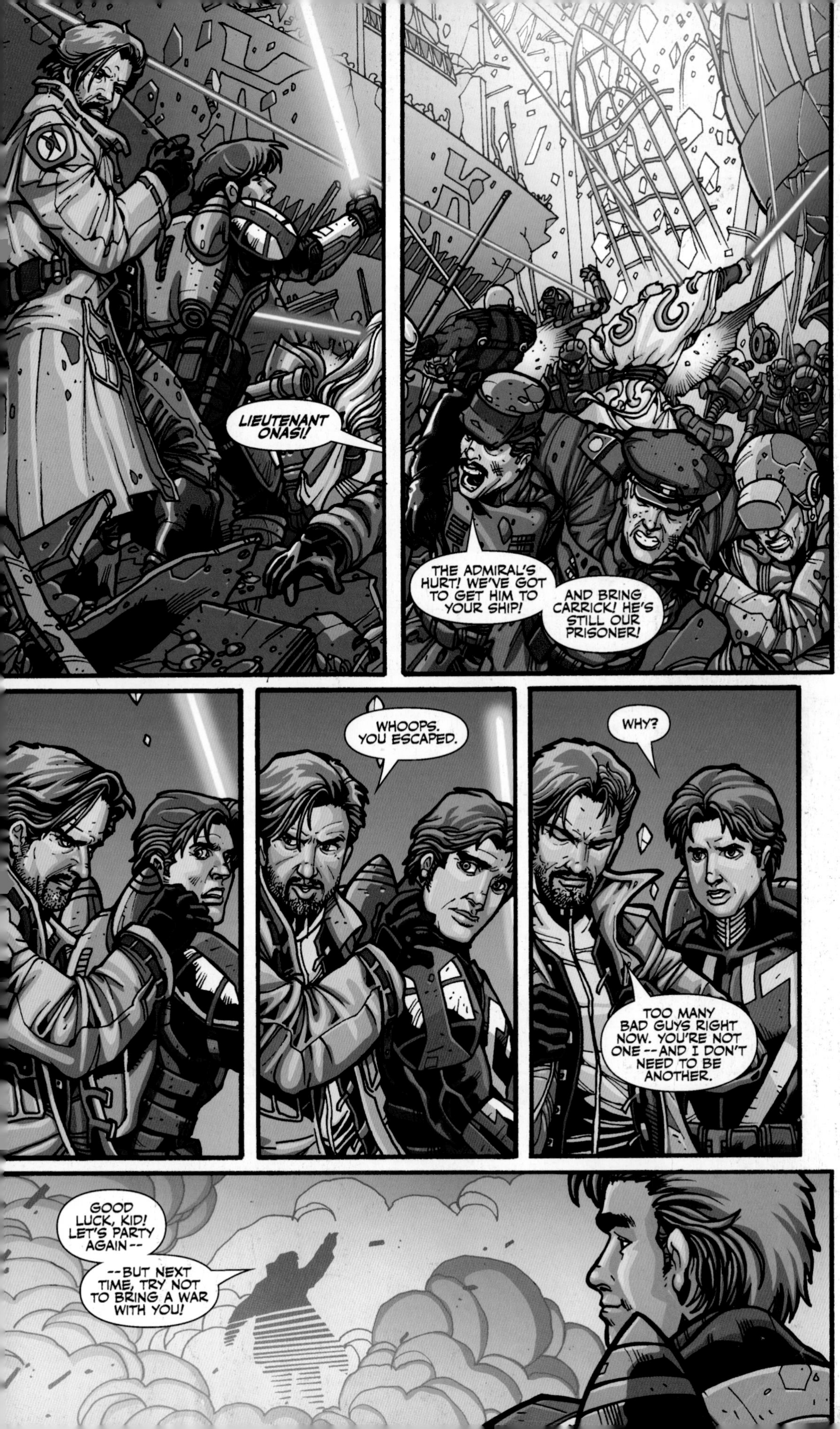
LIEUTENANT ONASI!
THE ADMIRAL'S HURT! WE'VE GOT TO GET HIM TO YOUR SHIP!
AND BRING CARRICK! HE'S STILL OUR PRISONER!
WHOOPS. YOU ESCAPED.
WHY?
TOO MANY BAD GUYS RIGHT NOW. YOU'RE NOT ONE --AND I DON'T NEED TO BE ANOTHER.
GOOD LUCK, KID! LET'S PARTY AGAIN--
--BUT NEXT TIME, TRY NOT TO BRING A WAR WITH YOU!

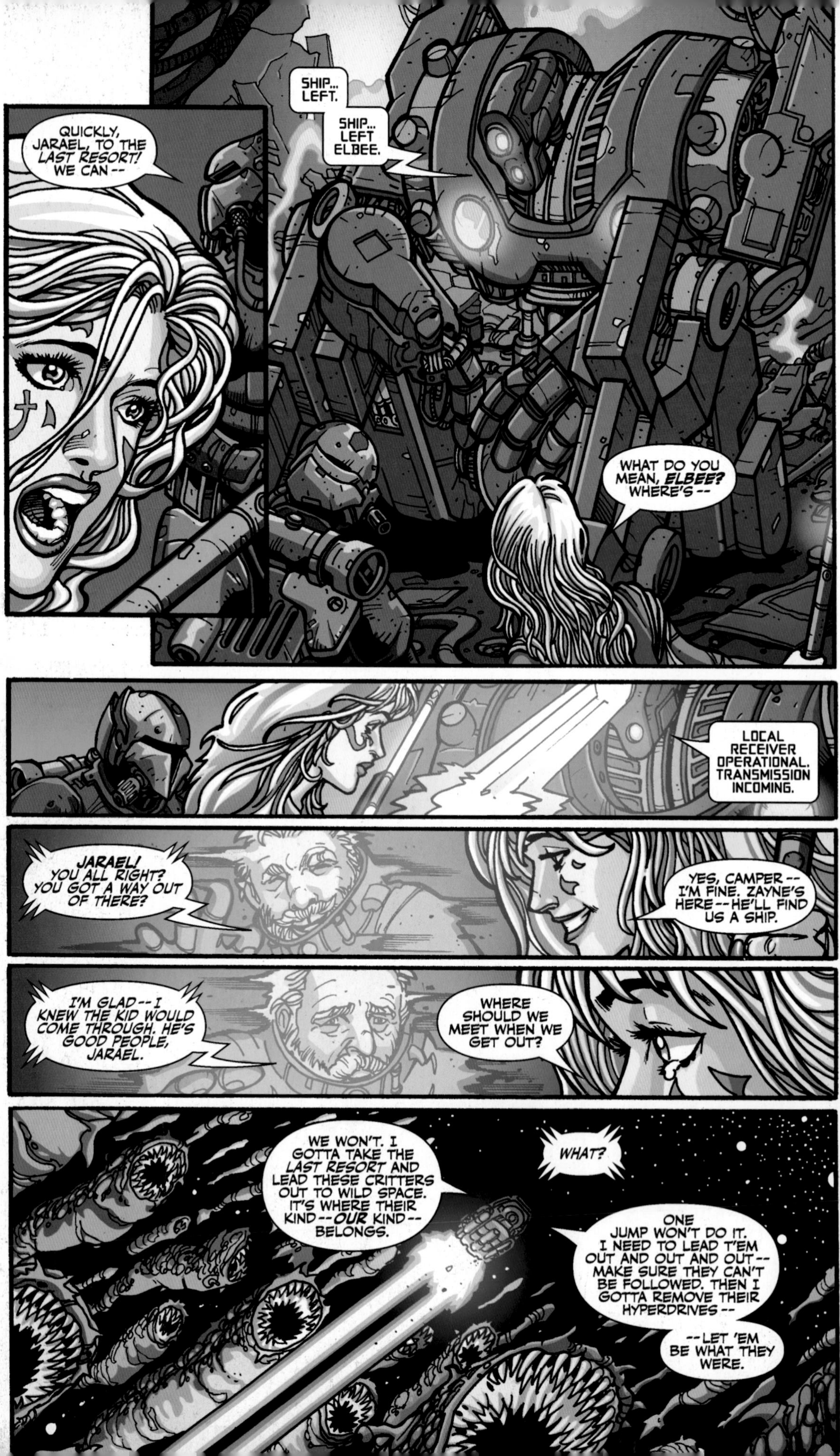
QUICKLY, JARAEL, TO THE LAST RESORT! WE CAN--
SHIP... LEFT.
SHIP... LEFT ELBEE.
WHAT DO YOU MEAN, ELBEE? WHERE'S--
LOCAL RECEIVER OPERATIONAL. TRANSMISSION INCOMING.
JARAEL! YOU ALL RIGHT? YOU GOT A WAY OUT OF THERE?
YES, CAMPER-- I'M FINE. ZAYNE'S HERE--HE'LL FIND US A SHIP.
I'M GLAD--I KNEW THE KID WOULD COME THROUGH. HE'S GOOD PEOPLE, JARAEL.
WHERE SHOULD WE MEET WHEN WE GET OUT?
WE WON'T. I GOTTA TAKE THE LAST RESORT AND LEAD THESE CRITTERS OUT TO WILD SPACE. IT'S WHERE THEIR KIND--OUR KIND--BELONGS.
WHAT?
ONE JUMP WON'T DO IT. I NEED TO LEAD T'EM OUT AND OUT AND OUT--MAKE SURE THEY CAN'T BE FOLLOWED. THEN I GOTTA REMOVE THEIR HYPERDRIVES--
--LET 'EM BE WHAT THEY WERE.

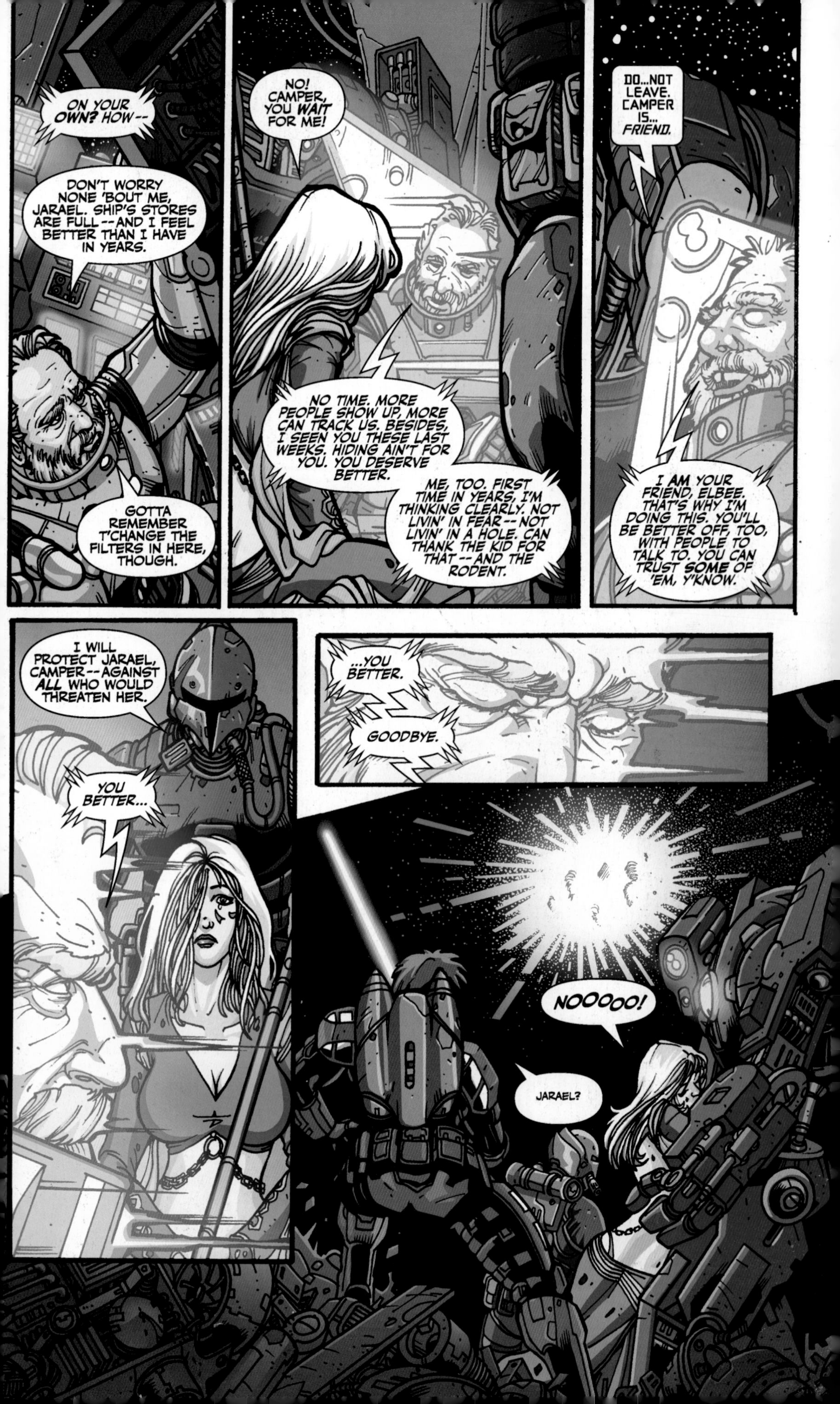

ON YOUR OWN? HOW--
DON'T WORRY NONE 'BOUT ME, JARAEL. SHIP'S STORES ARE FULL--AND I FEEL BETTER THAN I HAVE IN YEARS.
GOTTA REMEMBER T'CHANGE THE FILTERS IN HERE, THOUGH.
NO! CAMPER, YOU WAIT FOR ME!
NO TIME. MORE PEOPLE SHOW UP, MORE CAN TRACK US. BESIDES, I SEEN YOU THESE LAST WEEKS. HIDING AIN'T FOR YOU. YOU DESERVE BETTER.
ME, TOO. FIRST TIME IN YEARS, I'M THINKING CLEARLY. NOT LIVIN' IN FEAR--NOT LIVIN' IN A HOLE. CAN THANK THE KID FOR THAT--AND THE RODENT.
DO...NOT LEAVE. CAMPER IS... FRIEND.
I AM YOUR FRIEND, ELBEE. THAT'S WHY I'M DOING THIS. YOU'LL BE BETTER OFF, TOO, WITH PEOPLE TO TALK TO. YOU CAN TRUST SOME OF 'EM, Y'KNOW.
I WILL PROTECT JARAEL, CAMPER--AGAINST ALL WHO WOULD THREATEN HER.
YOU BETTER...
...YOU BETTER.
GOODBYE.
NOOOOO!
JARAEL?

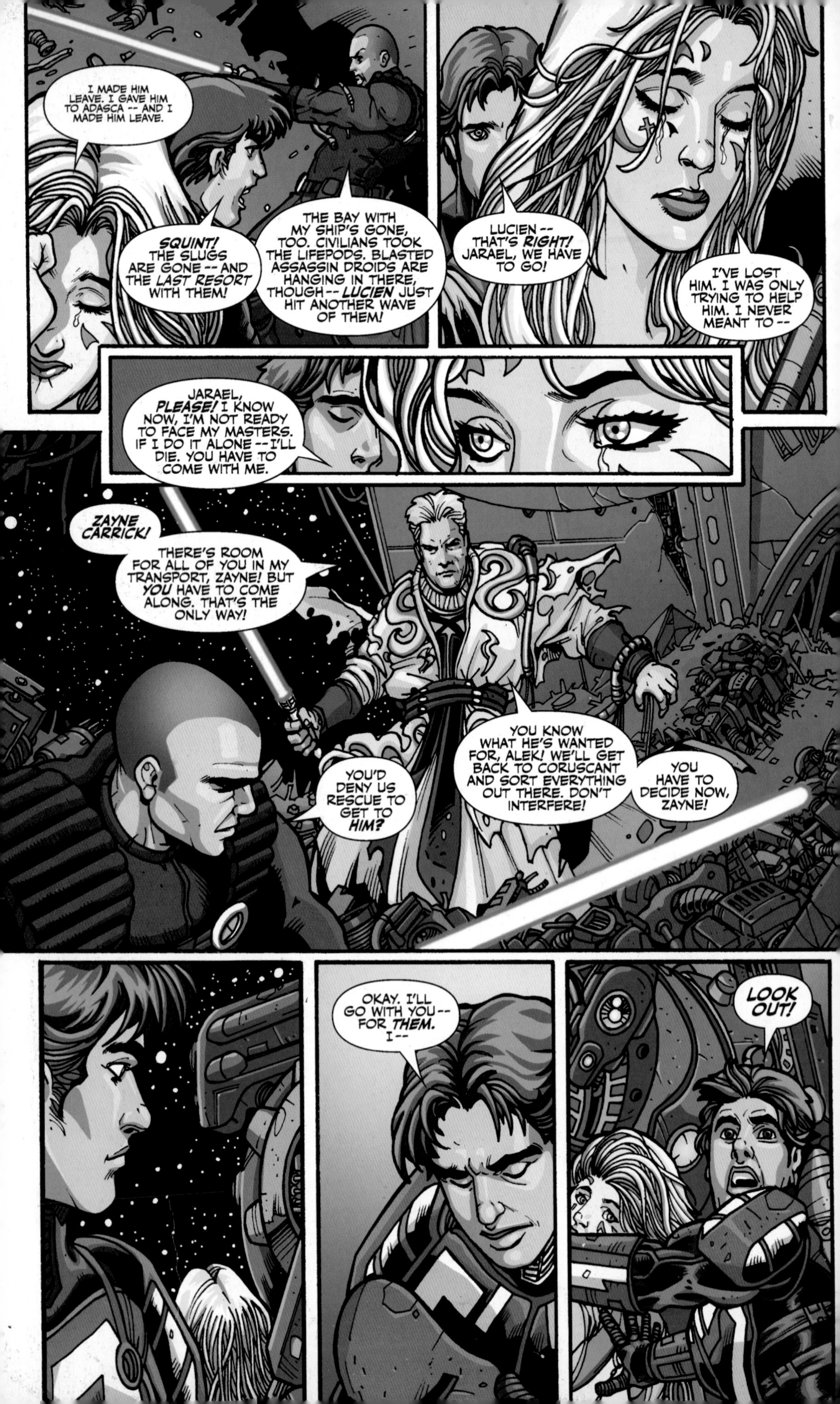

I MADE HIM LEAVE. I GAVE HIM TO ADASCA -- AND I MADE HIM LEAVE.
SQUINT! THE SLUGS ARE GONE -- AND THE LAST RESORT WITH THEM!
THE BAY WITH MY SHIP'S GONE, TOO. CIVILIANS TOOK THE LIFEPODS. BLASTED ASSASSIN DROIDS ARE HANGING IN THERE, THOUGH -- LUCIEN JUST HIT ANOTHER WAVE OF THEM!
LUCIEN -- THAT'S RIGHT! JARAEL, WE HAVE TO GO!
I'VE LOST HIM. I WAS ONLY TRYING TO HELP HIM. I NEVER MEANT TO --
JARAEL, PLEASE! I KNOW NOW, I'M NOT READY TO FACE MY MASTERS. IF I DO IT ALONE -- I'LL DIE. YOU HAVE TO COME WITH ME.
ZAYNE CARRICK!
THERE'S ROOM FOR ALL OF YOU IN MY TRANSPORT, ZAYNE! BUT YOU HAVE TO COME ALONG. THAT'S THE ONLY WAY!
YOU'D DENY US RESCUE TO GET TO HIM?
YOU KNOW WHAT HE'S WANTED FOR, ALEK! WE'LL GET BACK TO CORUSCANT AND SORT EVERYTHING OUT THERE. DON'T INTERFERE!
YOU HAVE TO DECIDE NOW, ZAYNE!
OKAY. I'LL GO WITH YOU -- FOR THEM. I --
LOOK OUT!

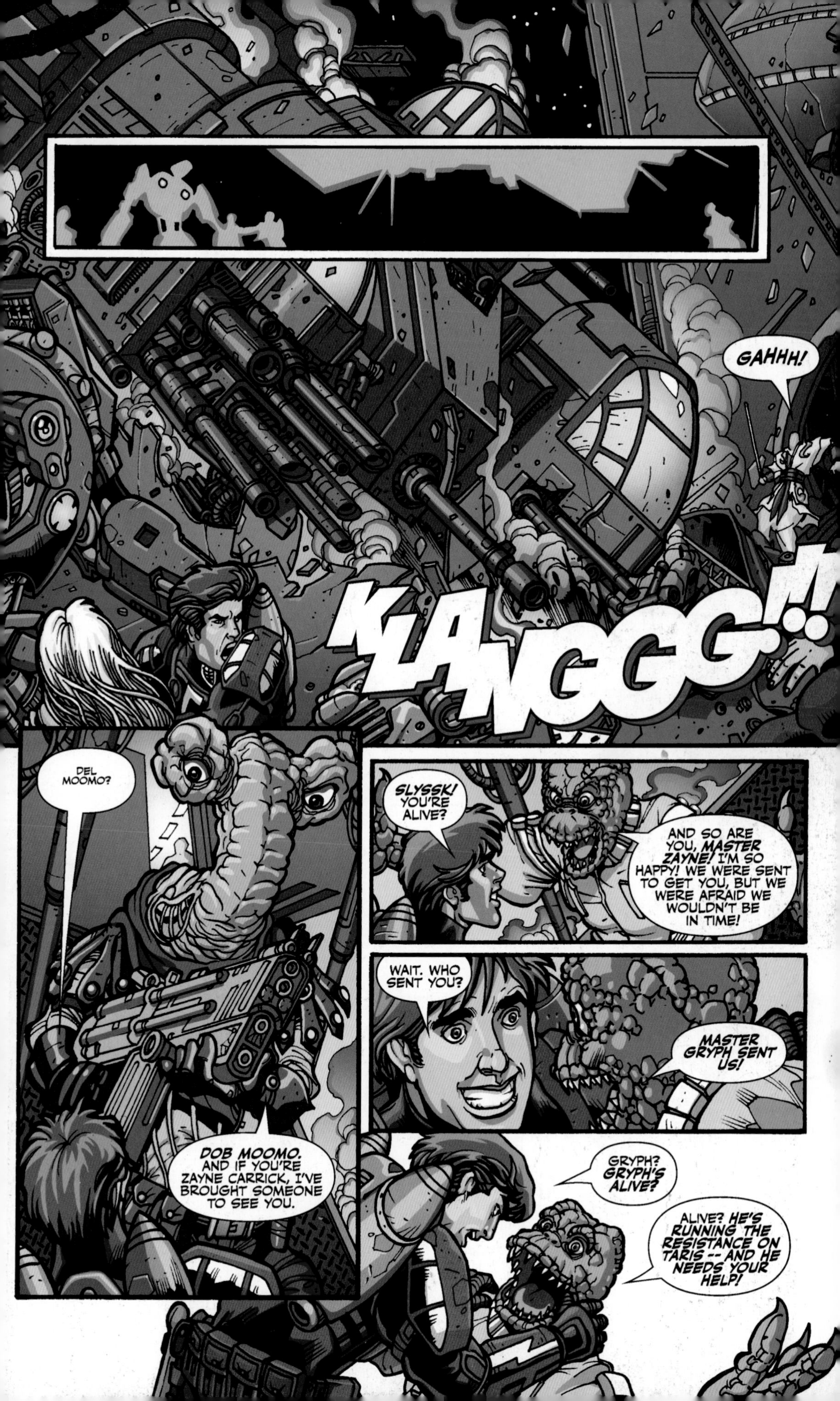
GAHHH!
KLANGGG!!
DEL MOOMO?
DOB MOOMO. AND IF YOU'RE ZAYNE CARRICK, I'VE BROUGHT SOMEONE TO SEE YOU.
SLYSSK! YOU'RE ALIVE?
AND SO ARE YOU, MASTER ZAYNE! I'M SO HAPPY! WE WERE SENT TO GET YOU, BUT WE WERE AFRAID WE WOULDN'T BE IN TIME!
WAIT. WHO SENT YOU?
MASTER GRYPH SENT US!
GRYPH? GRYPH'S ALIVE?
ALIVE? HE'S RUNNING THE RESISTANCE ON TARIS -- AND HE NEEDS YOUR HELP!

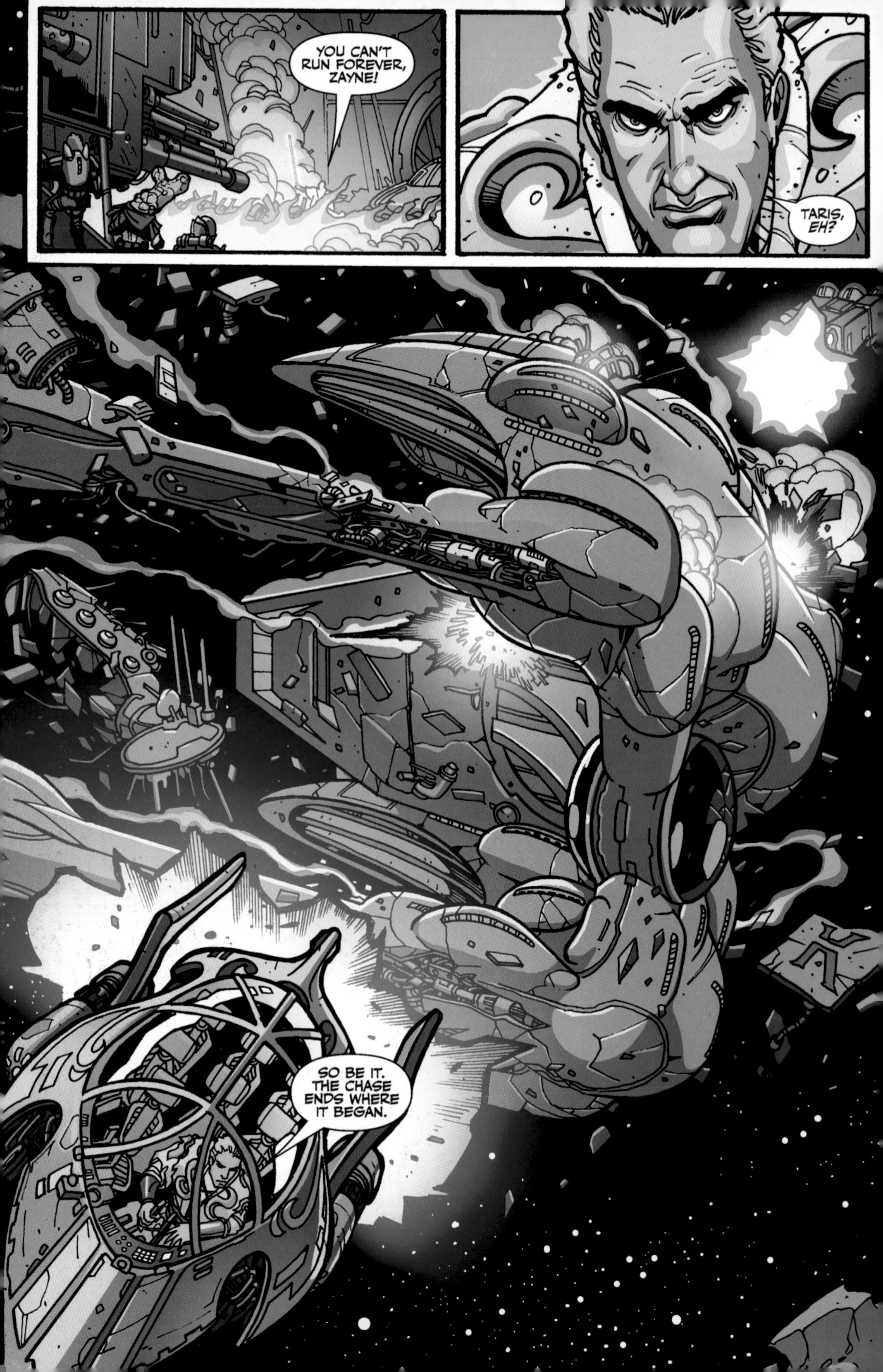
YOU CAN'T RUN FOREVER, ZAYNE!
TARIS, EH?
SO BE IT. THE CHASE ENDS WHERE IT BEGAN.

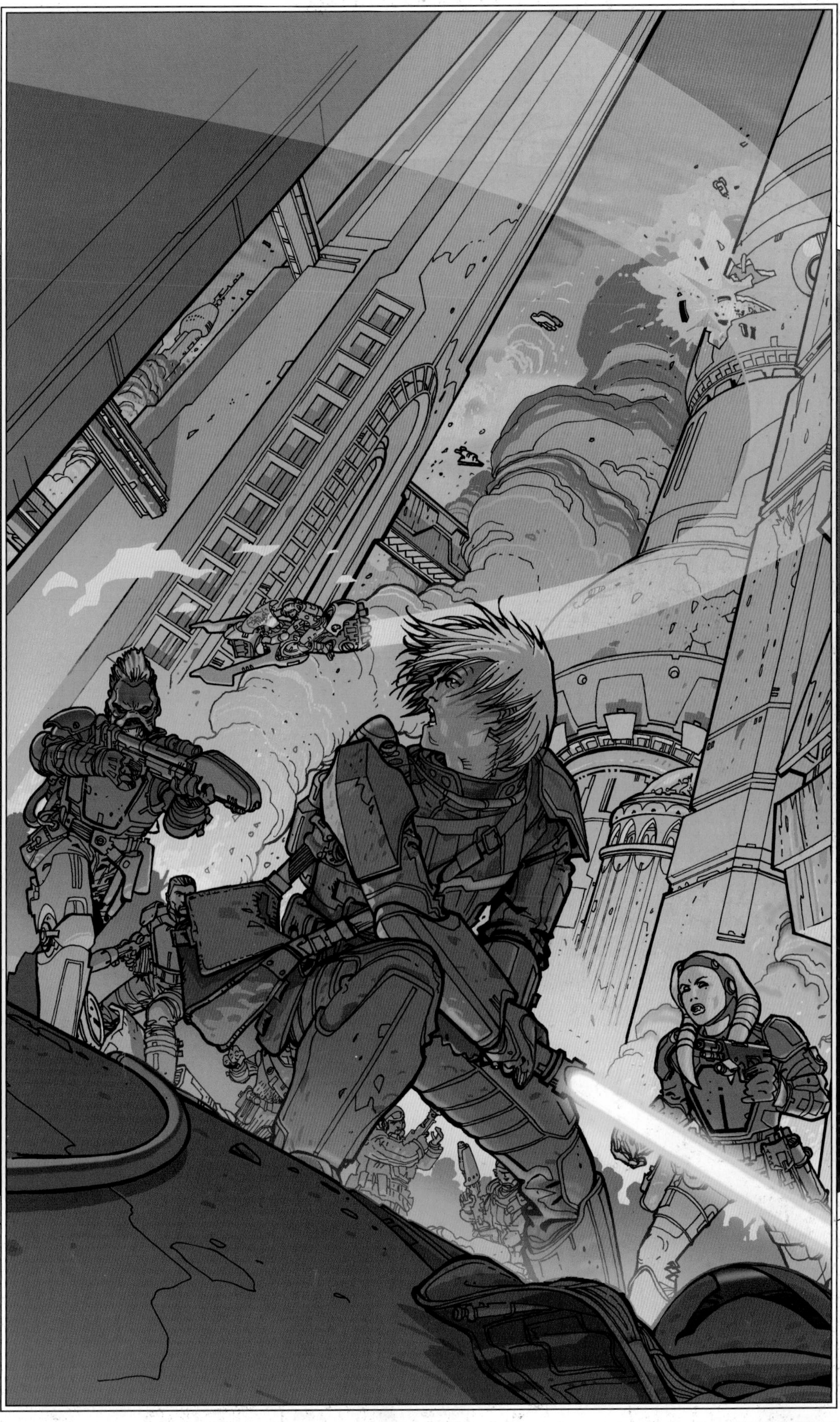

ILLUSTRATION BY COLIN WILSON

STAGING AREAS! PROCESSING! I *LEFT* THE REPUBLIC MILITARY BECAUSE OF THIS GARBAGE!

OH, YEAH? HAVE YOU EVER SEEN A SERPENT SWALLOWING A BANTHA?

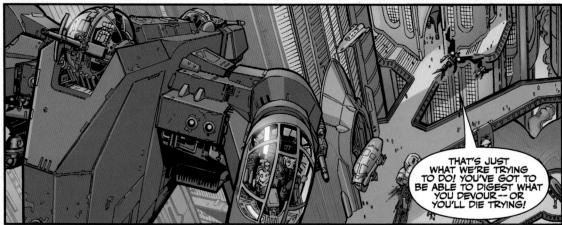

THAT'S JUST WHAT WE'RE TRYING TO DO! YOU'VE GOT TO BE ABLE TO DIGEST WHAT YOU DEVOUR -- OR YOU'LL DIE TRYING!

THAT'S WHY MAND'ALOR BROUGHT CASSUS IN ON TARIS. THIS PLACE IS JUST A TASTE OF WHAT WE'LL HAVE TO DEAL WITH WHEN WE GET TO CORUSCANT!

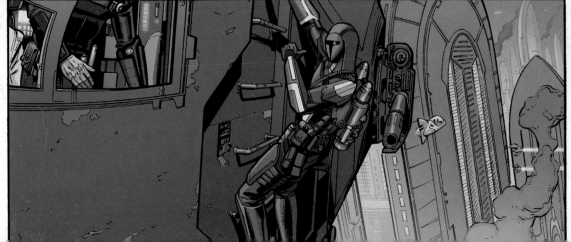

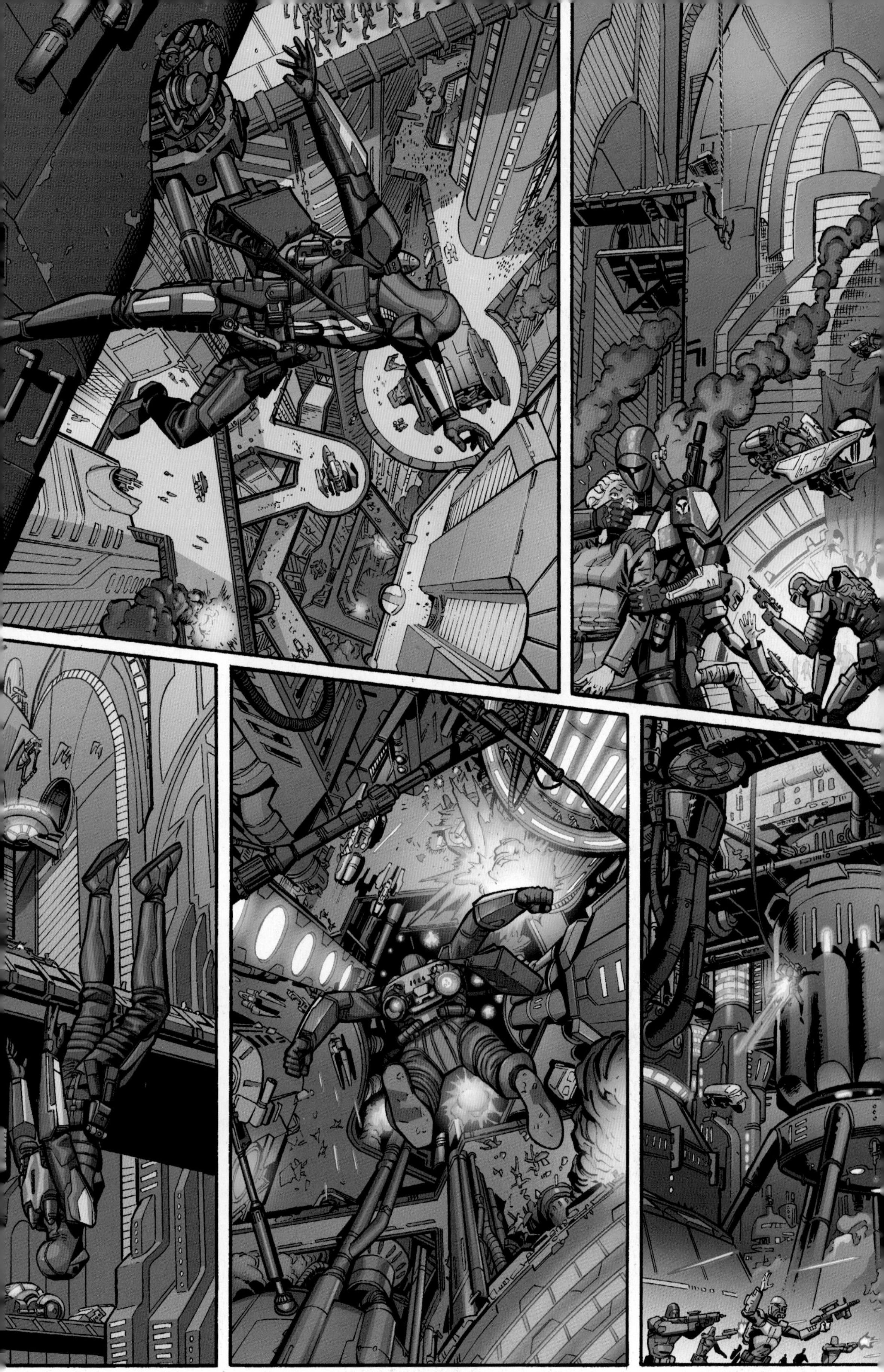

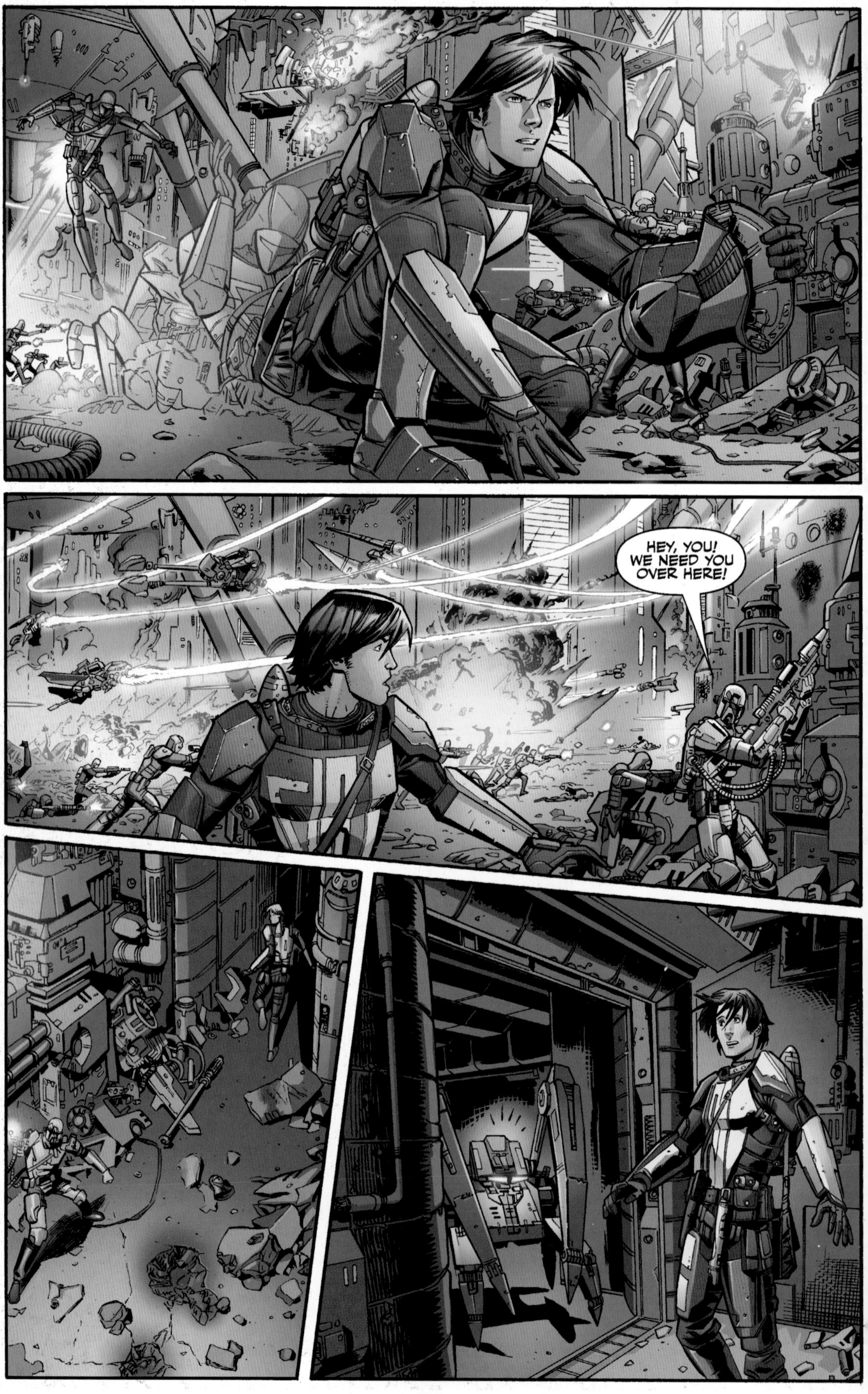
HEY, YOU! WE NEED YOU OVER HERE!

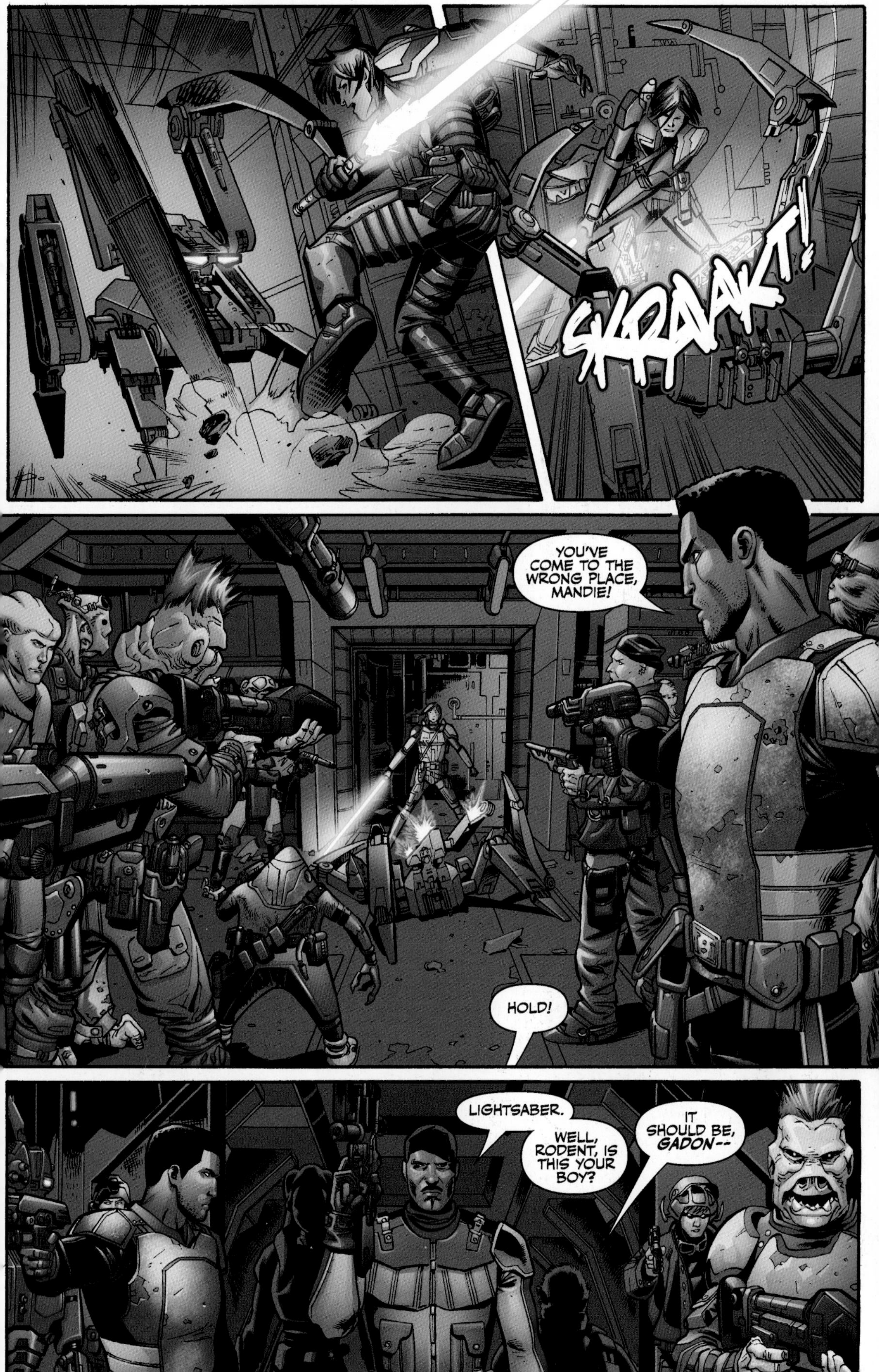
SKRAAKT!
YOU'VE COME TO THE WRONG PLACE, MANDIE!
HOLD!
LIGHTSABER.
WELL, RODENT, IS THIS YOUR BOY?
IT SHOULD BE, GADON--

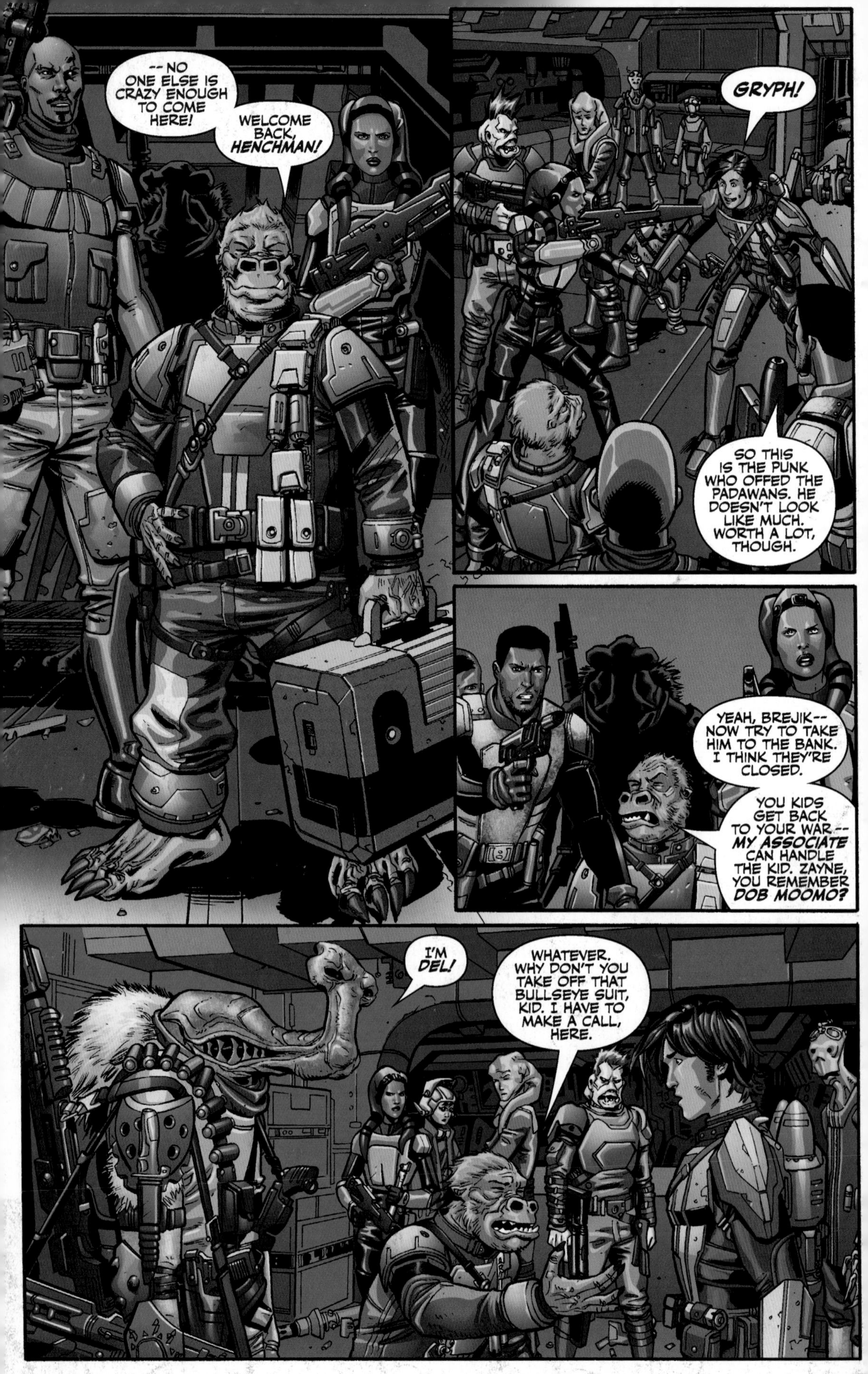
--NO ONE ELSE IS CRAZY ENOUGH TO COME HERE!
WELCOME BACK, HENCHMAN!
GRYPH!
SO THIS IS THE PUNK WHO OFFED THE PADAWANS. HE DOESN'T LOOK LIKE MUCH. WORTH A LOT, THOUGH.
YEAH, BREJIK-- NOW TRY TO TAKE HIM TO THE BANK. I THINK THEY'RE CLOSED.
YOU KIDS GET BACK TO YOUR WAR-- MY ASSOCIATE CAN HANDLE THE KID. ZAYNE, YOU REMEMBER DOB MOOMO?
I'M DEL!
WHATEVER. WHY DON'T YOU TAKE OFF THAT BULLSEYE SUIT, KID. I HAVE TO MAKE A CALL, HERE.

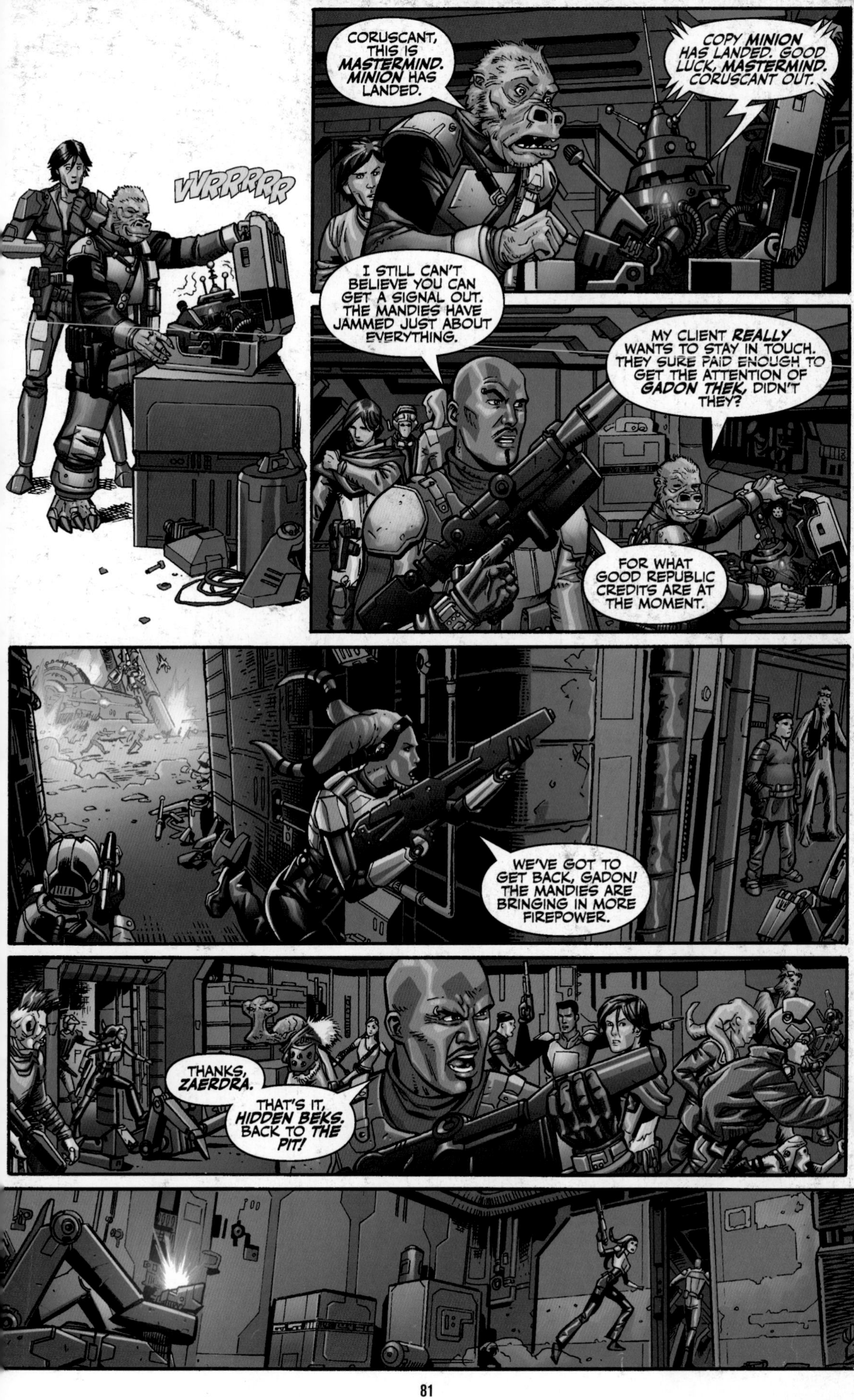
VVRRRRR
CORUSCANT, THIS IS MASTERMIND. MINION HAS LANDED.
COPY MINION HAS LANDED. GOOD LUCK, MASTERMIND. CORUSCANT OUT.
I STILL CAN'T BELIEVE YOU CAN GET A SIGNAL OUT. THE MANDIES HAVE JAMMED JUST ABOUT EVERYTHING.
MY CLIENT REALLY WANTS TO STAY IN TOUCH. THEY SURE PAID ENOUGH TO GET THE ATTENTION OF GADON THEK, DIDN'T THEY?
FOR WHAT GOOD REPUBLIC CREDITS ARE AT THE MOMENT.
WE'VE GOT TO GET BACK, GADON! THE MANDIES ARE BRINGING IN MORE FIREPOWER.
THANKS, ZAERDRA.
THAT'S IT, HIDDEN BEKS. BACK TO THE PIT!

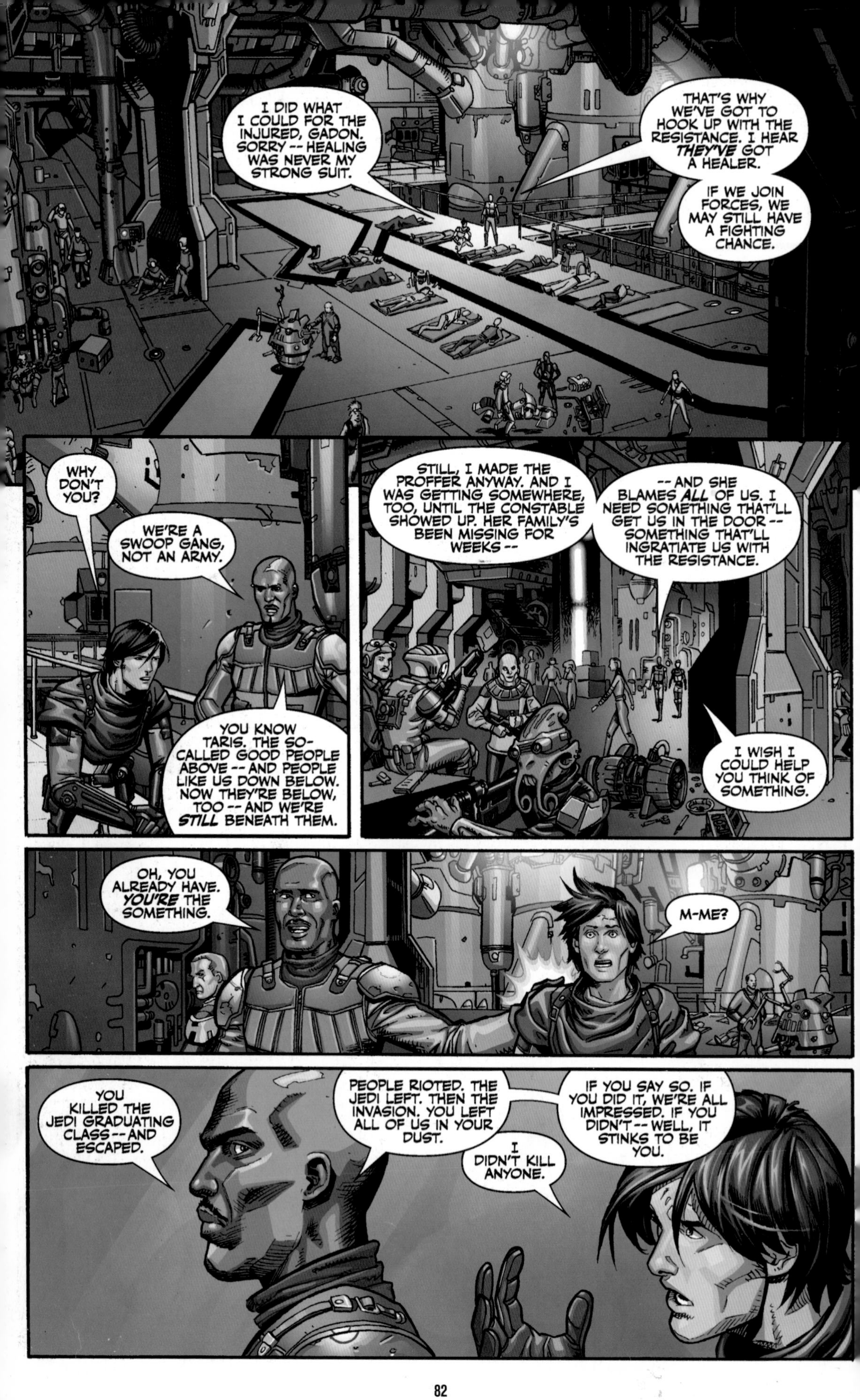
I DID WHAT I COULD FOR THE INJURED, GADON. SORRY -- HEALING WAS NEVER MY STRONG SUIT.
THAT'S WHY WE'VE GOT TO HOOK UP WITH THE RESISTANCE. I HEAR *THEY'VE* GOT A HEALER.
IF WE JOIN FORCES, WE MAY STILL HAVE A FIGHTING CHANCE.
WHY DON'T YOU?
WE'RE A SWOOP GANG, NOT AN ARMY.
YOU KNOW TARIS. THE SO-CALLED GOOD PEOPLE ABOVE -- AND PEOPLE LIKE US DOWN BELOW. NOW THEY'RE BELOW, TOO -- AND WE'RE *STILL* BENEATH THEM.
STILL, I MADE THE PROFFER ANYWAY. AND I WAS GETTING SOMEWHERE, TOO, UNTIL THE CONSTABLE SHOWED UP. HER FAMILY'S BEEN MISSING FOR WEEKS --
-- AND SHE BLAMES *ALL* OF US. I NEED SOMETHING THAT'LL GET US IN THE DOOR -- SOMETHING THAT'LL INGRATIATE US WITH THE RESISTANCE.
I WISH I COULD HELP YOU THINK OF SOMETHING.
OH, YOU ALREADY HAVE. *YOU'RE* THE SOMETHING.
M-ME?
YOU KILLED THE JEDI GRADUATING CLASS -- AND ESCAPED.
PEOPLE RIOTED. THE JEDI LEFT. THEN THE INVASION. YOU LEFT ALL OF US IN YOUR DUST.
I DIDN'T KILL ANYONE.
IF YOU SAY SO. IF YOU DID IT, WE'RE ALL IMPRESSED. IF YOU DIDN'T -- WELL, IT STINKS TO BE YOU.

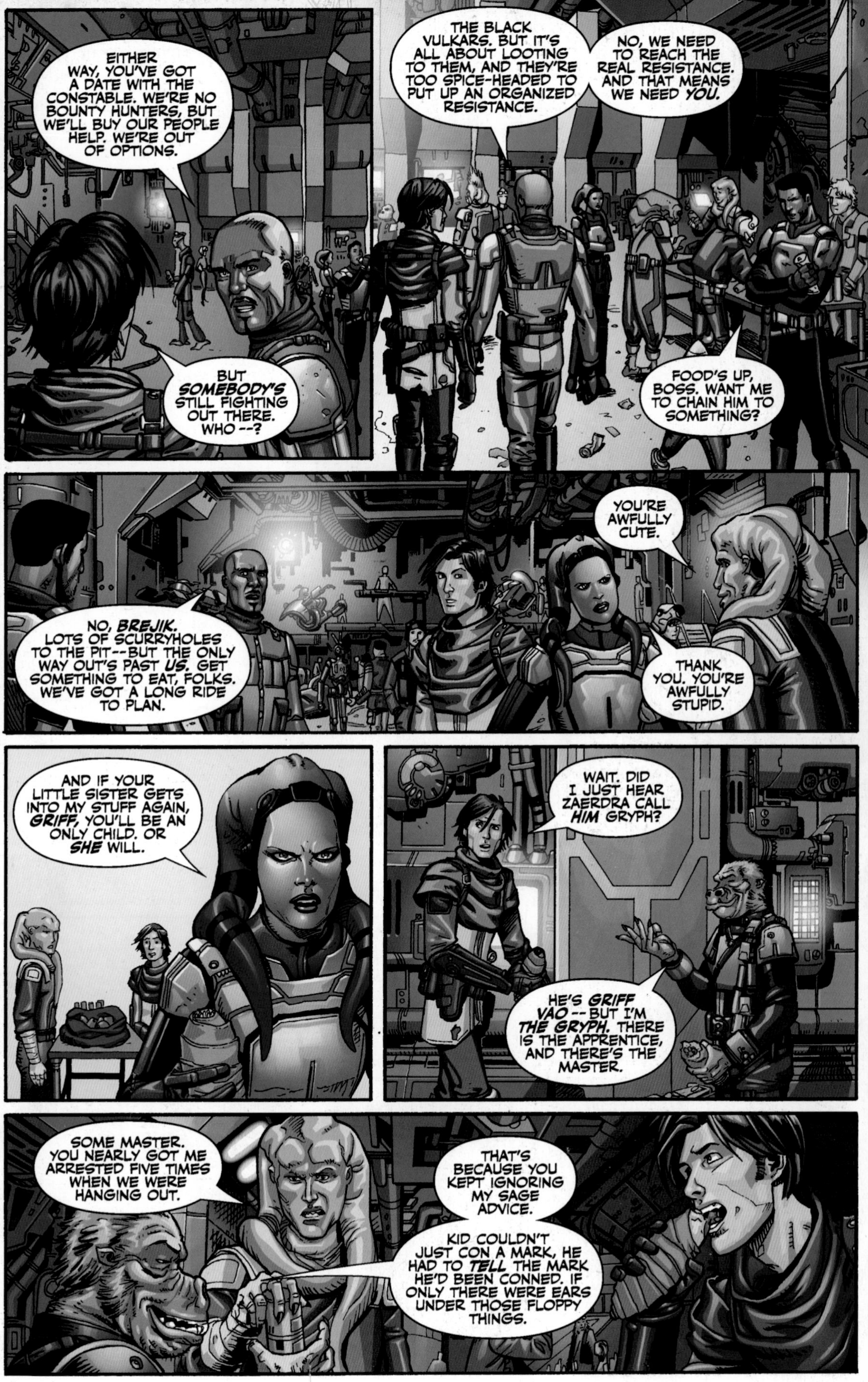
EITHER WAY, YOU'VE GOT A DATE WITH THE CONSTABLE. WE'RE NO BOUNTY HUNTERS, BUT WE'LL BUY OUR PEOPLE HELP. WE'RE OUT OF OPTIONS.
BUT SOMEBODY'S STILL FIGHTING OUT THERE. WHO --?
THE BLACK VULKARS. BUT IT'S ALL ABOUT LOOTING TO THEM, AND THEY'RE TOO SPICE-HEADED TO PUT UP AN ORGANIZED RESISTANCE.
NO, WE NEED TO REACH THE REAL RESISTANCE. AND THAT MEANS WE NEED YOU.
FOOD'S UP, BOSS. WANT ME TO CHAIN HIM TO SOMETHING?
NO, BREJIK. LOTS OF SCURRYHOLES TO THE PIT--BUT THE ONLY WAY OUT'S PAST US. GET SOMETHING TO EAT, FOLKS. WE'VE GOT A LONG RIDE TO PLAN.
YOU'RE AWFULLY CUTE.
THANK YOU. YOU'RE AWFULLY STUPID.
AND IF YOUR LITTLE SISTER GETS INTO MY STUFF AGAIN, GRIFF, YOU'LL BE AN ONLY CHILD. OR SHE WILL.
WAIT. DID I JUST HEAR ZAERDRA CALL HIM GRYPH?
HE'S GRIFF VAO -- BUT I'M THE GRYPH. THERE IS THE APPRENTICE, AND THERE'S THE MASTER.
SOME MASTER. YOU NEARLY GOT ME ARRESTED FIVE TIMES WHEN WE WERE HANGING OUT.
THAT'S BECAUSE YOU KEPT IGNORING MY SAGE ADVICE.
KID COULDN'T JUST CON A MARK, HE HAD TO TELL THE MARK HE'D BEEN CONNED. IF ONLY THERE WERE EARS UNDER THOSE FLOPPY THINGS.

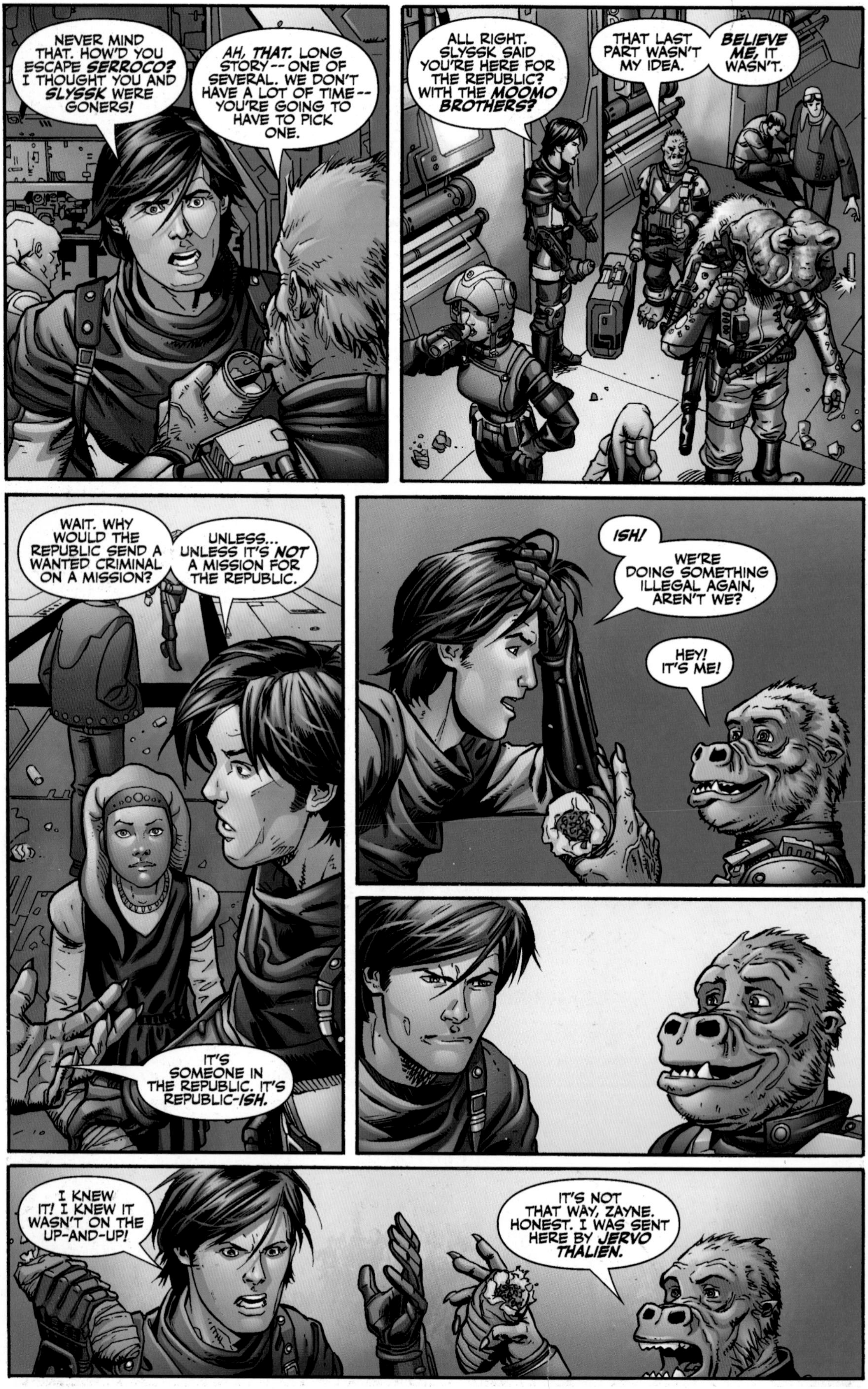
NEVER MIND THAT. HOW'D YOU ESCAPE SERROCO? I THOUGHT YOU AND SLYSSK WERE GONERS!
AH, THAT. LONG STORY -- ONE OF SEVERAL. WE DON'T HAVE A LOT OF TIME -- YOU'RE GOING TO HAVE TO PICK ONE.
ALL RIGHT. SLYSSK SAID YOU'RE HERE FOR THE REPUBLIC? WITH THE MOOMO BROTHERS?
THAT LAST PART WASN'T MY IDEA.
BELIEVE ME, IT WASN'T.
WAIT. WHY WOULD THE REPUBLIC SEND A WANTED CRIMINAL ON A MISSION?
UNLESS... UNLESS IT'S NOT A MISSION FOR THE REPUBLIC.
IT'S SOMEONE IN THE REPUBLIC. IT'S REPUBLIC-ISH.
ISH!
WE'RE DOING SOMETHING ILLEGAL AGAIN, AREN'T WE?
HEY! IT'S ME!
I KNEW IT! I KNEW IT WASN'T ON THE UP-AND-UP!
IT'S NOT THAT WAY, ZAYNE. HONEST. I WAS SENT HERE BY JERVO THALIEN.

JERVO *THALIEN?* THE HEAD OF *LHOSAN INDUSTRIES?* THE COMPANY THAT MAKES THE SWOOPBIKES?

AMONG OTHER THINGS. JERVO WANTED ME TO FIND *SENATOR GORAVVUS.*

HOW'D A PRIVATE COMPANY GET ITS HANDS ON REPUBLIC INTELLIGENCE?

HE'S A *ZILLIONAIRE,* HENCHMAN. HE CAN DO WHATEVER HE WANTS. HE ALSO LEARNED FROM THE ADMIRALTY THAT YOU AND KARATH HAD GONE TO OMONOTH.

THAT'S HOW I WAS ABLE TO SEND SLYSSK AND DOB FOR YOU!

OUR SENATOR? I MEAN, *TARIS'* SENATOR?

UNTIL RECENTLY. HE VANISHED RIGHT AFTER YOU AND I LEFT TARIS.

BUT JERVO FOUND OUT FROM REPUBLIC INTEL THAT THE SENATOR WAS ACTUALLY STILL *HERE,* RUNNING THE RESISTANCE IN THE LOWER CITY!

WHY DIDN'T JERVO SEND SOMEONE OFFICIAL AFTER THE SENATOR? SOMEONE *BETTER?*

I MISSED YOU, TOO. NO, I ASKED ABOUT THAT.

AFTER SERROCO, THE CHANCELLOR STARTED AN INQUIRY INTO JUST HOW TARIS GOT INTO THE REPUBLIC SO EASILY, BEING SO FAR OUT HERE AND ALL.

WELL, BEFORE HE WAS A SENATOR, GORAVVUS WAS KEY IN ESTABLISHING LHOSAN ON TARIS -- AND JERVO THANKED HIM WITH A SENATE SEAT.

LHOSAN'S STOCK PRICE GOES UP -- AND EVERYONE'S HAPPY. UNTIL THE INVASION, ANYWAY. NOW, I FIGURE JERVO WANTS TO SAVE HIS FRIEND --

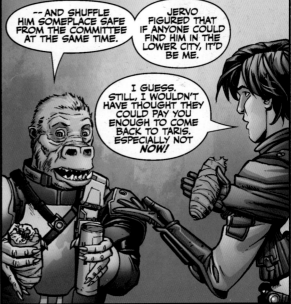

-- AND SHUFFLE HIM SOMEPLACE SAFE FROM THE COMMITTEE AT THE SAME TIME.

JERVO FIGURED THAT IF ANYONE COULD FIND HIM IN THE LOWER CITY, IT'D BE ME.

I GUESS. STILL, I WOULDN'T HAVE THOUGHT THEY COULD PAY YOU ENOUGH TO COME BACK TO TARIS. ESPECIALLY NOT *NOW!*

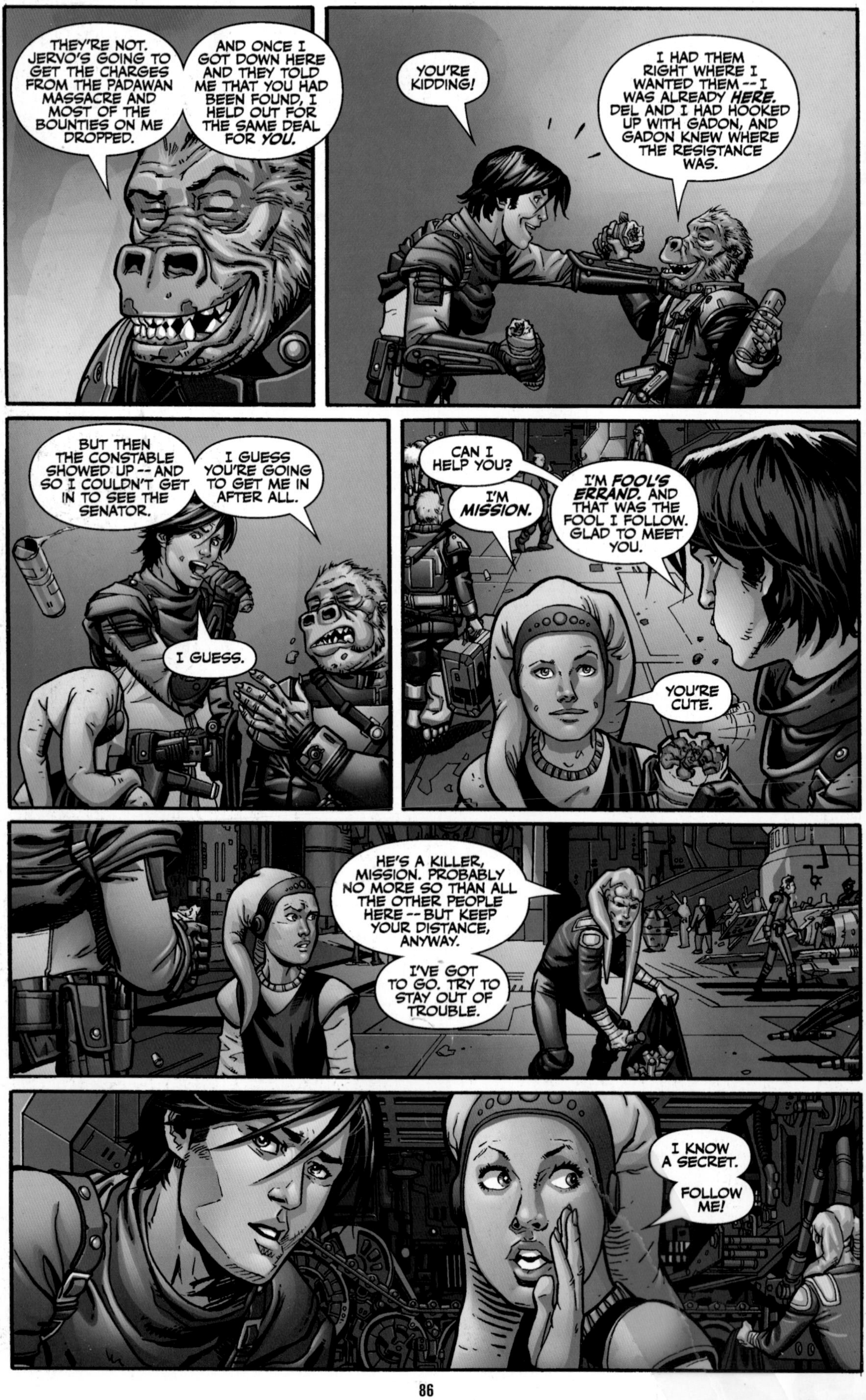
THEY'RE NOT. JERVO'S GOING TO GET THE CHARGES FROM THE PADAWAN MASSACRE AND MOST OF THE BOUNTIES ON ME DROPPED.
AND ONCE I GOT DOWN HERE AND THEY TOLD ME THAT YOU HAD BEEN FOUND, I HELD OUT FOR THE SAME DEAL FOR *YOU.*
YOU'RE KIDDING!
I HAD THEM RIGHT WHERE I WANTED THEM -- I WAS ALREADY *HERE.* DEL AND I HAD HOOKED UP WITH GADON, AND GADON KNEW WHERE THE RESISTANCE WAS.
BUT THEN THE CONSTABLE SHOWED UP -- AND SO I COULDN'T GET IN TO SEE THE SENATOR.
I GUESS YOU'RE GOING TO GET ME IN AFTER ALL.
I GUESS.
CAN I HELP YOU?
I'M *MISSION.*
I'M *FOOL'S ERRAND.* AND THAT WAS THE FOOL I FOLLOW. GLAD TO MEET YOU.
YOU'RE CUTE.
HE'S A KILLER, MISSION. PROBABLY NO MORE SO THAN ALL THE OTHER PEOPLE HERE -- BUT KEEP YOUR DISTANCE, ANYWAY.
I'VE GOT TO GO. TRY TO STAY OUT OF TROUBLE.
I KNOW A SECRET.
FOLLOW ME!

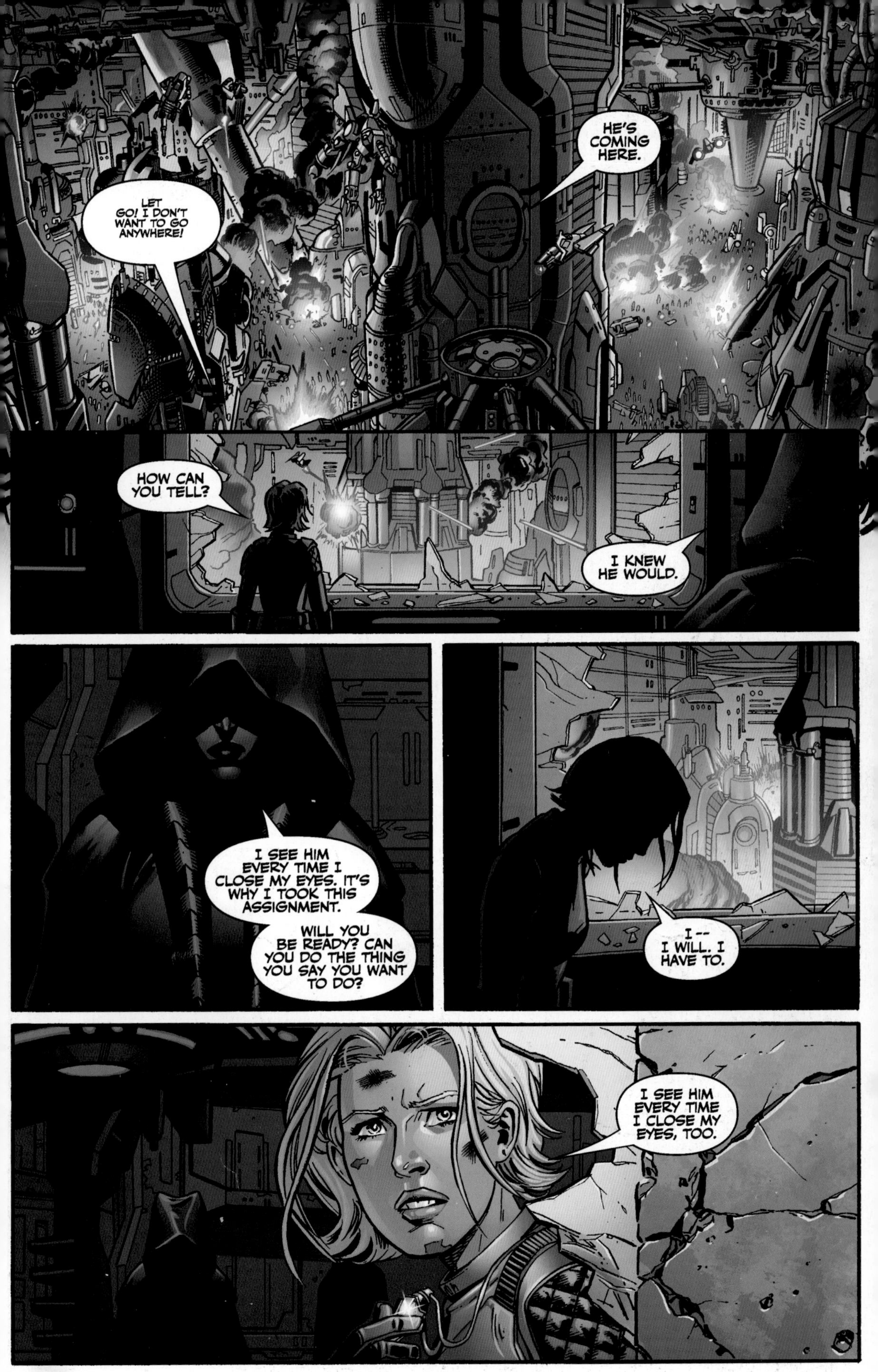
HE'S COMING HERE.
LET GO! I DON'T WANT TO GO ANYWHERE!
HOW CAN YOU TELL?
I KNEW HE WOULD.
I SEE HIM EVERY TIME I CLOSE MY EYES. IT'S WHY I TOOK THIS ASSIGNMENT.
WILL YOU BE READY? CAN YOU DO THE THING YOU SAY YOU WANT TO DO?
I -- I WILL. I HAVE TO.
I SEE HIM EVERY TIME I CLOSE MY EYES, TOO.

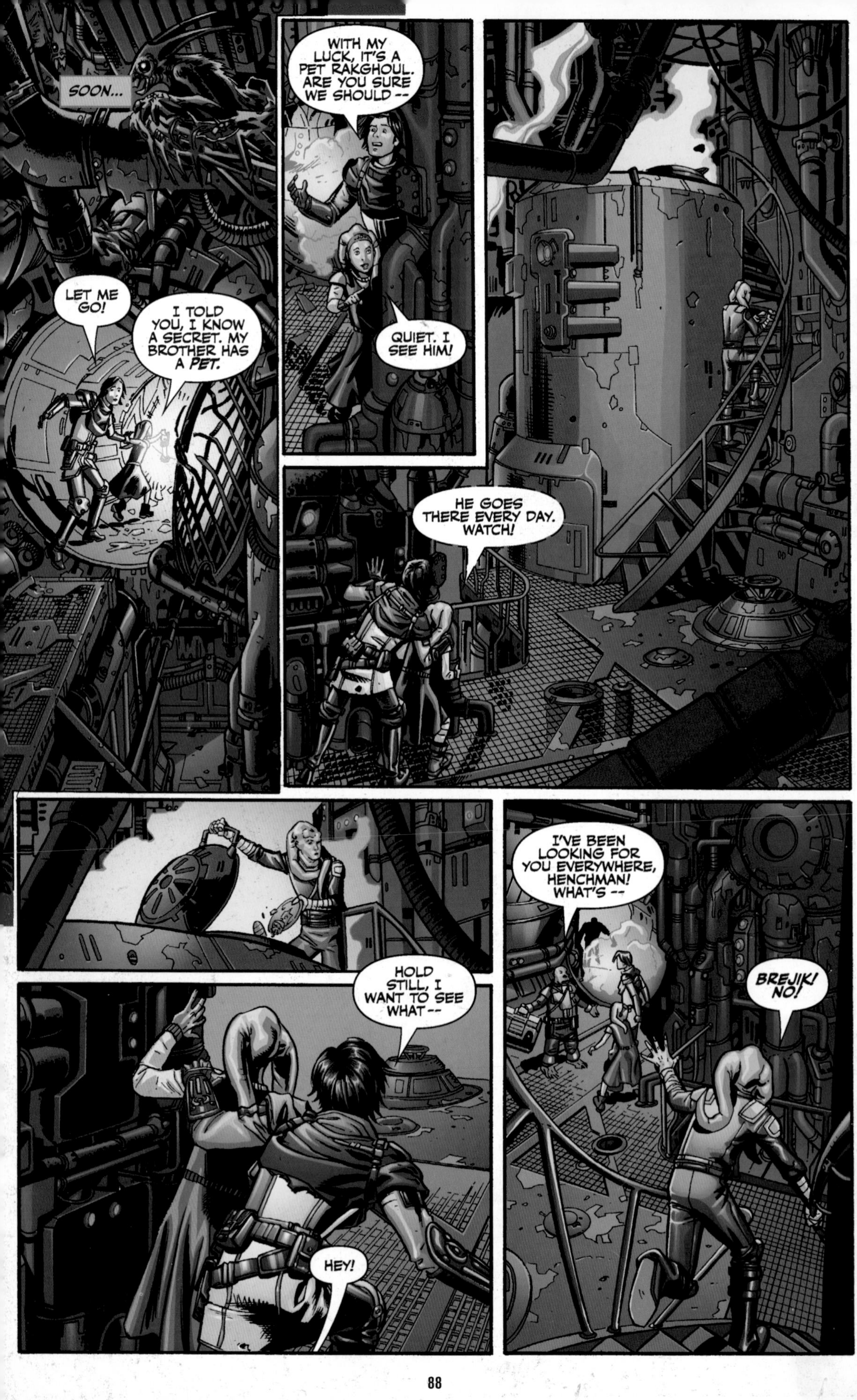
SOON...
LET ME GO!
I TOLD YOU, I KNOW A SECRET. MY BROTHER HAS A PET.
WITH MY LUCK, IT'S A PET RAKGHOUL. ARE YOU SURE WE SHOULD --
QUIET. I SEE HIM!
HE GOES THERE EVERY DAY. WATCH!
HOLD STILL, I WANT TO SEE WHAT --
HEY!
I'VE BEEN LOOKING FOR YOU EVERYWHERE, HENCHMAN! WHAT'S --
BREJIK! NO!

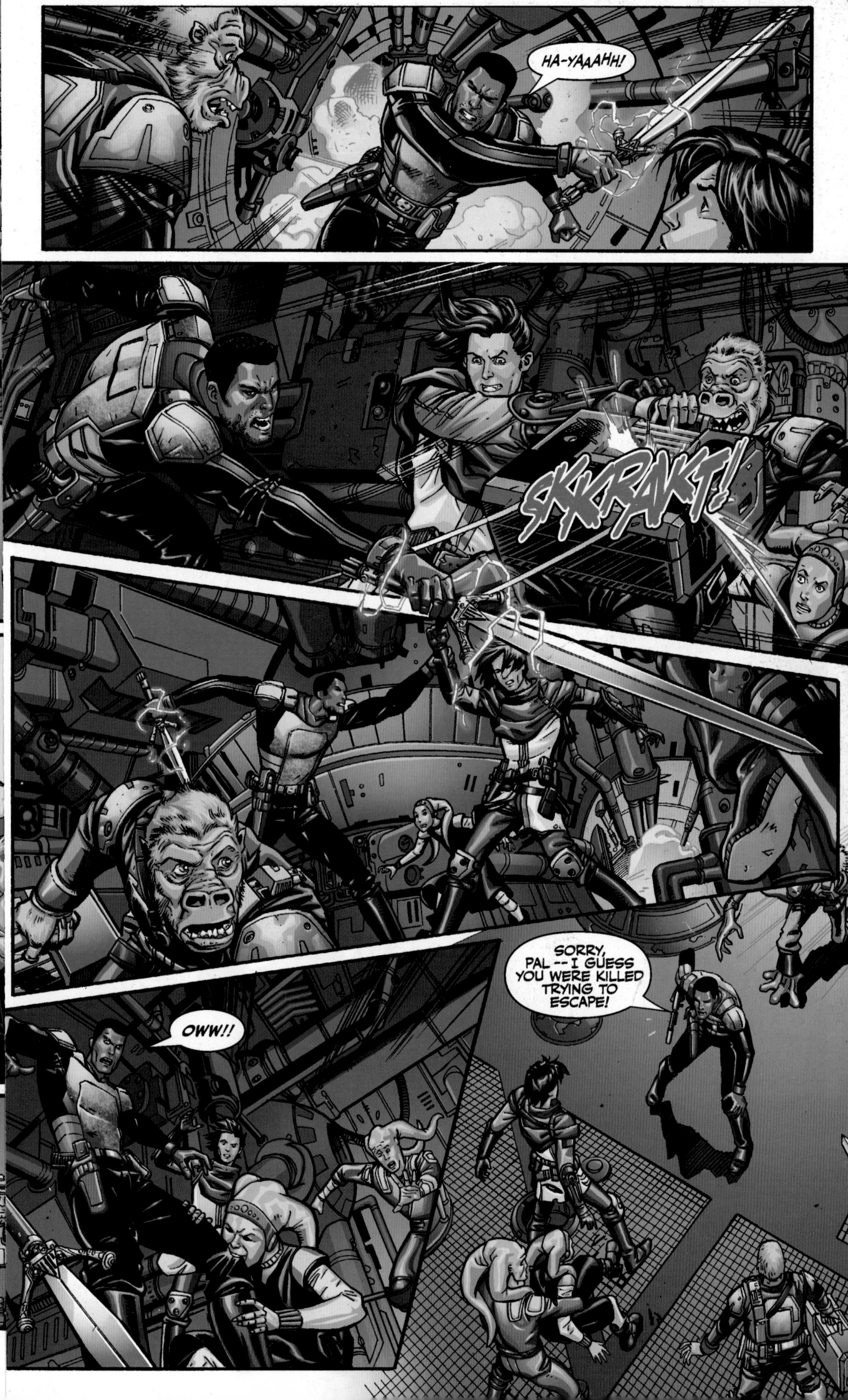
HA-YAAAHH!
SKKRAKT!
SORRY, PAL -- I GUESS YOU WERE KILLED TRYING TO ESCAPE!
OWW!!

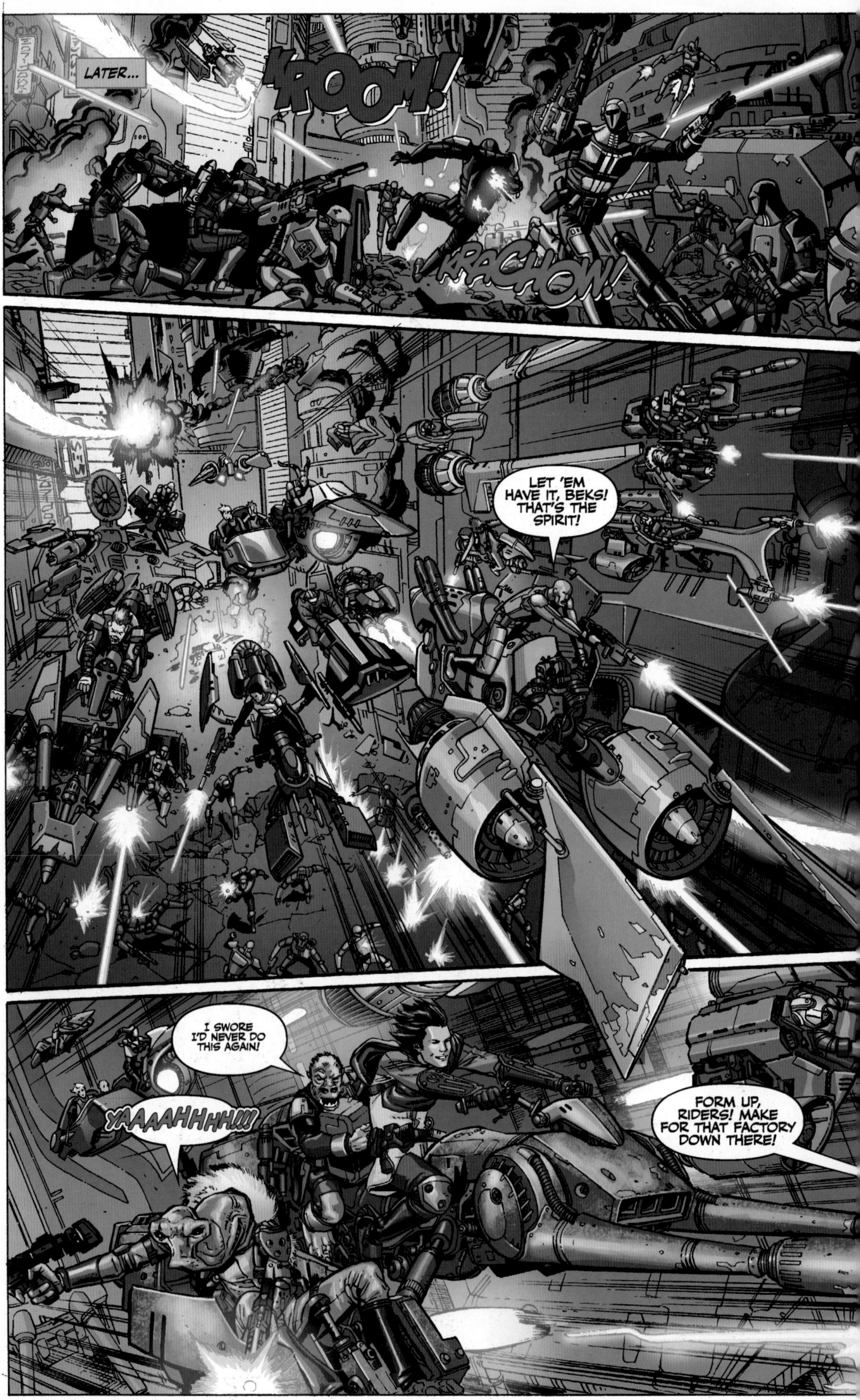
LATER...
KROOM!
KRACHOW!
LET 'EM HAVE IT, BEKS! THAT'S THE SPIRIT!
I SWORE I'D NEVER DO THIS AGAIN!
YAAAAHHHH!!!
FORM UP, RIDERS! MAKE FOR THAT FACTORY DOWN THERE!

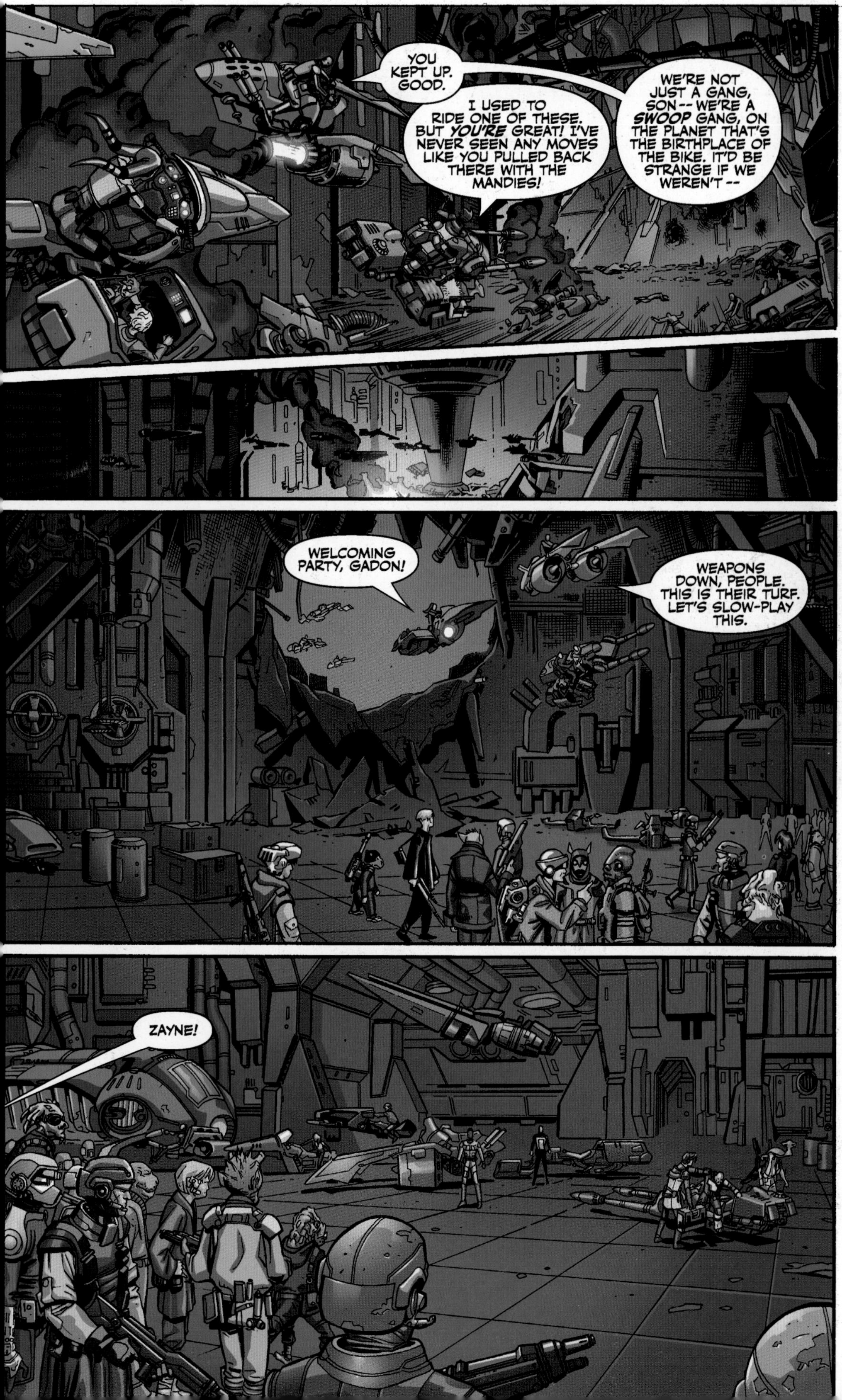
YOU KEPT UP. GOOD.
I USED TO RIDE ONE OF THESE. BUT YOU'RE GREAT! I'VE NEVER SEEN ANY MOVES LIKE YOU PULLED BACK THERE WITH THE MANDIES!
WE'RE NOT JUST A GANG, SON -- WE'RE A SWOOP GANG, ON THE PLANET THAT'S THE BIRTHPLACE OF THE BIKE. IT'D BE STRANGE IF WE WEREN'T --
WELCOMING PARTY, GADON!
WEAPONS DOWN, PEOPLE. THIS IS THEIR TURF. LET'S SLOW-PLAY THIS.
ZAYNE!

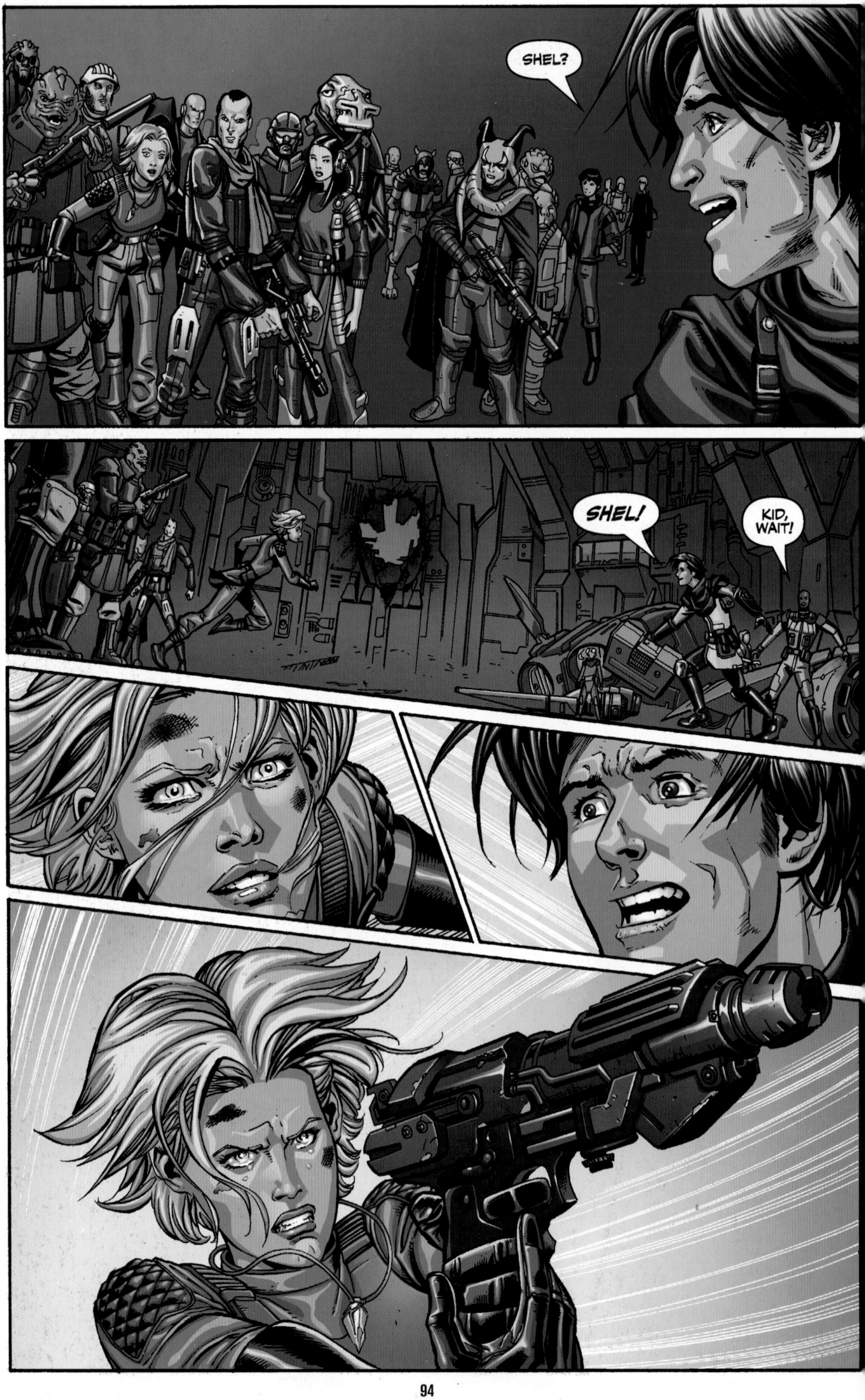
SHEL?
SHEL!
KID, WAIT!

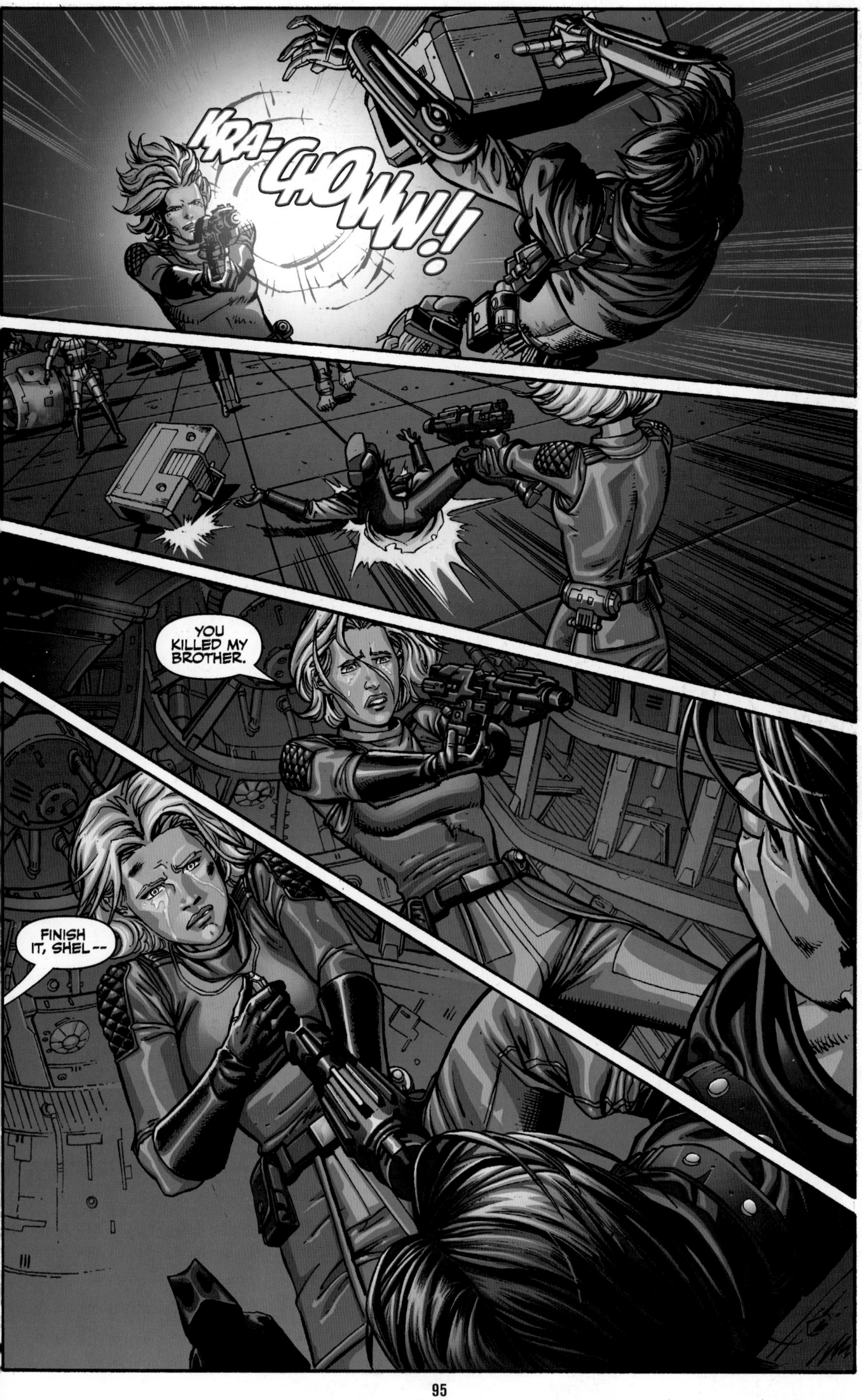
KRA-CHOWW!!
YOU KILLED MY BROTHER.
FINISH IT, SHEL--

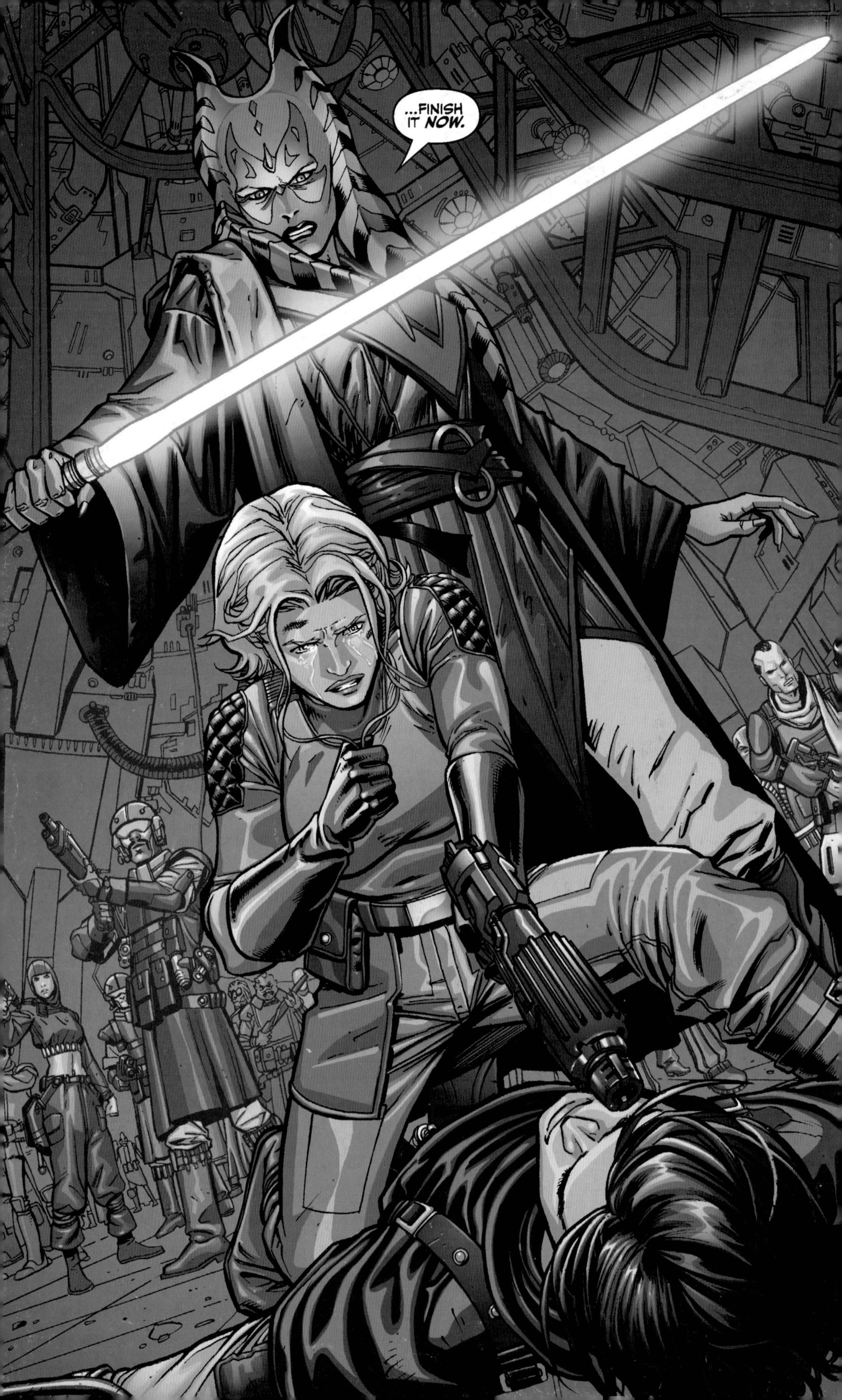
...FINISH IT NOW.

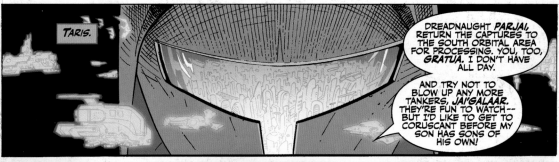

TARIS.

DREADNAUGHT *PARJAI*, RETURN THE CAPTURES TO THE SOUTH ORBITAL AREA FOR PROCESSING. YOU, TOO, *GRATUA*. I DON'T HAVE ALL DAY.

AND TRY NOT TO BLOW UP ANY MORE TANKERS, *JAI'GALAAR*. THEY'RE FUN TO WATCH-- BUT I'D LIKE TO GET TO CORUSCANT BEFORE MY SON HAS SONS OF HIS OWN!

I CAN SEE WHY I WAS BROUGHT IN. THE REPUBLIC DOESN'T NEED TO FIGHT BACK WHEN WE HAVE OUR OWN FORCES SLAMMING INTO EACH OTHER.

I'M TRYING TO GET THE WORD OUT, *CASSUS*--

--BUT A LOT ARE BUCKING YOUR SYSTEM. WE'RE THE *MANDO'ADE!* WE DON'T *HAVE* SYSTEMS!

OH, WE HAVE SYSTEMS--WE JUST NEVER *KEEP* THEM FOR LONG. IT'S THE NOMAD'S CURSE. WE MOVE ON BEFORE WE'RE FINISHED.

BUT I'LL MAKE YOU A DEAL, *GORMER*--

--YOU LISTEN TO *CASSUS FETT*, AND *YOUR* SON'S SONS WILL HAVE NOTHING TO DO--BECAUSE YOU'LL HAVE CONQUERED EVERYTHING!

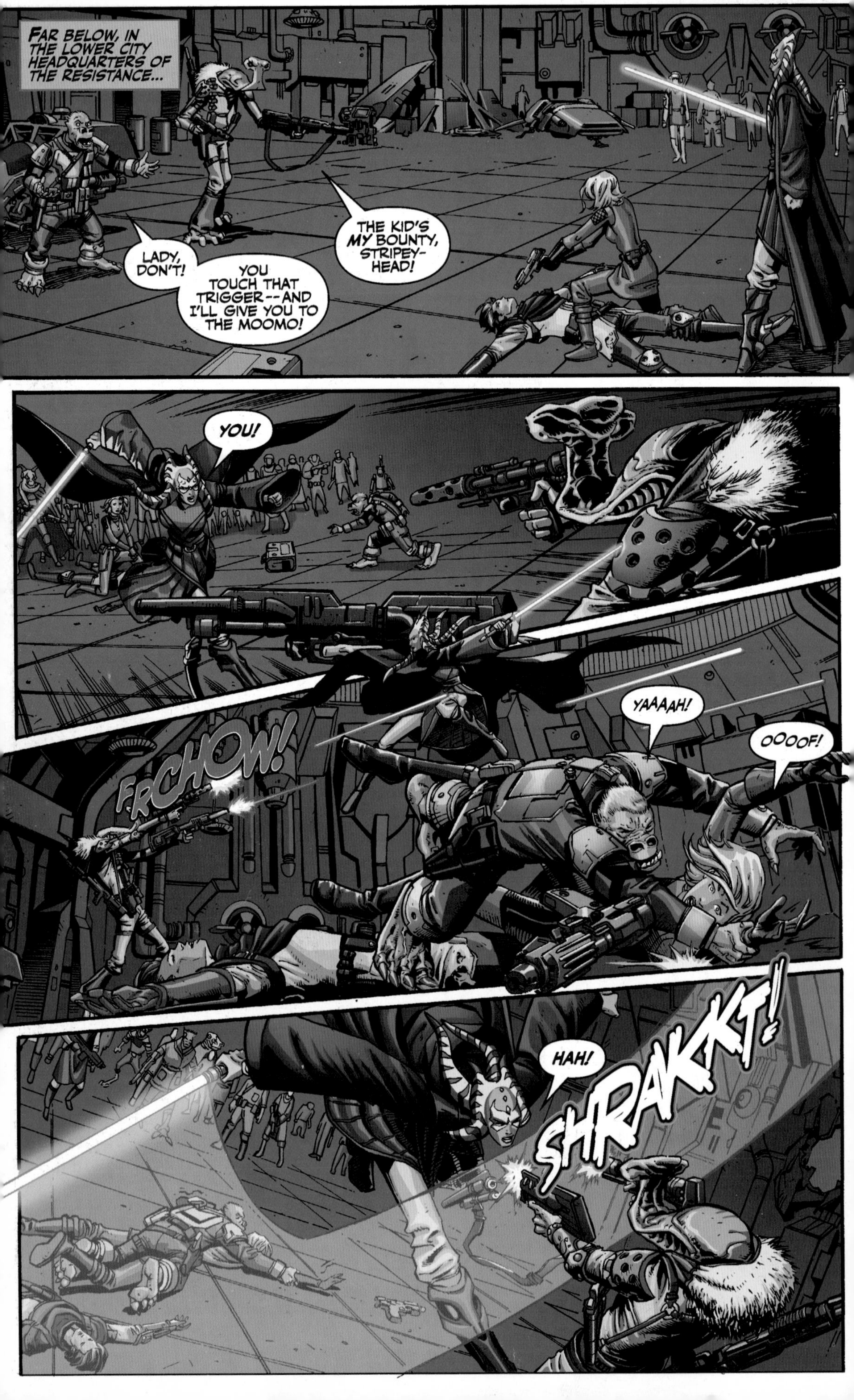
FAR BELOW, IN THE LOWER CITY HEADQUARTERS OF THE RESISTANCE...
LADY, DON'T!
YOU TOUCH THAT TRIGGER--AND I'LL GIVE YOU TO THE MOOMO!
THE KID'S MY BOUNTY, STRIPEY-HEAD!
YOU!
YAAAAH!
OOOOF!
FRCHOW!
HAH!
SHRAKKT!

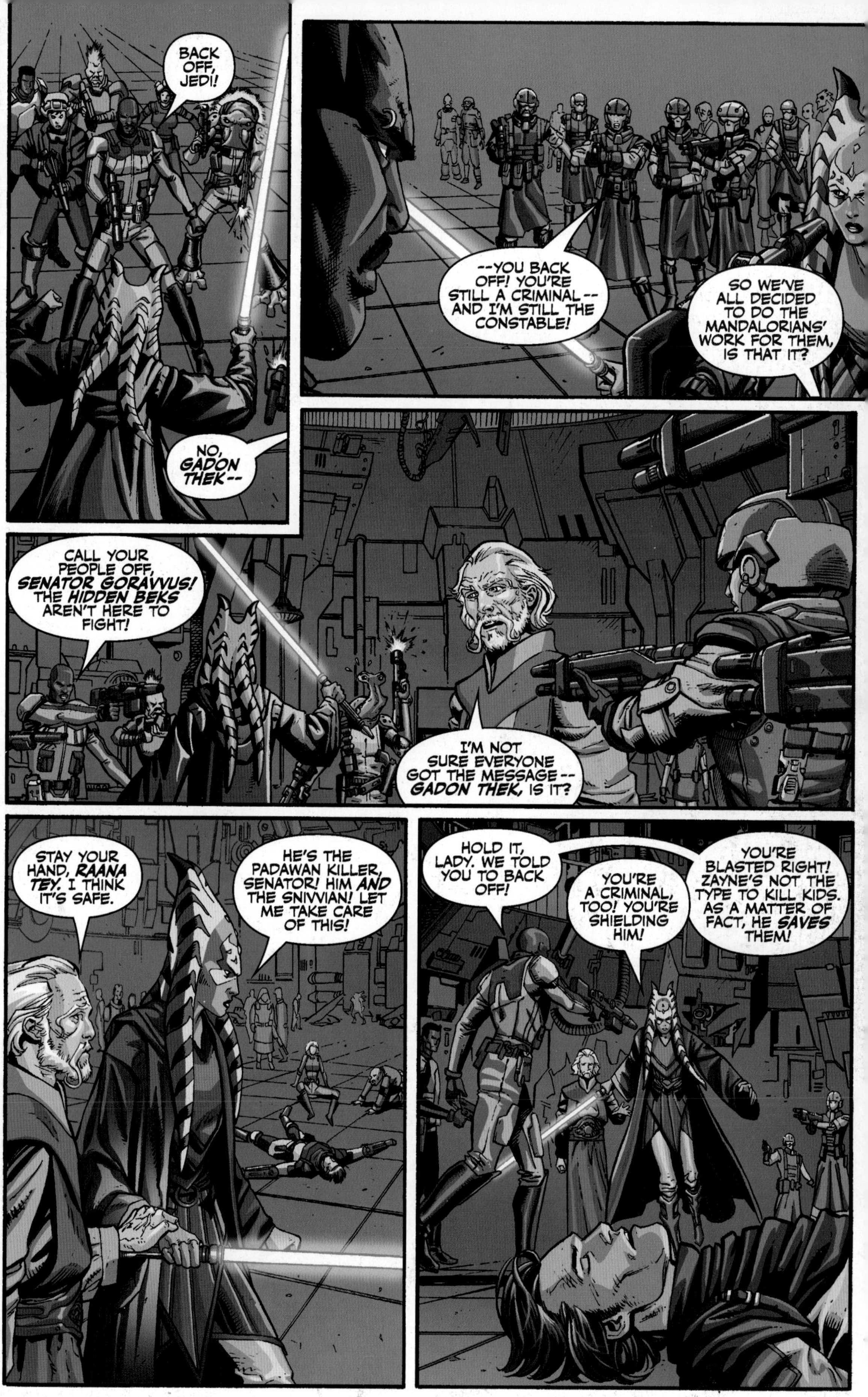
BACK OFF, JEDI!
--YOU BACK OFF! YOU'RE STILL A CRIMINAL-- AND I'M STILL THE CONSTABLE!
SO WE'VE ALL DECIDED TO DO THE MANDALORIANS' WORK FOR THEM, IS THAT IT?
NO, GADON THEK--
CALL YOUR PEOPLE OFF, SENATOR GORAVVUS! THE HIDDEN BEKS AREN'T HERE TO FIGHT!
I'M NOT SURE EVERYONE GOT THE MESSAGE-- GADON THEK, IS IT?
STAY YOUR HAND, RAANA TEY. I THINK IT'S SAFE.
HE'S THE PADAWAN KILLER, SENATOR! HIM AND THE SNIVVIAN! LET ME TAKE CARE OF THIS!
HOLD IT, LADY. WE TOLD YOU TO BACK OFF!
YOU'RE A CRIMINAL, TOO! YOU'RE SHIELDING HIM!
YOU'RE BLASTED RIGHT! ZAYNE'S NOT THE TYPE TO KILL KIDS. AS A MATTER OF FACT, HE SAVES THEM!

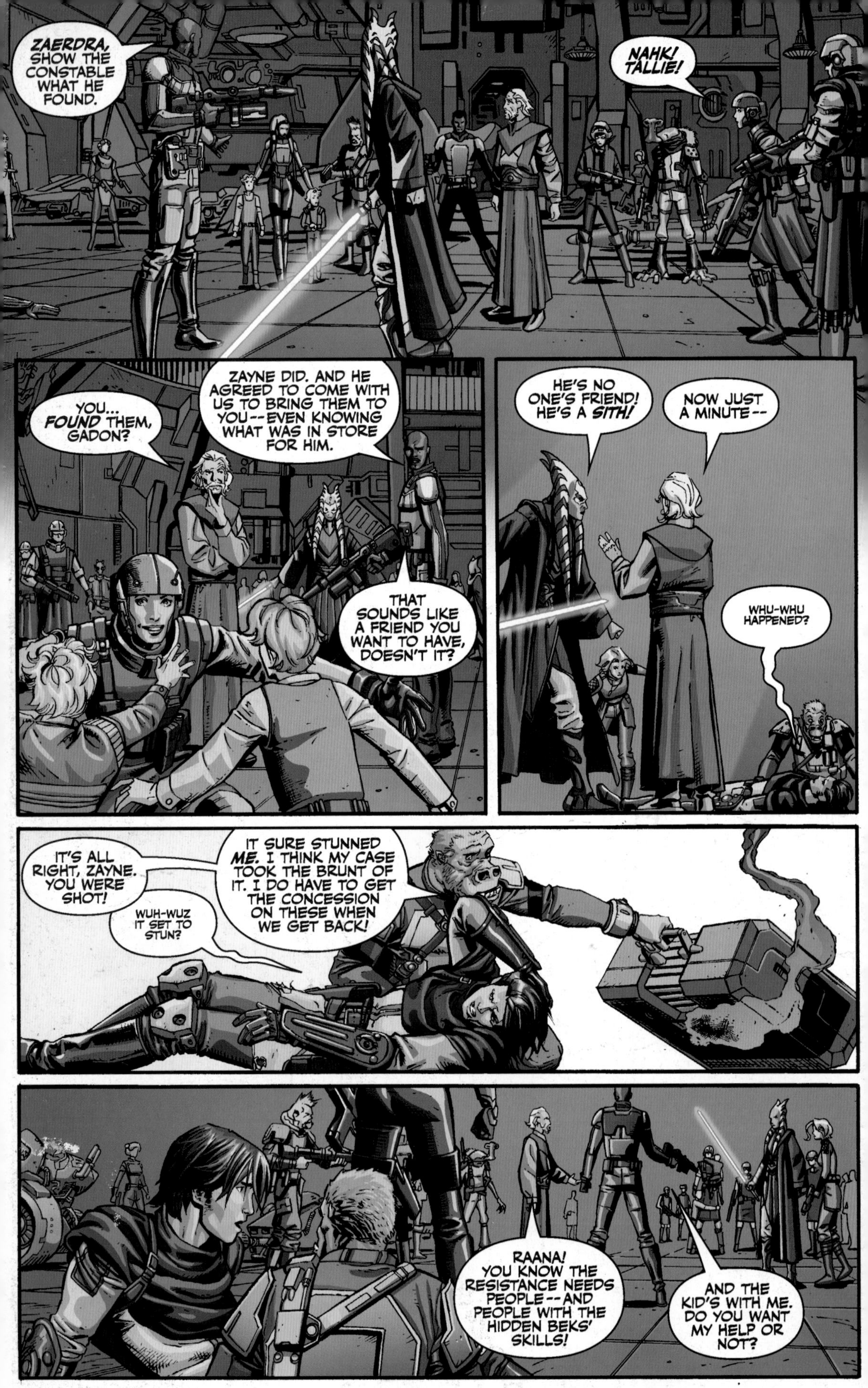
ZAERDRA, SHOW THE CONSTABLE WHAT HE FOUND.
NAHK! TALLIE!
YOU... FOUND THEM, GADON?
ZAYNE DID. AND HE AGREED TO COME WITH US TO BRING THEM TO YOU--EVEN KNOWING WHAT WAS IN STORE FOR HIM.
THAT SOUNDS LIKE A FRIEND YOU WANT TO HAVE, DOESN'T IT?
HE'S NO ONE'S FRIEND! HE'S A SITH!
NOW JUST A MINUTE--
WHU-WHU HAPPENED?
IT'S ALL RIGHT, ZAYNE. YOU WERE SHOT!
WUH-WUZ IT SET TO STUN?
IT SURE STUNNED ME. I THINK MY CASE TOOK THE BRUNT OF IT. I DO HAVE TO GET THE CONCESSION ON THESE WHEN WE GET BACK!
RAANA! YOU KNOW THE RESISTANCE NEEDS PEOPLE--AND PEOPLE WITH THE HIDDEN BEKS' SKILLS!
AND THE KID'S WITH ME. DO YOU WANT MY HELP OR NOT?

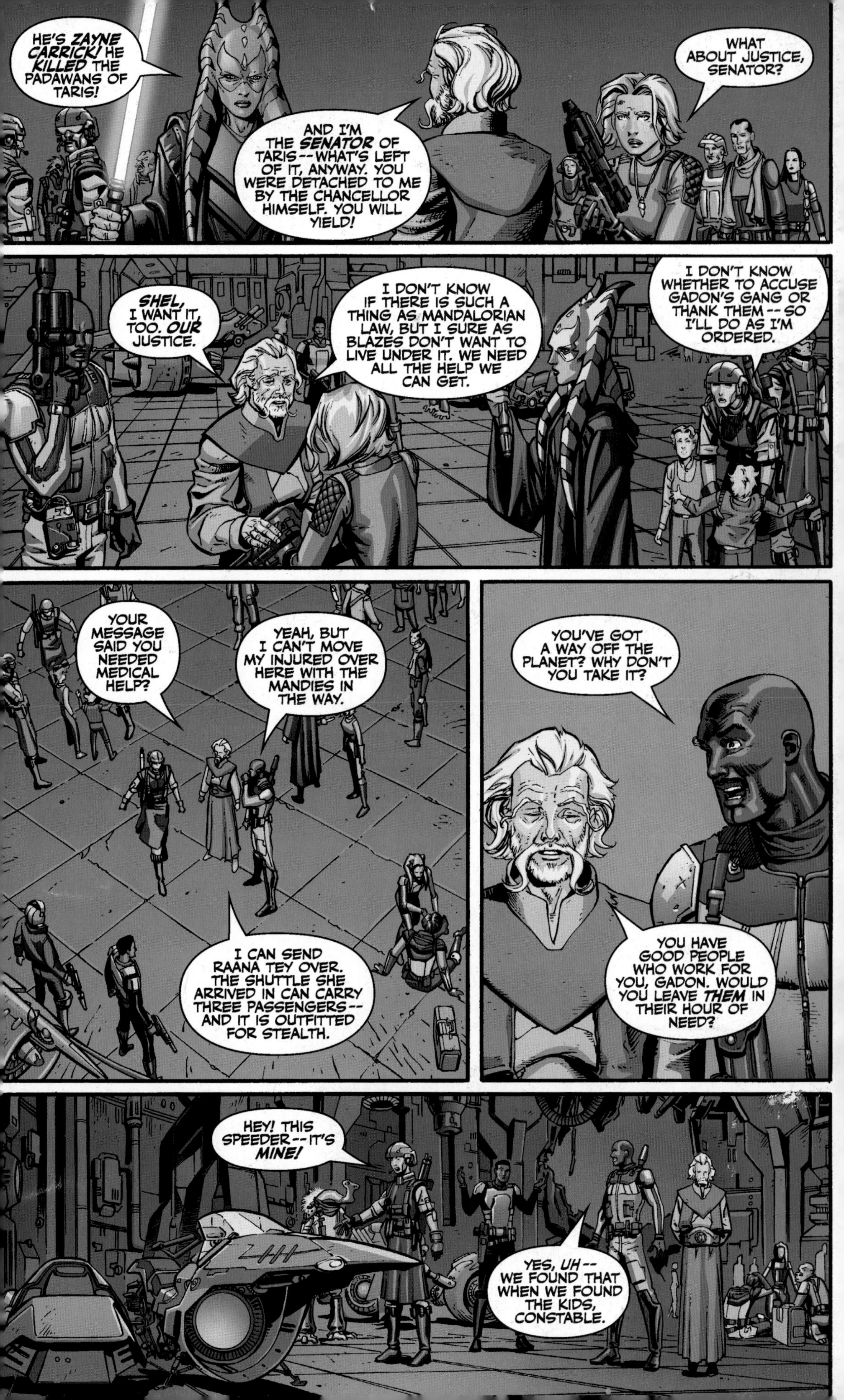
HE'S ZAYNE CARRICK! HE KILLED THE PADAWANS OF TARIS!
AND I'M THE SENATOR OF TARIS--WHAT'S LEFT OF IT, ANYWAY. YOU WERE DETACHED TO ME BY THE CHANCELLOR HIMSELF. YOU WILL YIELD!
WHAT ABOUT JUSTICE, SENATOR?
SHEL, I WANT IT, TOO. OUR JUSTICE.
I DON'T KNOW IF THERE IS SUCH A THING AS MANDALORIAN LAW, BUT I SURE AS BLAZES DON'T WANT TO LIVE UNDER IT. WE NEED ALL THE HELP WE CAN GET.
I DON'T KNOW WHETHER TO ACCUSE GADON'S GANG OR THANK THEM--SO I'LL DO AS I'M ORDERED.
YOUR MESSAGE SAID YOU NEEDED MEDICAL HELP?
YEAH, BUT I CAN'T MOVE MY INJURED OVER HERE WITH THE MANDIES IN THE WAY.
I CAN SEND RAANA TEY OVER. THE SHUTTLE SHE ARRIVED IN CAN CARRY THREE PASSENGERS--AND IT IS OUTFITTED FOR STEALTH.
YOU'VE GOT A WAY OFF THE PLANET? WHY DON'T YOU TAKE IT?
YOU HAVE GOOD PEOPLE WHO WORK FOR YOU, GADON. WOULD YOU LEAVE THEM IN THEIR HOUR OF NEED?
HEY! THIS SPEEDER--IT'S MINE!
YES, UH--WE FOUND THAT WHEN WE FOUND THE KIDS, CONSTABLE.

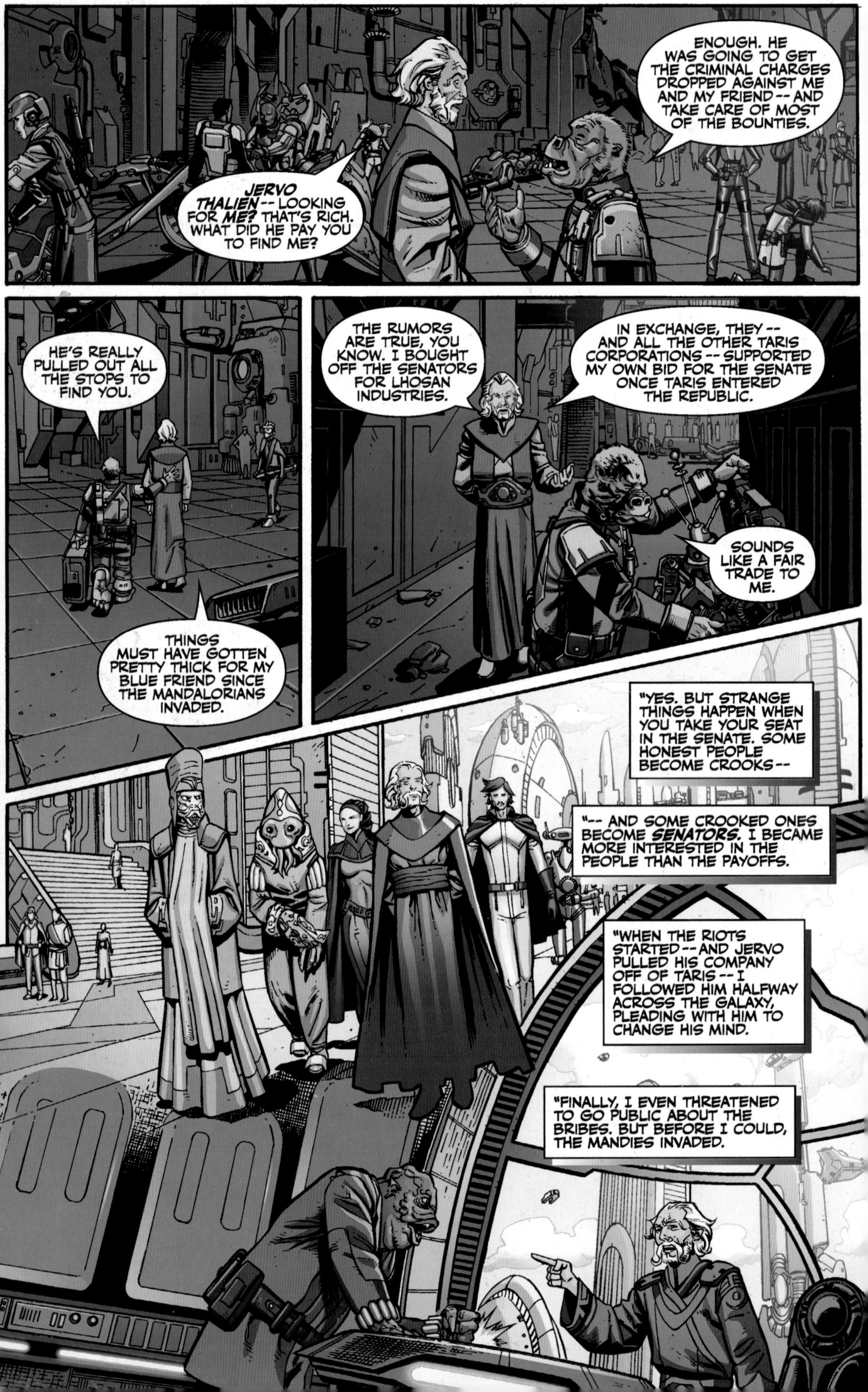
JERVO THALIEN-- LOOKING FOR ME? THAT'S RICH. WHAT DID HE PAY YOU TO FIND ME?
ENOUGH. HE WAS GOING TO GET THE CRIMINAL CHARGES DROPPED AGAINST ME AND MY FRIEND-- AND TAKE CARE OF MOST OF THE BOUNTIES.
HE'S REALLY PULLED OUT ALL THE STOPS TO FIND YOU.
THINGS MUST HAVE GOTTEN PRETTY THICK FOR MY BLUE FRIEND SINCE THE MANDALORIANS INVADED.
THE RUMORS ARE TRUE, YOU KNOW. I BOUGHT OFF THE SENATORS FOR LHOSAN INDUSTRIES.
IN EXCHANGE, THEY-- AND ALL THE OTHER TARIS CORPORATIONS-- SUPPORTED MY OWN BID FOR THE SENATE ONCE TARIS ENTERED THE REPUBLIC.
SOUNDS LIKE A FAIR TRADE TO ME.
"YES. BUT STRANGE THINGS HAPPEN WHEN YOU TAKE YOUR SEAT IN THE SENATE. SOME HONEST PEOPLE BECOME CROOKS--
"-- AND SOME CROOKED ONES BECOME SENATORS. I BECAME MORE INTERESTED IN THE PEOPLE THAN THE PAYOFFS.
"WHEN THE RIOTS STARTED-- AND JERVO PULLED HIS COMPANY OFF OF TARIS-- I FOLLOWED HIM HALFWAY ACROSS THE GALAXY, PLEADING WITH HIM TO CHANGE HIS MIND.
"FINALLY, I EVEN THREATENED TO GO PUBLIC ABOUT THE BRIBES. BUT BEFORE I COULD, THE MANDIES INVADED.

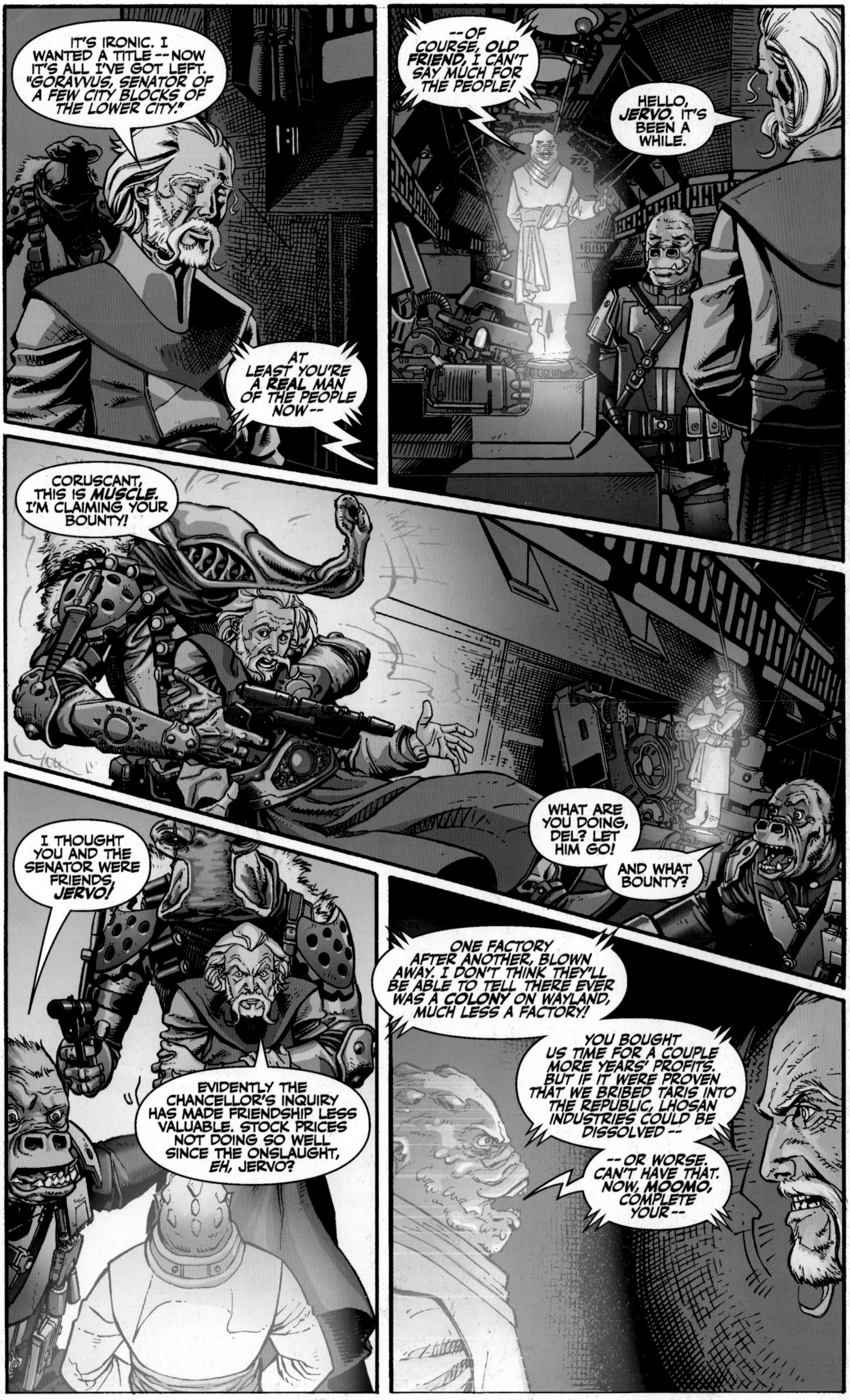
IT'S IRONIC. I WANTED A TITLE--NOW IT'S ALL I'VE GOT LEFT. "GORAVVUS, SENATOR OF A FEW CITY BLOCKS OF THE LOWER CITY."
AT LEAST YOU'RE A REAL MAN OF THE PEOPLE NOW--
--OF COURSE, OLD FRIEND, I CAN'T SAY MUCH FOR THE PEOPLE!
HELLO, JERVO. IT'S BEEN A WHILE.
CORUSCANT, THIS IS MUSCLE. I'M CLAIMING YOUR BOUNTY!
WHAT ARE YOU DOING, DEL? LET HIM GO!
AND WHAT BOUNTY?
I THOUGHT YOU AND THE SENATOR WERE FRIENDS, JERVO!
EVIDENTLY THE CHANCELLOR'S INQUIRY HAS MADE FRIENDSHIP LESS VALUABLE. STOCK PRICES NOT DOING SO WELL SINCE THE ONSLAUGHT, EH, JERVO?
ONE FACTORY AFTER ANOTHER, BLOWN AWAY. I DON'T THINK THEY'LL BE ABLE TO TELL THERE EVER WAS A COLONY ON WAYLAND, MUCH LESS A FACTORY!
YOU BOUGHT US TIME FOR A COUPLE MORE YEARS' PROFITS. BUT IF IT WERE PROVEN THAT WE BRIBED TARIS INTO THE REPUBLIC, LHOSAN INDUSTRIES COULD BE DISSOLVED--
--OR WORSE. CAN'T HAVE THAT. NOW, MOOMO, COMPLETE YOUR--

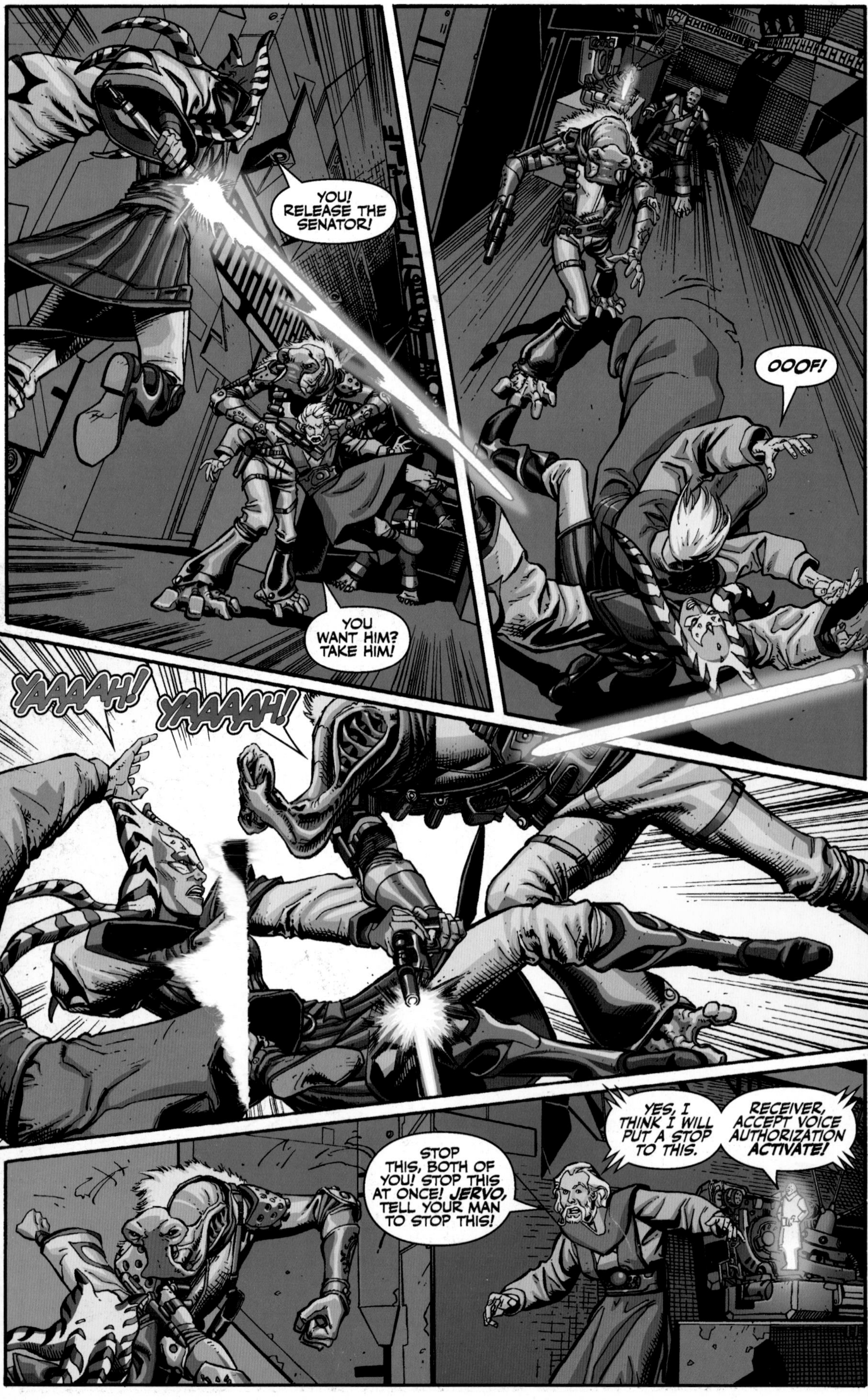
YOU! RELEASE THE SENATOR!
YOU WANT HIM? TAKE HIM!
OOOF!
YAAAAH!
YAAAAH!
STOP THIS, BOTH OF YOU! STOP THIS AT ONCE! JERVO, TELL YOUR MAN TO STOP THIS!
YES, I THINK I WILL PUT A STOP TO THIS.
RECEIVER, ACCEPT VOICE AUTHORIZATION ACTIVATE!

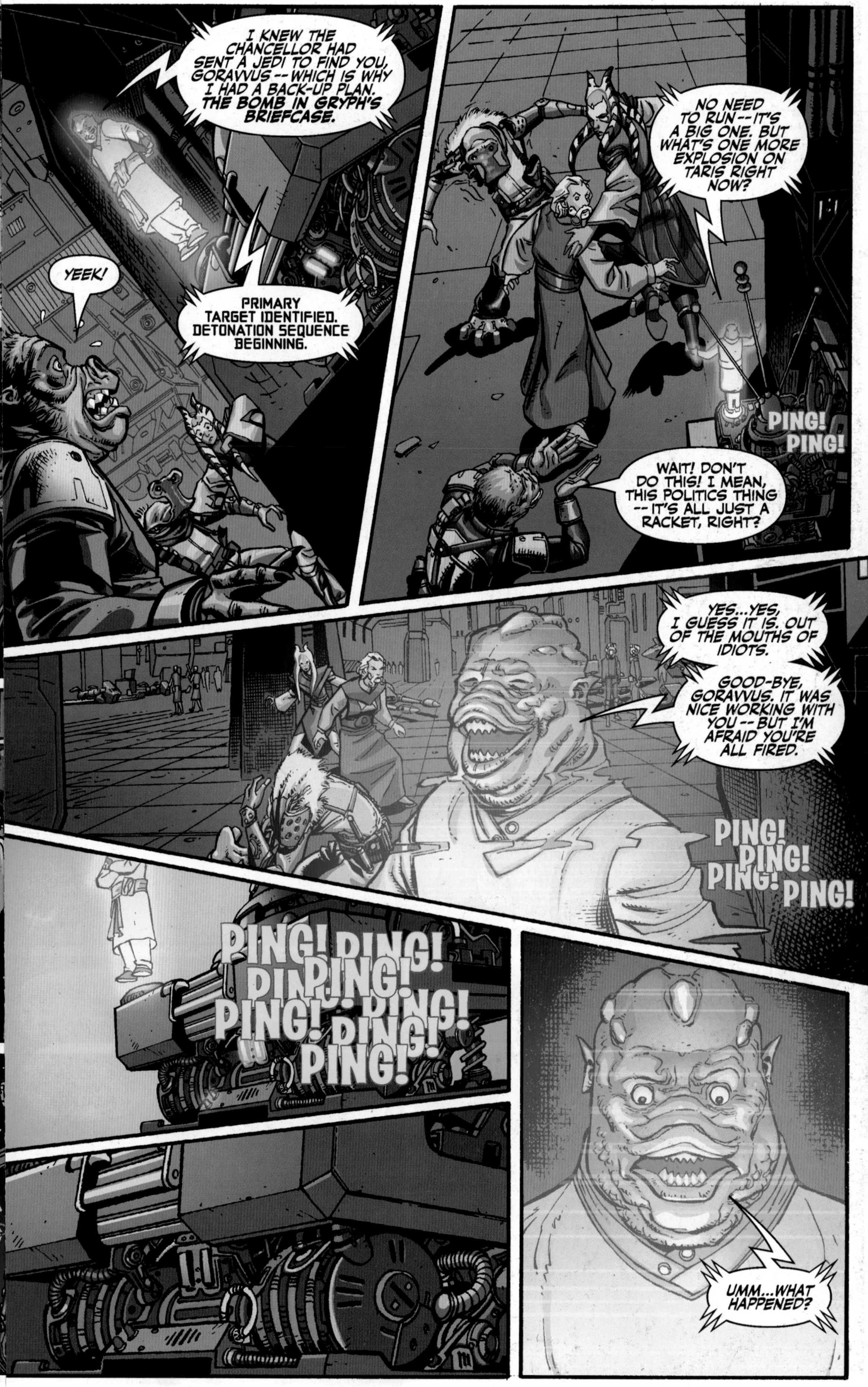
I KNEW THE CHANCELLOR HAD SENT A JEDI TO FIND YOU, GORAVVUS -- WHICH IS WHY I HAD A BACK-UP PLAN. THE BOMB IN GRYPH'S BRIEFCASE.
YEEK!
PRIMARY TARGET IDENTIFIED. DETONATION SEQUENCE BEGINNING.
NO NEED TO RUN -- IT'S A BIG ONE. BUT WHAT'S ONE MORE EXPLOSION ON TARIS RIGHT NOW?
PING! PING!
WAIT! DON'T DO THIS! I MEAN, THIS POLITICS THING -- IT'S ALL JUST A RACKET, RIGHT?
YES...YES, I GUESS IT IS. OUT OF THE MOUTHS OF IDIOTS.
GOOD-BYE, GORAVVUS. IT WAS NICE WORKING WITH YOU -- BUT I'M AFRAID YOU'RE ALL FIRED.
PING! PING! PING! PING!
PING! PING! PING! PING! PING! PING! PING!
UMM...WHAT HAPPENED?

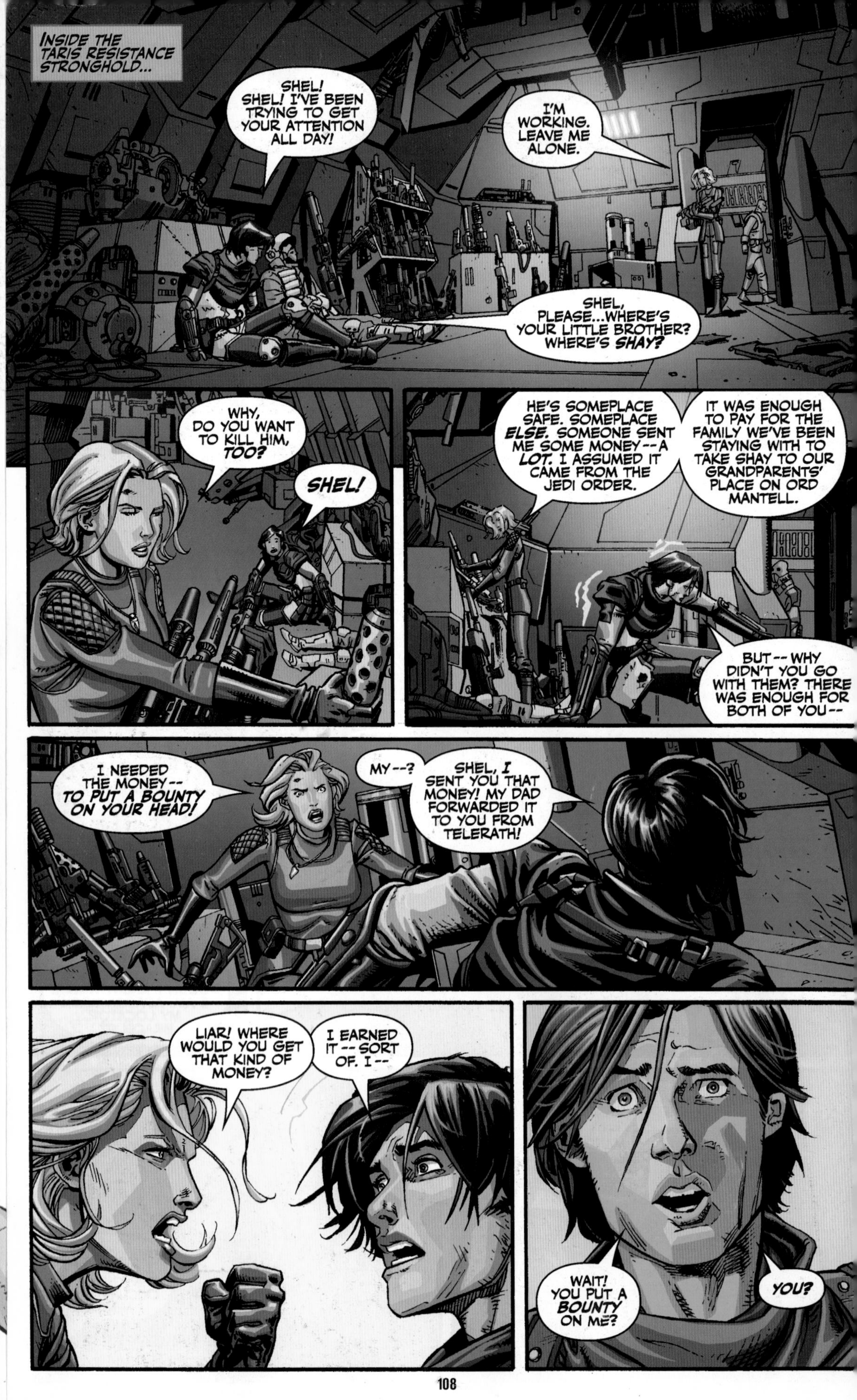
INSIDE THE TARIS RESISTANCE STRONGHOLD...
SHEL! SHEL! I'VE BEEN TRYING TO GET YOUR ATTENTION ALL DAY!
I'M WORKING. LEAVE ME ALONE.
SHEL, PLEASE...WHERE'S YOUR LITTLE BROTHER? WHERE'S SHAY?
WHY, DO YOU WANT TO KILL HIM, TOO?
SHEL!
HE'S SOMEPLACE SAFE. SOMEPLACE ELSE. SOMEONE SENT ME SOME MONEY--A LOT. I ASSUMED IT CAME FROM THE JEDI ORDER.
IT WAS ENOUGH TO PAY FOR THE FAMILY WE'VE BEEN STAYING WITH TO TAKE SHAY TO OUR GRANDPARENTS' PLACE ON ORD MANTELL.
BUT--WHY DIDN'T YOU GO WITH THEM? THERE WAS ENOUGH FOR BOTH OF YOU--
I NEEDED THE MONEY--TO PUT A BOUNTY ON YOUR HEAD!
MY--?
SHEL, I SENT YOU THAT MONEY! MY DAD FORWARDED IT TO YOU FROM TELERATH!
LIAR! WHERE WOULD YOU GET THAT KIND OF MONEY?
I EARNED IT--SORT OF. I--
WAIT! YOU PUT A BOUNTY ON ME?
YOU?

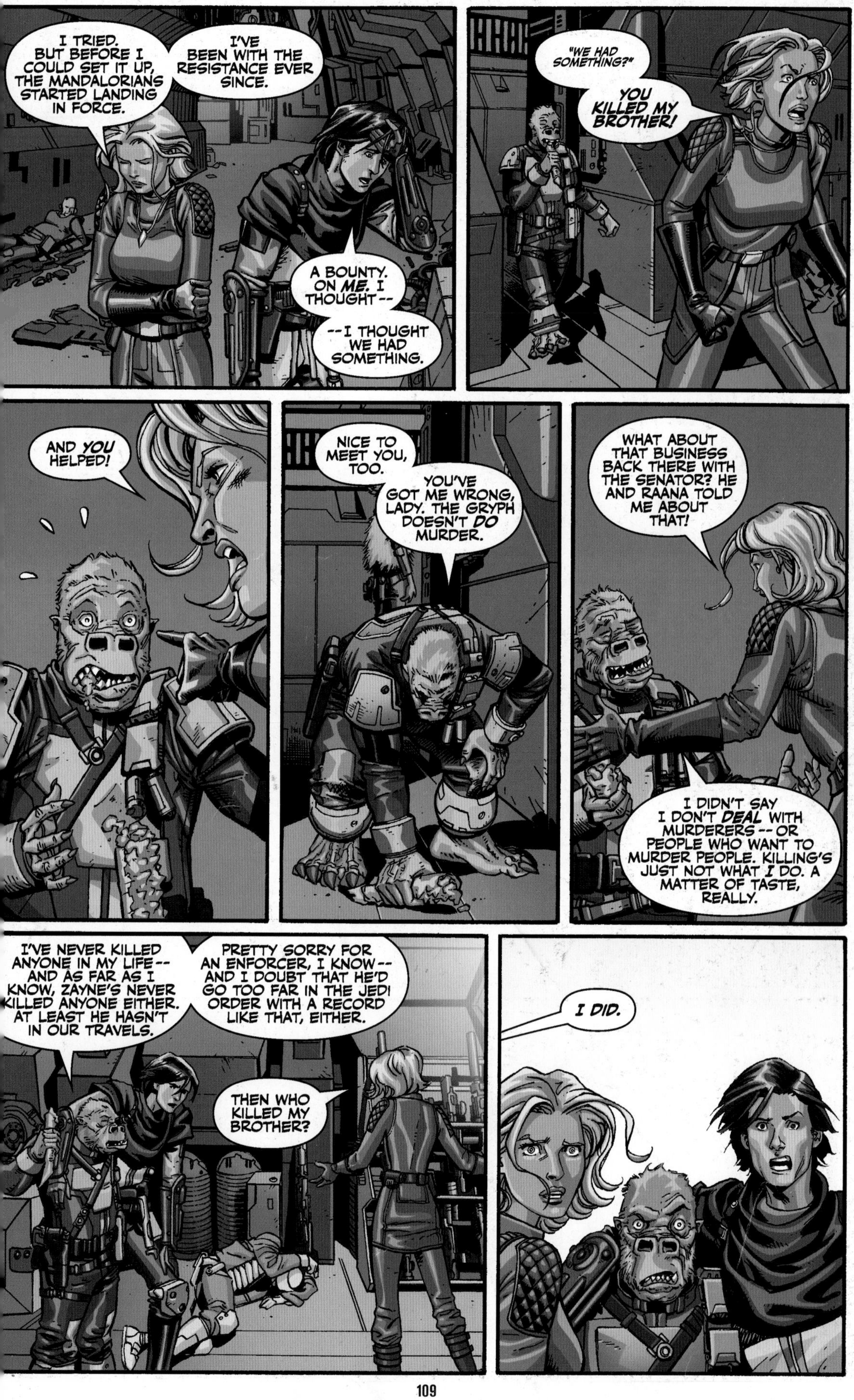

I TRIED. BUT BEFORE I COULD SET IT UP, THE MANDALORIANS STARTED LANDING IN FORCE.
I'VE BEEN WITH THE RESISTANCE EVER SINCE.
A BOUNTY. ON *ME.* I THOUGHT--
--I THOUGHT WE HAD SOMETHING.
"WE HAD SOMETHING?"
YOU KILLED MY BROTHER!
AND *YOU* HELPED!
NICE TO MEET YOU, TOO.
YOU'VE GOT ME WRONG, LADY. THE GRYPH DOESN'T *DO* MURDER.
WHAT ABOUT THAT BUSINESS BACK THERE WITH THE SENATOR? HE AND RAANA TOLD ME ABOUT THAT!
I DIDN'T SAY I DON'T *DEAL* WITH MURDERERS--OR PEOPLE WHO WANT TO MURDER PEOPLE. KILLING'S JUST NOT WHAT *I* DO. A MATTER OF TASTE, REALLY.
I'VE NEVER KILLED ANYONE IN MY LIFE--AND AS FAR AS I KNOW, ZAYNE'S NEVER KILLED ANYONE EITHER. AT LEAST HE HASN'T IN OUR TRAVELS.
PRETTY SORRY FOR AN ENFORCER, I KNOW--AND I DOUBT THAT HE'D GO TOO FAR IN THE JEDI ORDER WITH A RECORD LIKE THAT, EITHER.
THEN WHO KILLED MY BROTHER?
I DID.

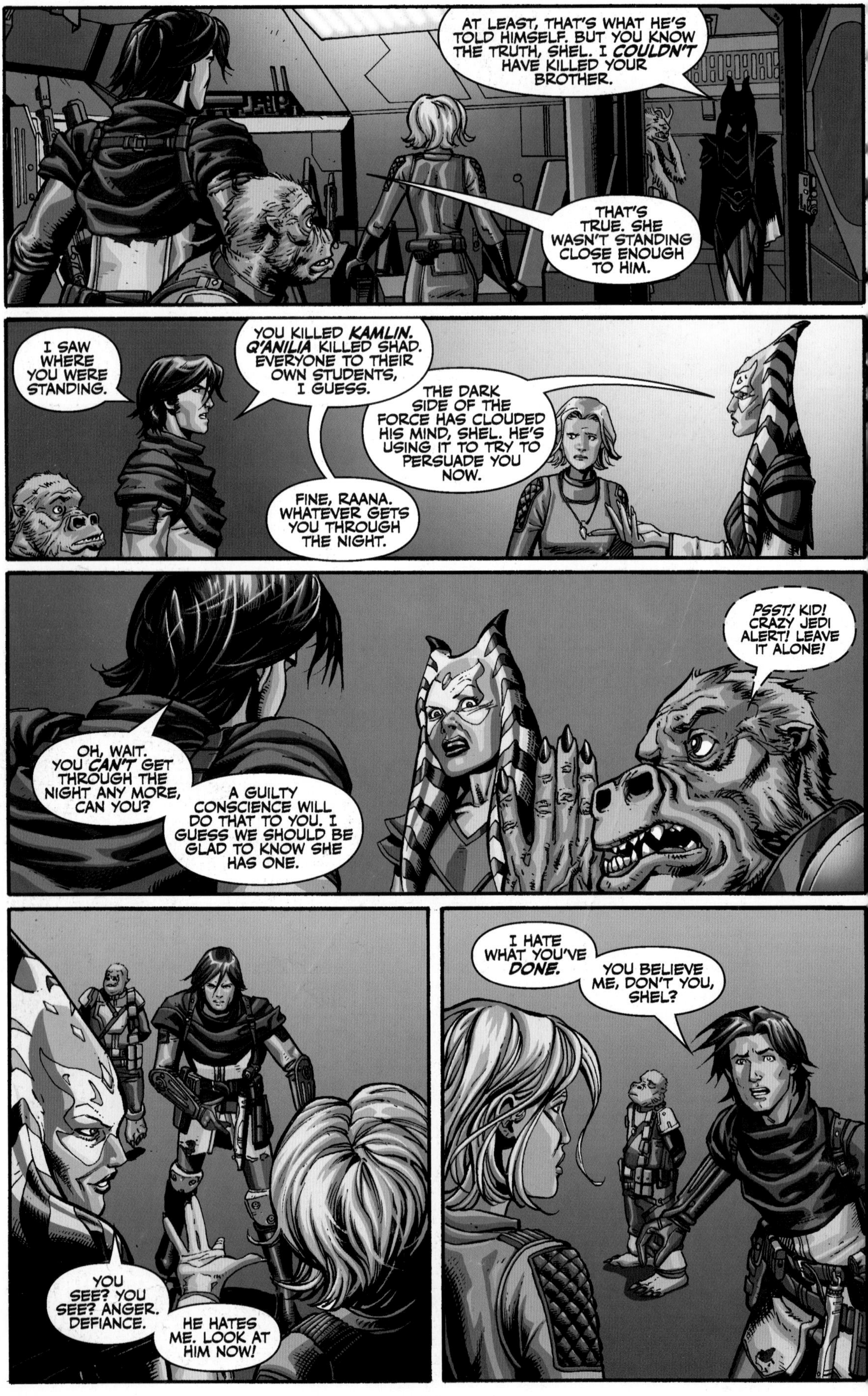

AT LEAST, THAT'S WHAT HE'S TOLD HIMSELF. BUT YOU KNOW THE TRUTH, SHEL. I COULDN'T HAVE KILLED YOUR BROTHER.
THAT'S TRUE. SHE WASN'T STANDING CLOSE ENOUGH TO HIM.
I SAW WHERE YOU WERE STANDING.
YOU KILLED KAMLIN. Q'ANILIA KILLED SHAD. EVERYONE TO THEIR OWN STUDENTS, I GUESS.
THE DARK SIDE OF THE FORCE HAS CLOUDED HIS MIND, SHEL. HE'S USING IT TO TRY TO PERSUADE YOU NOW.
FINE, RAANA. WHATEVER GETS YOU THROUGH THE NIGHT.
OH, WAIT. YOU CAN'T GET THROUGH THE NIGHT ANY MORE, CAN YOU?
A GUILTY CONSCIENCE WILL DO THAT TO YOU. I GUESS WE SHOULD BE GLAD TO KNOW SHE HAS ONE.
PSST! KID! CRAZY JEDI ALERT! LEAVE IT ALONE!
YOU SEE? YOU SEE? ANGER. DEFIANCE.
HE HATES ME. LOOK AT HIM NOW!
I HATE WHAT YOU'VE DONE.
YOU BELIEVE ME, DON'T YOU, SHEL?

I WISH I'D NEVER MET ANY OF YOU!

SORRY TO INTERRUPT... BUT BEFORE WE ALL KILL EACH OTHER, MAYBE WE SHOULD LOOK FOR ANOTHER TARGET-- A MILITARY TARGET.

WE'VE JUST LEARNED THAT CASSUS FETT HIMSELF HAS COME TO REVIEW THE OPERATIONS FROM HIGHPORT.

HE'S USING YOUR JEDI TOWER AS HIS COMMAND CENTER.

SHOULD THAT MEAN SOMETHING TO ME?

I DON'T KNOW WHAT YOU'VE HEARD, SENATOR, BUT THE JEDI ARE NOT INVOLVED IN MILITARY ACTIONS. AND YOU DON'T HAVE ENOUGH PEOPLE TO STORM IT.

MAYBE. BUT MAYBE WE DON'T HAVE TO STORM IT.

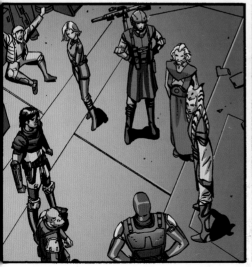

HEY, YOU GUYS MIND IF I KEEP THIS BOMB? MY BROTHER KEEPS STEALING MINE.

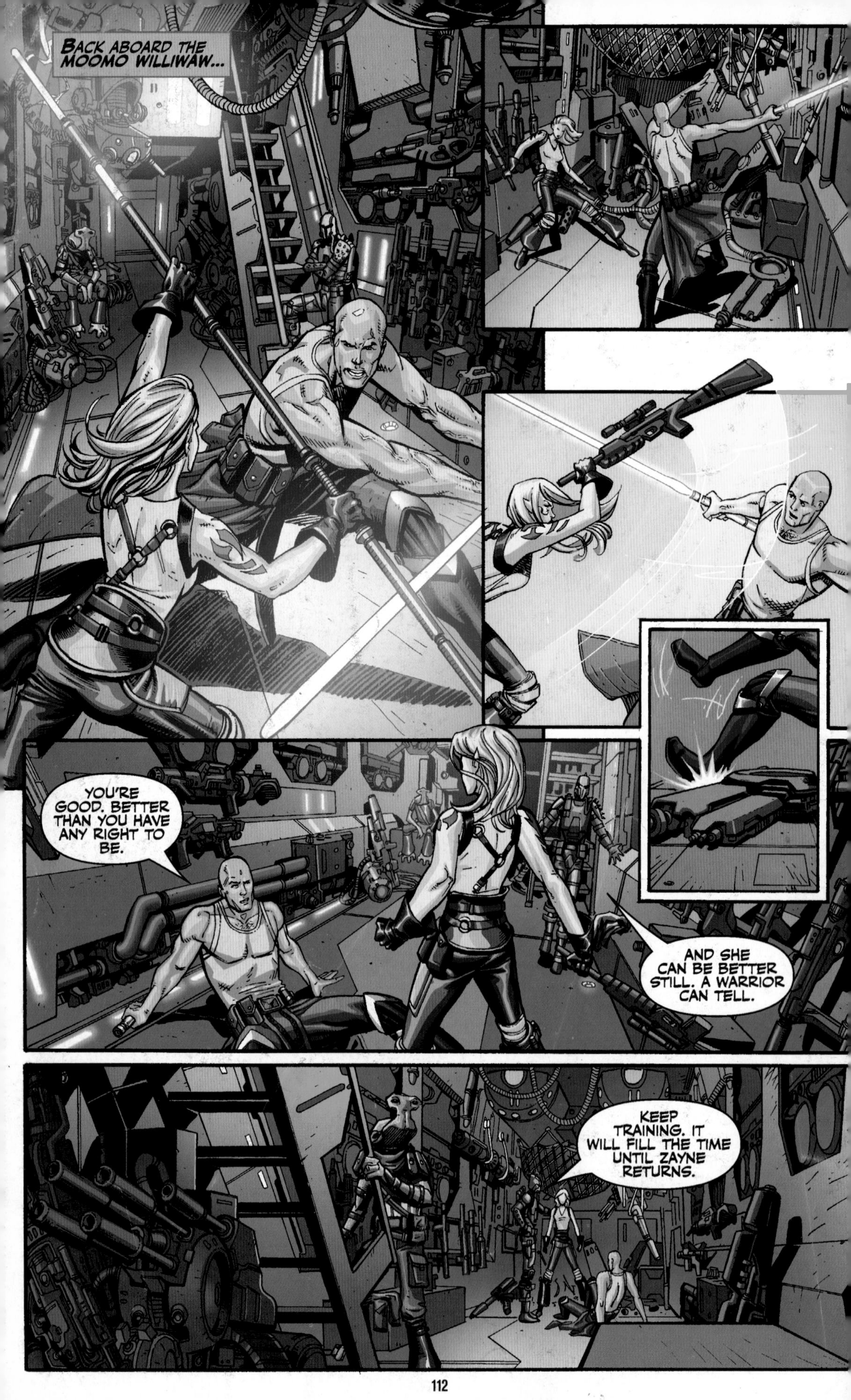

BACK ABOARD THE MOOMO WILLIWAW...
YOU'RE GOOD. BETTER THAN YOU HAVE ANY RIGHT TO BE.
AND SHE CAN BE BETTER STILL. A WARRIOR CAN TELL.
KEEP TRAINING. IT WILL FILL THE TIME UNTIL ZAYNE RETURNS.

MANDALORIANS. WHO CAN FIGURE THEM?

HE'S BEEN WONDERFUL TO ME.

OH, I KNOW--

-- INTELLECTUALLY, I KNOW. BUT MY SENSES ARE ALL TWISTED WHEN IT COMES TO THAT GUY. SEEING HIM JUST REMINDS ME OF *FLASHPOINT* --

-- AND WHAT *DEMAGOL* DID TO ME THERE.

WELL, REMEMBER WHAT ROHLAN DID *FOR* YOU THERE. HE SAVED YOUR LIFE.

YOU SAID HIS PEOPLE ARE CALLING HIM *"THE QUESTIONER"* AFTER THAT.

YEAH, AND NOW PEOPLE ARE CALLING MY MASTER *"THE REVANCHIST."* WE'RE LIVING IN THE DAYS OF THE SNAPPY SOBRIQUET.

ALMOST MAKES YOU FORGET HOW DEADLY SERIOUS IT'S ALL BECOME...

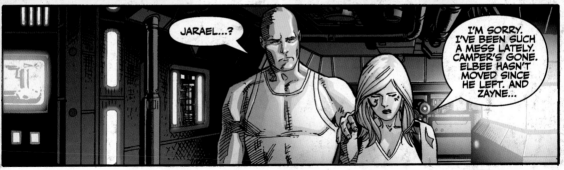

JARAEL...?

I'M SORRY. I'VE BEEN SUCH A MESS LATELY. CAMPER'S GONE. ELBEE HASN'T MOVED SINCE HE LEFT. AND ZAYNE...

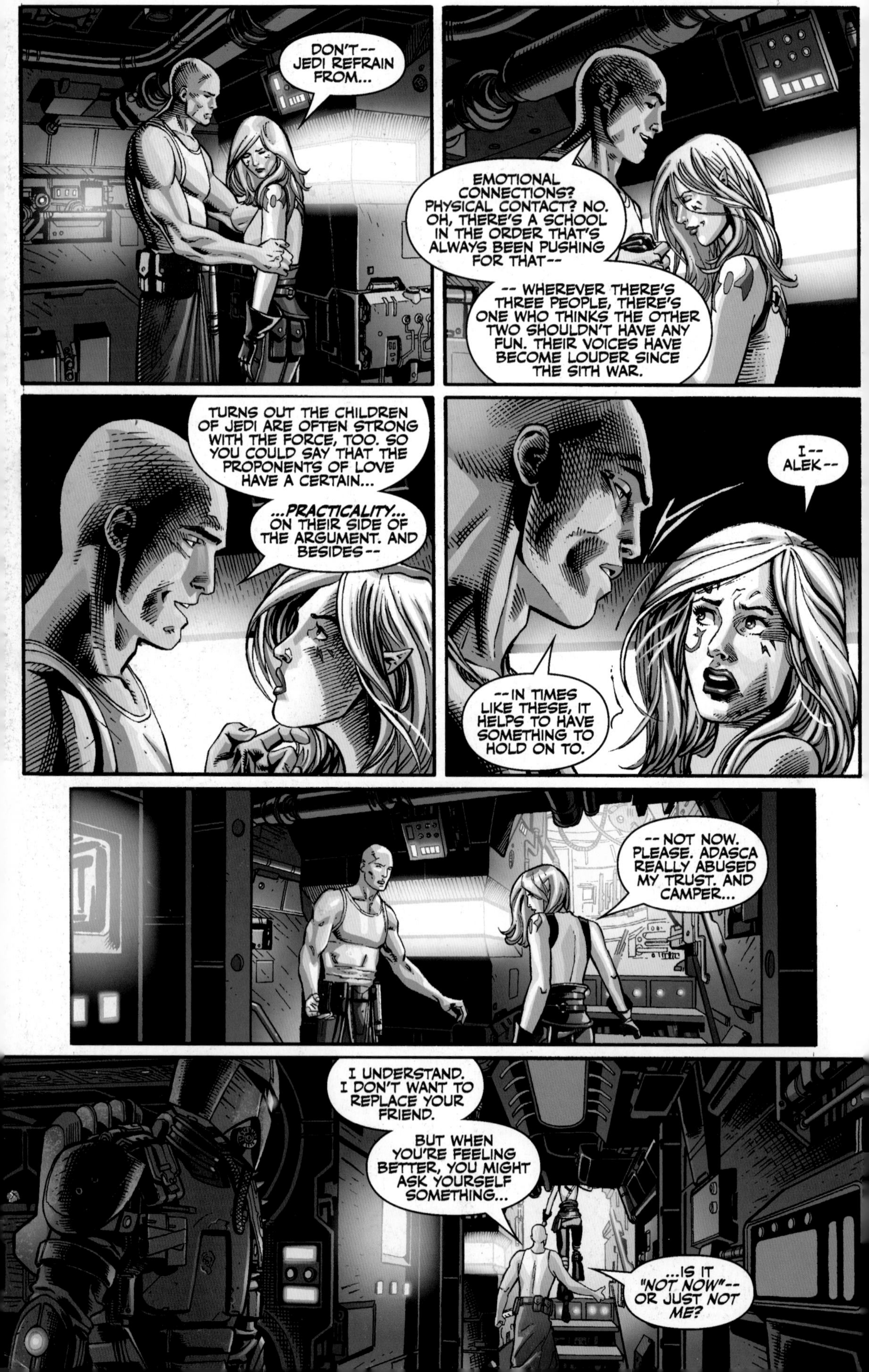
DON'T-- JEDI REFRAIN FROM...
EMOTIONAL CONNECTIONS? PHYSICAL CONTACT? NO. OH, THERE'S A SCHOOL IN THE ORDER THAT'S ALWAYS BEEN PUSHING FOR THAT--
-- WHEREVER THERE'S THREE PEOPLE, THERE'S ONE WHO THINKS THE OTHER TWO SHOULDN'T HAVE ANY FUN. THEIR VOICES HAVE BECOME LOUDER SINCE THE SITH WAR.
TURNS OUT THE CHILDREN OF JEDI ARE OFTEN STRONG WITH THE FORCE, TOO. SO YOU COULD SAY THAT THE PROPONENTS OF LOVE HAVE A CERTAIN...
...PRACTICALITY... ON THEIR SIDE OF THE ARGUMENT. AND BESIDES--
--IN TIMES LIKE THESE, IT HELPS TO HAVE SOMETHING TO HOLD ON TO.
I-- ALEK--
-- NOT NOW. PLEASE. ADASCA REALLY ABUSED MY TRUST. AND CAMPER...
I UNDERSTAND. I DON'T WANT TO REPLACE YOUR FRIEND.
BUT WHEN YOU'RE FEELING BETTER, YOU MIGHT ASK YOURSELF SOMETHING...
...IS IT "NOT NOW"-- OR JUST NOT ME?

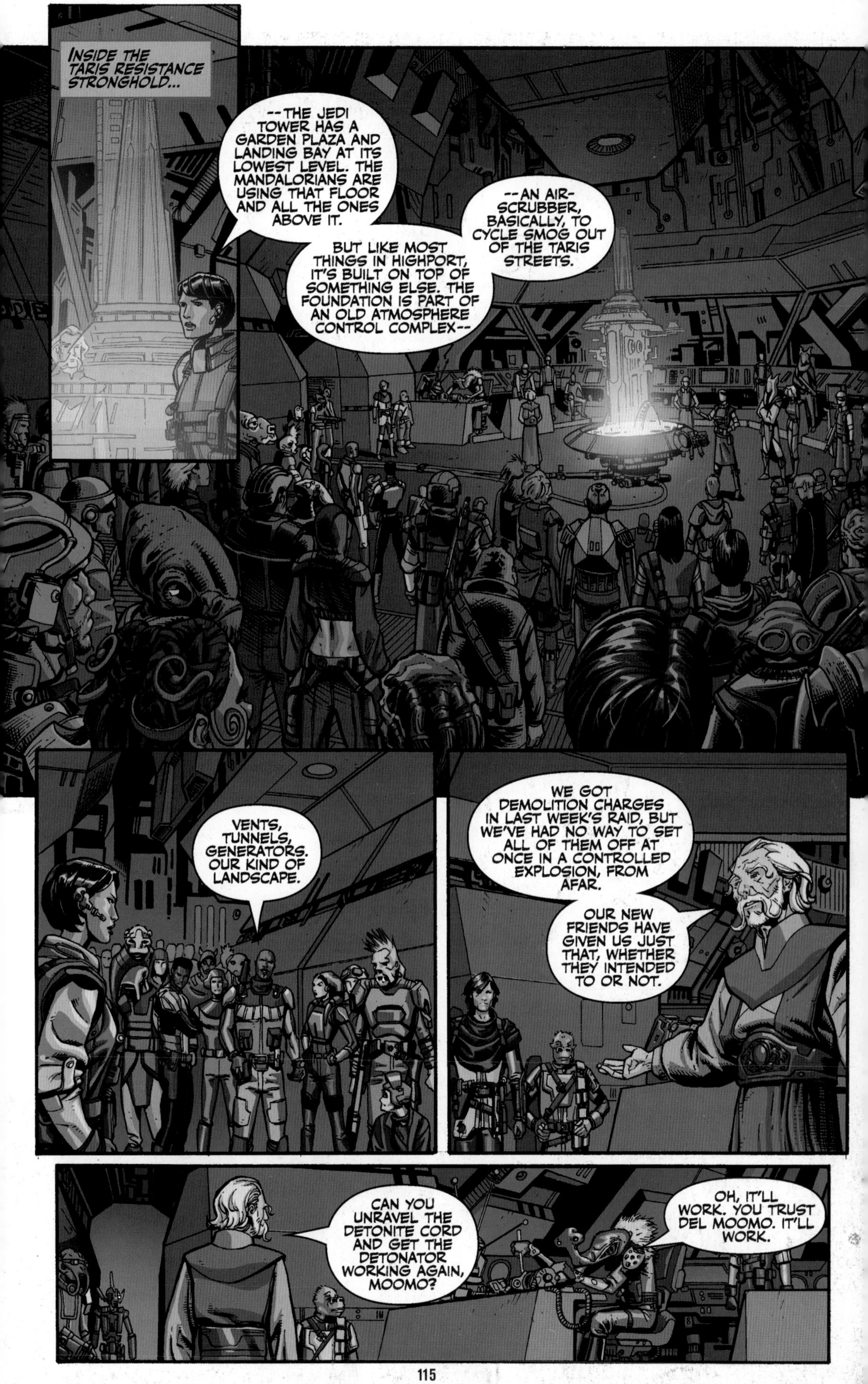
Inside the Taris Resistance stronghold...
--The Jedi tower has a garden plaza and landing bay at its lowest level. The Mandalorians are using that floor and all the ones above it.
But like most things in Highport, it's built on top of something else. The foundation is part of an old atmosphere control complex--
--An air-scrubber, basically, to cycle smog out of the Taris streets.
Vents, tunnels, generators. Our kind of landscape.
We got demolition charges in last week's raid, but we've had no way to set all of them off at once in a controlled explosion, from afar.
Our new friends have given us just that, whether they intended to or not.
Can you unravel the detonite cord and get the detonator working again, Moomo?
Oh, it'll work. You trust Del Moomo. It'll work.

CAN I PRESS THE BUTTON? I REALLY, *REALLY* WANT TO PRESS THE BUTTON.

IT'S OKAY. DESTRUCTION IS THE ONE THING HE *IS* GOOD AT.

SENATOR, ARE YOU SURE YOU WANT TO DO THIS? WHAT ABOUT THE PEOPLE WHO LIVE NEAR THE TOWER?

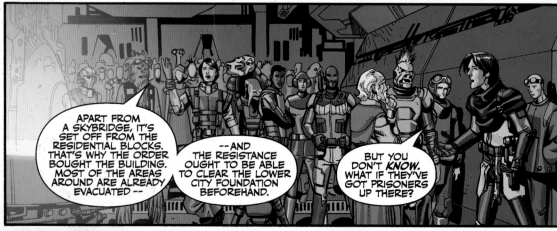

APART FROM A SKYBRIDGE, IT'S SET OFF FROM THE RESIDENTIAL BLOCKS. THAT'S WHY THE ORDER BOUGHT THE BUILDING. MOST OF THE AREAS AROUND ARE ALREADY EVACUATED --

-- AND THE RESISTANCE OUGHT TO BE ABLE TO CLEAR THE LOWER CITY FOUNDATION BEFOREHAND.

BUT YOU DON'T *KNOW.* WHAT IF THEY'VE GOT PRISONERS UP THERE?

IT'S A *WAR,* KID!

THEN WHAT IF CASSUS ISN'T THERE? YOU'VE WASTED YOUR MUNITIONS.

I AGREE. WE NEED A SAME-DAY RECON, THEN.

RAANA TEY, IS THERE A WAY FROM THE FOUNDATION INTO THE JEDI TOWER PROPER?

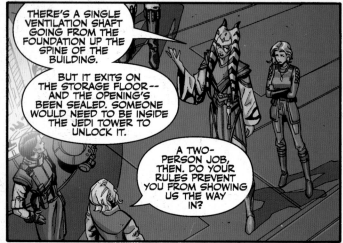

THERE'S A SINGLE VENTILATION SHAFT GOING FROM THE FOUNDATION UP THE SPINE OF THE BUILDING.

BUT IT EXITS ON THE STORAGE FLOOR -- AND THE OPENING'S BEEN SEALED. SOMEONE WOULD NEED TO BE INSIDE THE JEDI TOWER TO UNLOCK IT.

A TWO-PERSON JOB, THEN. DO YOUR RULES PREVENT YOU FROM SHOWING US THE WAY IN?

SENATOR, I'VE TOLD YOU --

I'LL DO IT.

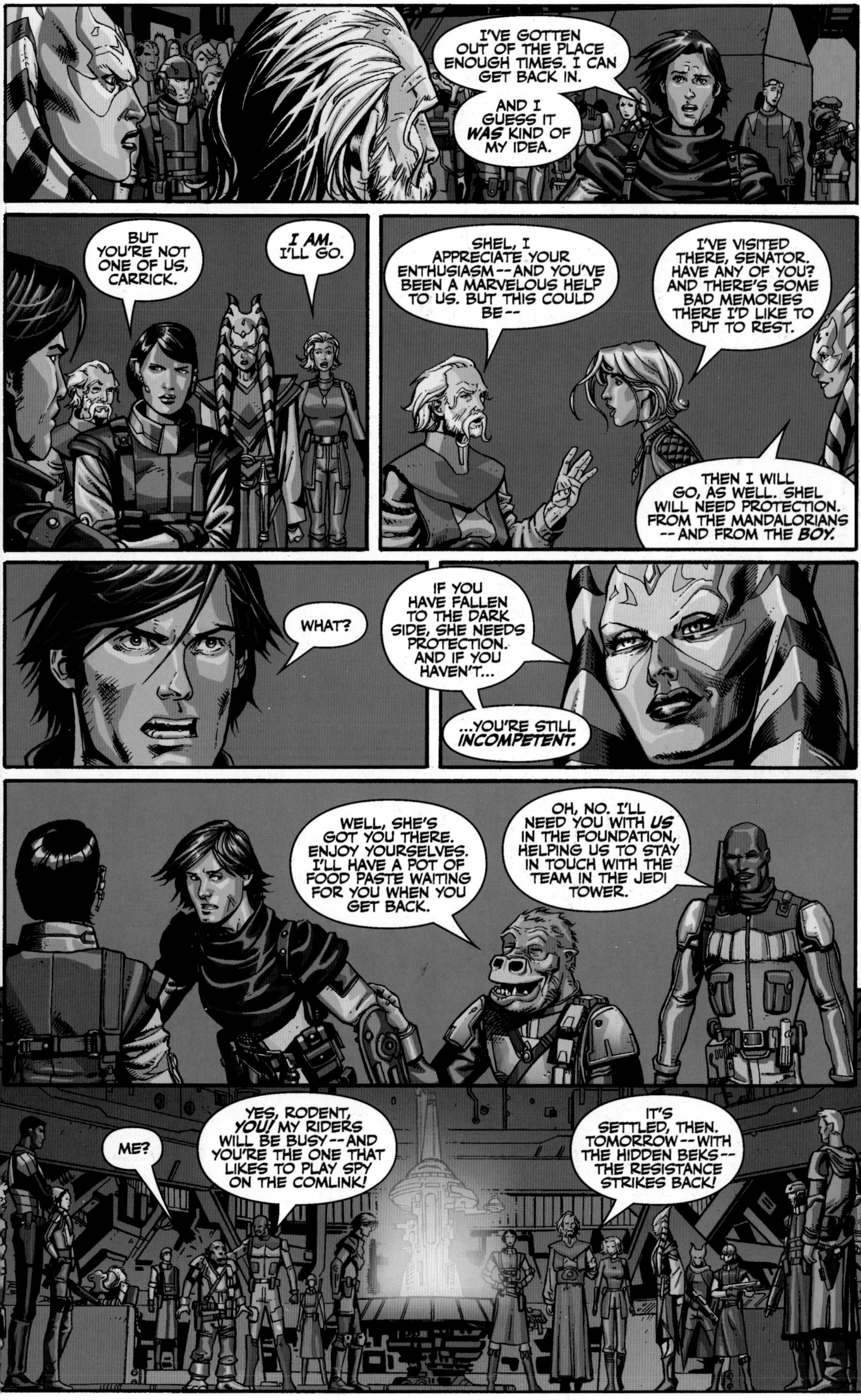
I'VE GOTTEN OUT OF THE PLACE ENOUGH TIMES. I CAN GET BACK IN.
AND I GUESS IT *WAS* KIND OF MY IDEA.
BUT YOU'RE NOT ONE OF US, CARRICK.
I AM. I'LL GO.
SHEL, I APPRECIATE YOUR ENTHUSIASM--AND YOU'VE BEEN A MARVELOUS HELP TO US. BUT THIS COULD BE--
I'VE VISITED THERE, SENATOR. HAVE ANY OF YOU? AND THERE'S SOME BAD MEMORIES THERE I'D LIKE TO PUT TO REST.
THEN I WILL GO, AS WELL. SHEL WILL NEED PROTECTION. FROM THE MANDALORIANS --AND FROM THE *BOY.*
WHAT?
IF YOU HAVE FALLEN TO THE DARK SIDE, SHE NEEDS PROTECTION. AND IF YOU HAVEN'T...
...YOU'RE STILL *INCOMPETENT.*
WELL, SHE'S GOT YOU THERE. ENJOY YOURSELVES. I'LL HAVE A POT OF FOOD PASTE WAITING FOR YOU WHEN YOU GET BACK.
OH, NO. I'LL NEED YOU WITH *US* IN THE FOUNDATION, HELPING US TO STAY IN TOUCH WITH THE TEAM IN THE JEDI TOWER.
ME?
YES, RODENT, *YOU!* MY RIDERS WILL BE BUSY--AND YOU'RE THE ONE THAT LIKES TO PLAY SPY ON THE COMLINK!
IT'S SETTLED, THEN. TOMORROW--WITH THE HIDDEN BEKS--THE RESISTANCE STRIKES BACK!

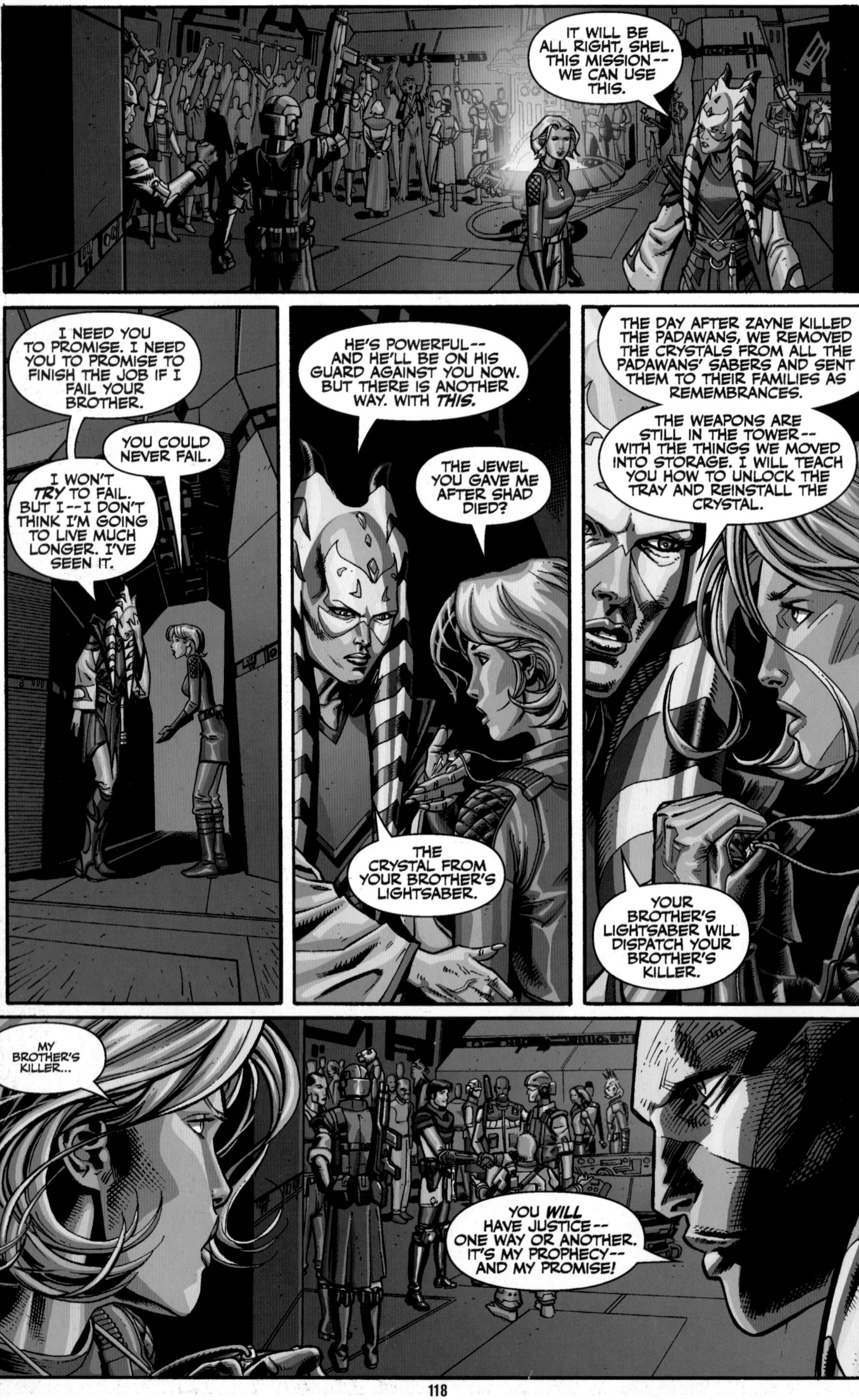
IT WILL BE ALL RIGHT, SHEL. THIS MISSION-- WE CAN USE THIS.
I NEED YOU TO PROMISE. I NEED YOU TO PROMISE TO FINISH THE JOB IF I FAIL YOUR BROTHER.
YOU COULD NEVER FAIL.
I WON'T TRY TO FAIL. BUT I--I DON'T THINK I'M GOING TO LIVE MUCH LONGER. I'VE SEEN IT.
HE'S POWERFUL-- AND HE'LL BE ON HIS GUARD AGAINST YOU NOW. BUT THERE IS ANOTHER WAY. WITH THIS.
THE JEWEL YOU GAVE ME AFTER SHAD DIED?
THE CRYSTAL FROM YOUR BROTHER'S LIGHTSABER.
THE DAY AFTER ZAYNE KILLED THE PADAWANS, WE REMOVED THE CRYSTALS FROM ALL THE PADAWANS' SABERS AND SENT THEM TO THEIR FAMILIES AS REMEMBRANCES.
THE WEAPONS ARE STILL IN THE TOWER-- WITH THE THINGS WE MOVED INTO STORAGE. I WILL TEACH YOU HOW TO UNLOCK THE TRAY AND REINSTALL THE CRYSTAL.
YOUR BROTHER'S LIGHTSABER WILL DISPATCH YOUR BROTHER'S KILLER.
MY BROTHER'S KILLER...
YOU WILL HAVE JUSTICE-- ONE WAY OR ANOTHER. IT'S MY PROPHECY-- AND MY PROMISE!

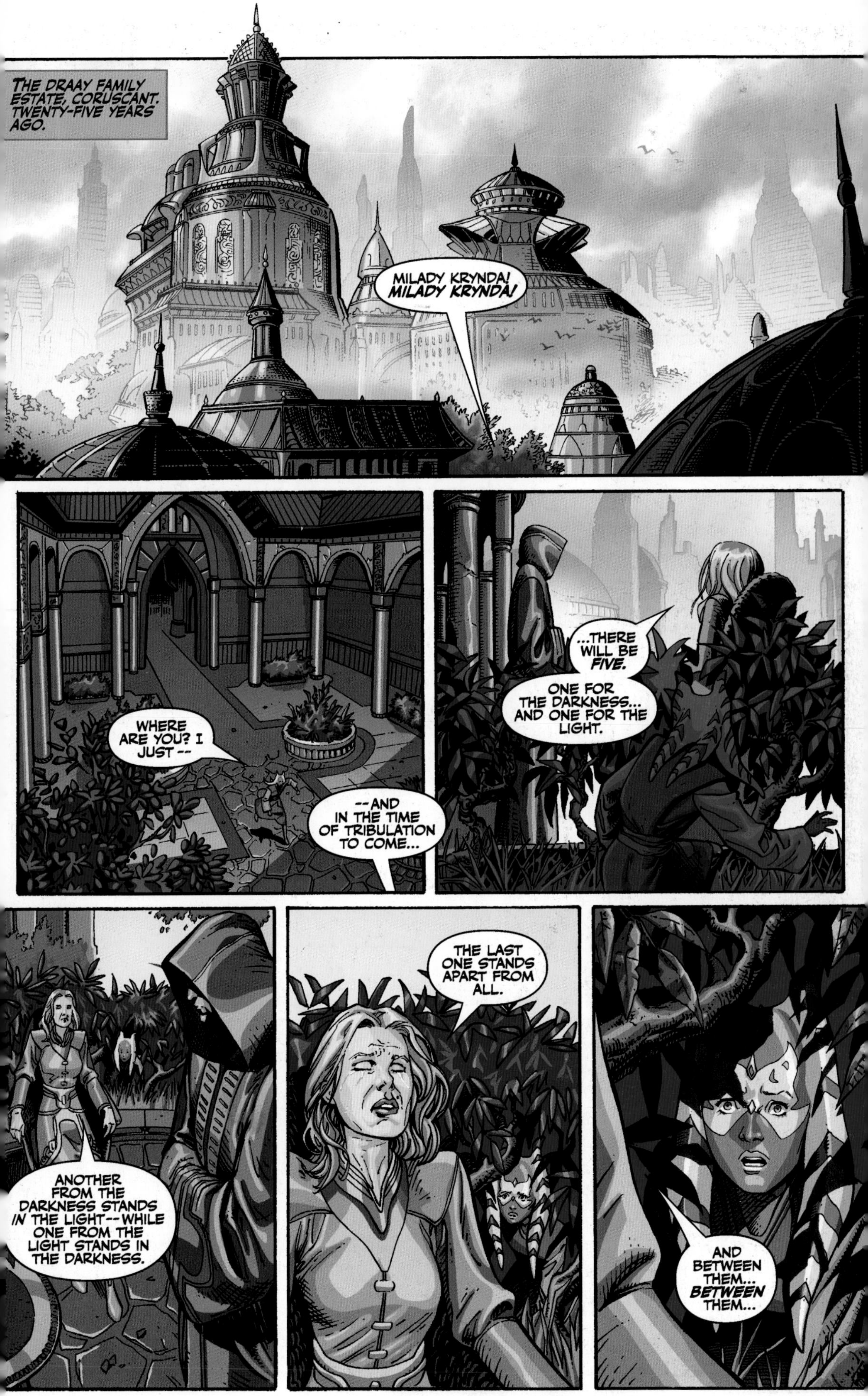
THE DRAAY FAMILY ESTATE, CORUSCANT. TWENTY-FIVE YEARS AGO.
MILADY KRYNDA! MILADY KRYNDA!
WHERE ARE YOU? I JUST --
--AND IN THE TIME OF TRIBULATION TO COME...
...THERE WILL BE FIVE.
ONE FOR THE DARKNESS... AND ONE FOR THE LIGHT.
ANOTHER FROM THE DARKNESS STANDS IN THE LIGHT--WHILE ONE FROM THE LIGHT STANDS IN THE DARKNESS.
THE LAST ONE STANDS APART FROM ALL.
AND BETWEEN THEM... BETWEEN THEM...

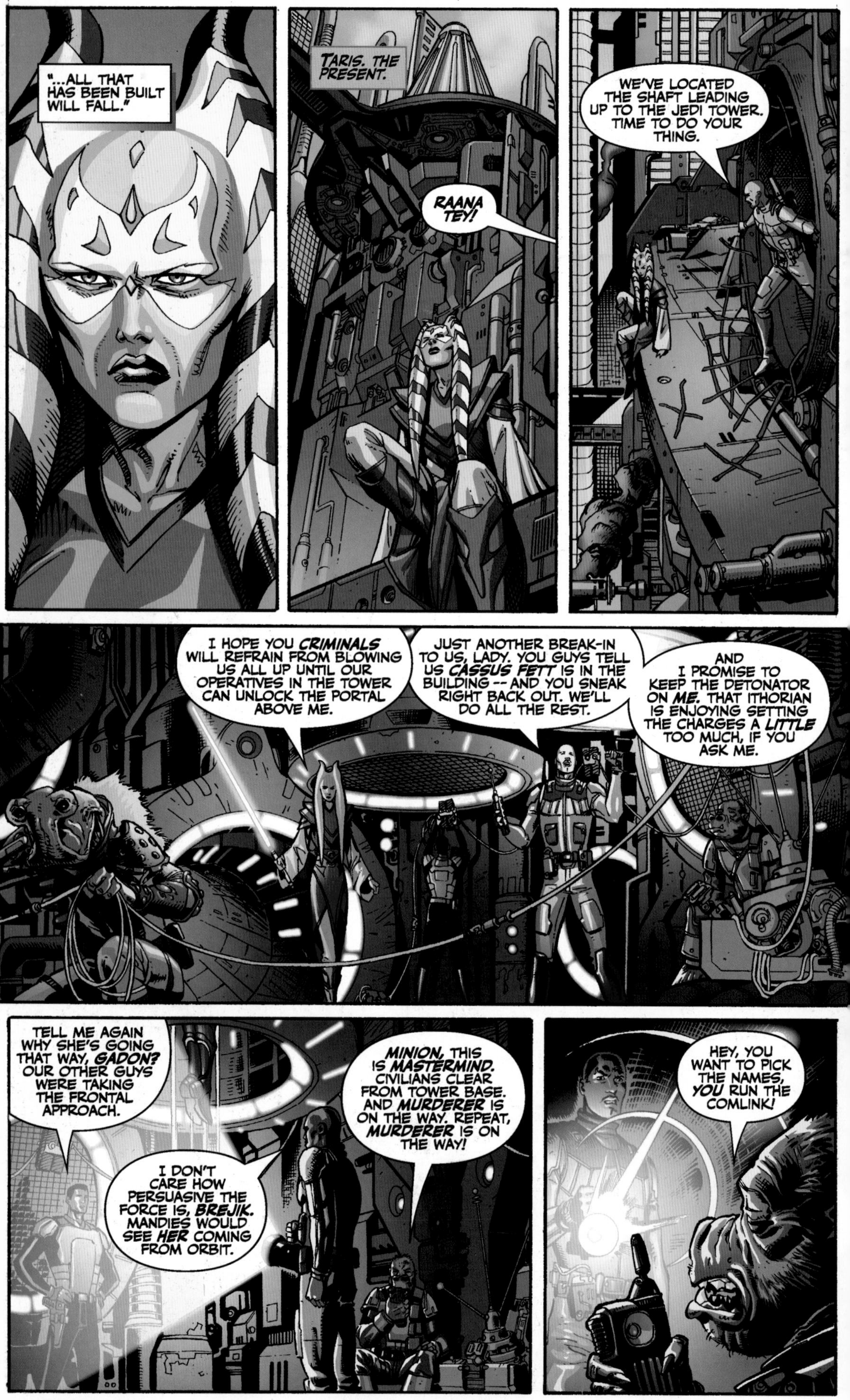
"...ALL THAT HAS BEEN BUILT WILL FALL."
TARIS. THE PRESENT.
RAANA TEY!
WE'VE LOCATED THE SHAFT LEADING UP TO THE JEDI TOWER. TIME TO DO YOUR THING.
I HOPE YOU CRIMINALS WILL REFRAIN FROM BLOWING US ALL UP UNTIL OUR OPERATIVES IN THE TOWER CAN UNLOCK THE PORTAL ABOVE ME.
JUST ANOTHER BREAK-IN TO US, LADY. YOU GUYS TELL US CASSUS FETT IS IN THE BUILDING -- AND YOU SNEAK RIGHT BACK OUT. WE'LL DO ALL THE REST.
AND I PROMISE TO KEEP THE DETONATOR ON ME. THAT ITHORIAN IS ENJOYING SETTING THE CHARGES A LITTLE TOO MUCH, IF YOU ASK ME.
TELL ME AGAIN WHY SHE'S GOING THAT WAY, GADON? OUR OTHER GUYS WERE TAKING THE FRONTAL APPROACH.
I DON'T CARE HOW PERSUASIVE THE FORCE IS, BREJIK. MANDIES WOULD SEE HER COMING FROM ORBIT.
MINION, THIS IS MASTERMIND. CIVILIANS CLEAR FROM TOWER BASE. AND MURDERER IS ON THE WAY. REPEAT, MURDERER IS ON THE WAY!
HEY, YOU WANT TO PICK THE NAMES, YOU RUN THE COMLINK!

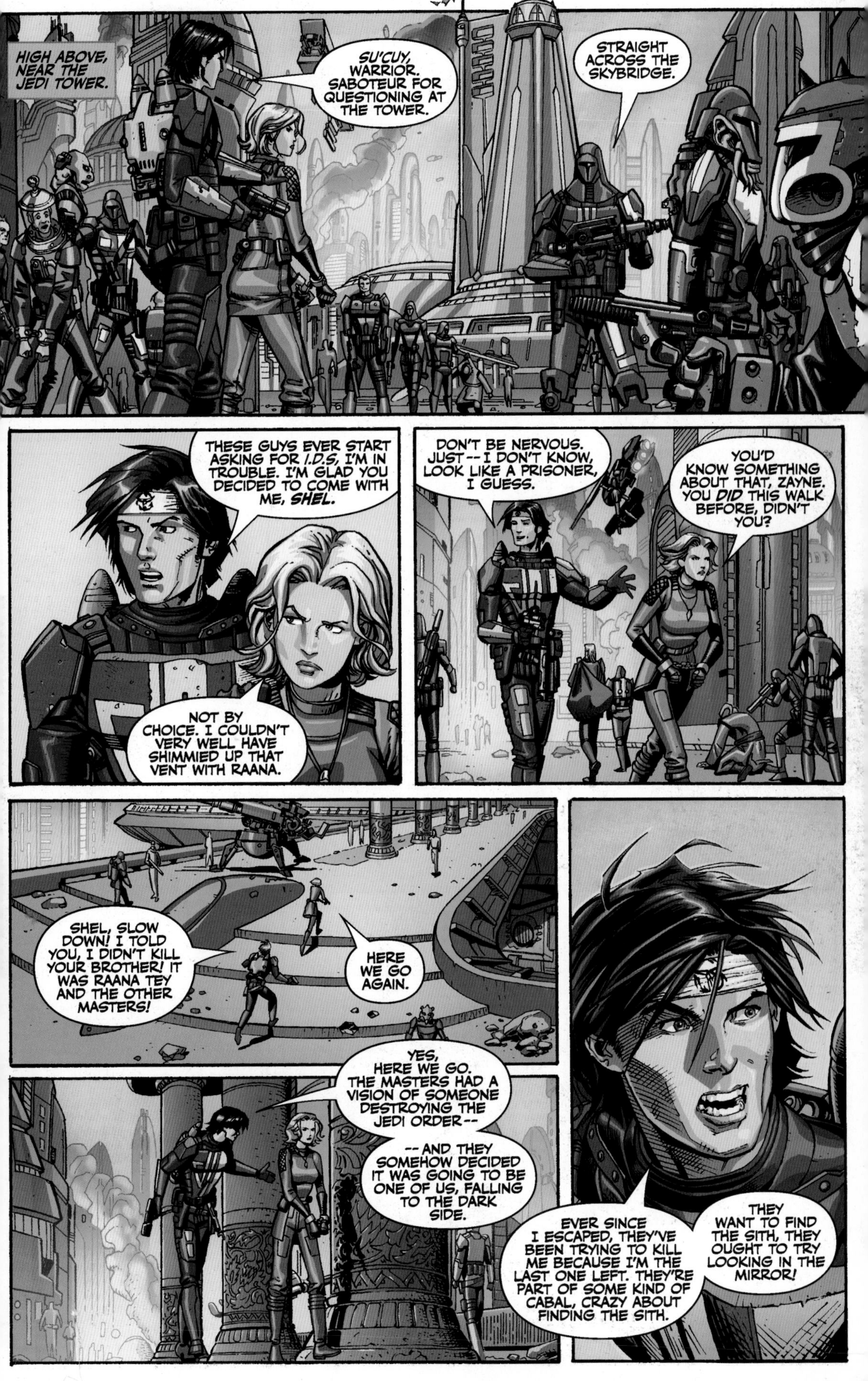

HIGH ABOVE, NEAR THE JEDI TOWER.
SU'CUY, WARRIOR. SABOTEUR FOR QUESTIONING AT THE TOWER.
STRAIGHT ACROSS THE SKYBRIDGE.
THESE GUYS EVER START ASKING FOR I.D.S, I'M IN TROUBLE. I'M GLAD YOU DECIDED TO COME WITH ME, SHEL.
NOT BY CHOICE. I COULDN'T VERY WELL HAVE SHIMMIED UP THAT VENT WITH RAANA.
DON'T BE NERVOUS. JUST-- I DON'T KNOW, LOOK LIKE A PRISONER, I GUESS.
YOU'D KNOW SOMETHING ABOUT THAT, ZAYNE. YOU DID THIS WALK BEFORE, DIDN'T YOU?
SHEL, SLOW DOWN! I TOLD YOU, I DIDN'T KILL YOUR BROTHER! IT WAS RAANA TEY AND THE OTHER MASTERS!
HERE WE GO AGAIN.
YES, HERE WE GO. THE MASTERS HAD A VISION OF SOMEONE DESTROYING THE JEDI ORDER--
-- AND THEY SOMEHOW DECIDED IT WAS GOING TO BE ONE OF US, FALLING TO THE DARK SIDE.
EVER SINCE I ESCAPED, THEY'VE BEEN TRYING TO KILL ME BECAUSE I'M THE LAST ONE LEFT. THEY'RE PART OF SOME KIND OF CABAL, CRAZY ABOUT FINDING THE SITH.
THEY WANT TO FIND THE SITH, THEY OUGHT TO TRY LOOKING IN THE MIRROR!

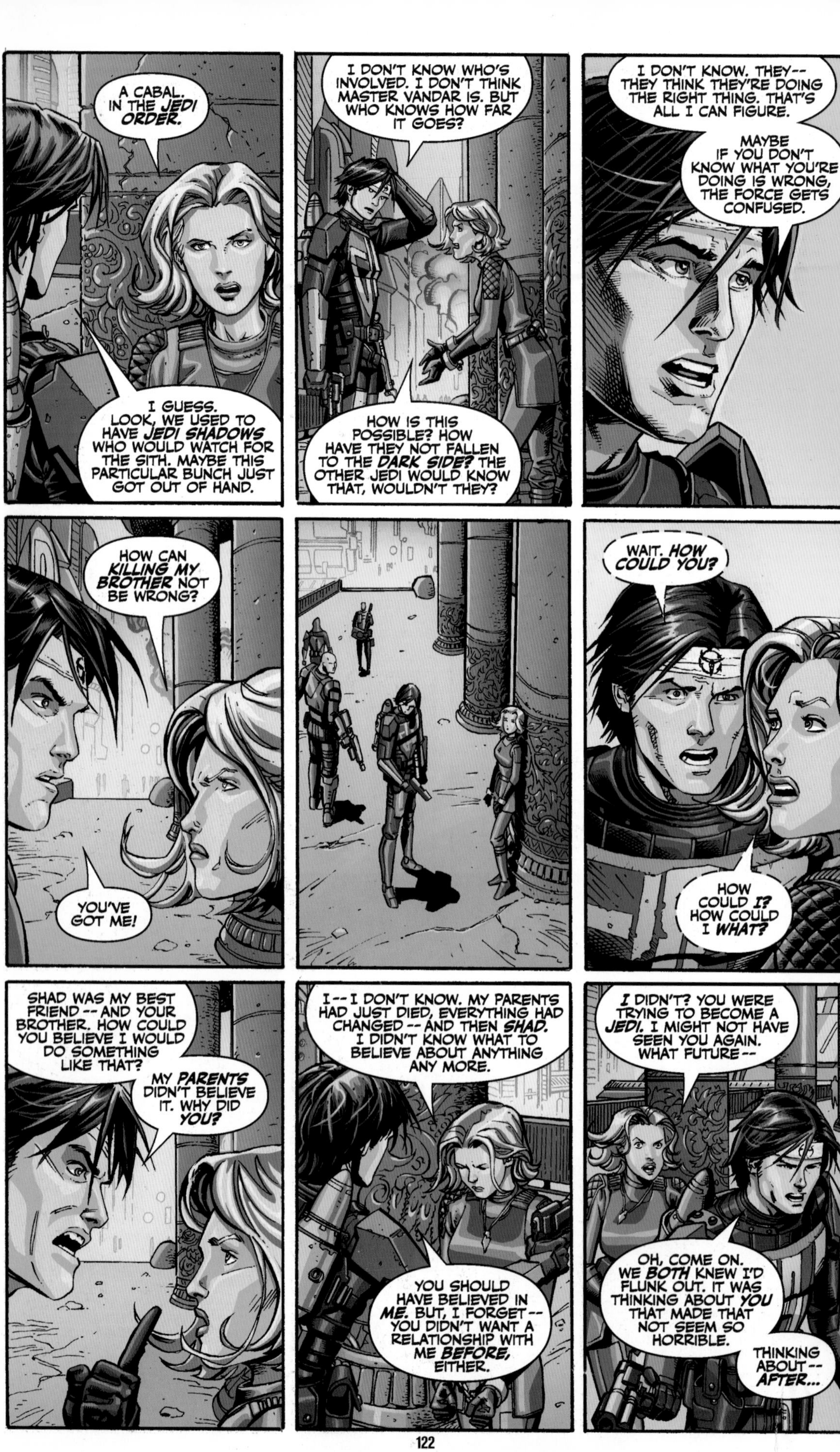
A CABAL. IN THE JEDI ORDER.
I GUESS. LOOK, WE USED TO HAVE JEDI SHADOWS WHO WOULD WATCH FOR THE SITH. MAYBE THIS PARTICULAR BUNCH JUST GOT OUT OF HAND.
I DON'T KNOW WHO'S INVOLVED. I DON'T THINK MASTER VANDAR IS. BUT WHO KNOWS HOW FAR IT GOES?
HOW IS THIS POSSIBLE? HOW HAVE THEY NOT FALLEN TO THE DARK SIDE? THE OTHER JEDI WOULD KNOW THAT, WOULDN'T THEY?
I DON'T KNOW. THEY-- THEY THINK THEY'RE DOING THE RIGHT THING. THAT'S ALL I CAN FIGURE.
MAYBE IF YOU DON'T KNOW WHAT YOU'RE DOING IS WRONG, THE FORCE GETS CONFUSED.
HOW CAN KILLING MY BROTHER NOT BE WRONG?
YOU'VE GOT ME!
WAIT. HOW COULD YOU?
HOW COULD I? HOW COULD I WHAT?
SHAD WAS MY BEST FRIEND -- AND YOUR BROTHER. HOW COULD YOU BELIEVE I WOULD DO SOMETHING LIKE THAT?
MY PARENTS DIDN'T BELIEVE IT. WHY DID YOU?
I -- I DON'T KNOW. MY PARENTS HAD JUST DIED, EVERYTHING HAD CHANGED -- AND THEN SHAD. I DIDN'T KNOW WHAT TO BELIEVE ABOUT ANYTHING ANY MORE.
YOU SHOULD HAVE BELIEVED IN ME. BUT, I FORGET -- YOU DIDN'T WANT A RELATIONSHIP WITH ME BEFORE, EITHER.
I DIDN'T? YOU WERE TRYING TO BECOME A JEDI. I MIGHT NOT HAVE SEEN YOU AGAIN. WHAT FUTURE --
OH, COME ON. WE BOTH KNEW I'D FLUNK OUT. IT WAS THINKING ABOUT YOU THAT MADE THAT NOT SEEM SO HORRIBLE.
THINKING ABOUT -- AFTER...

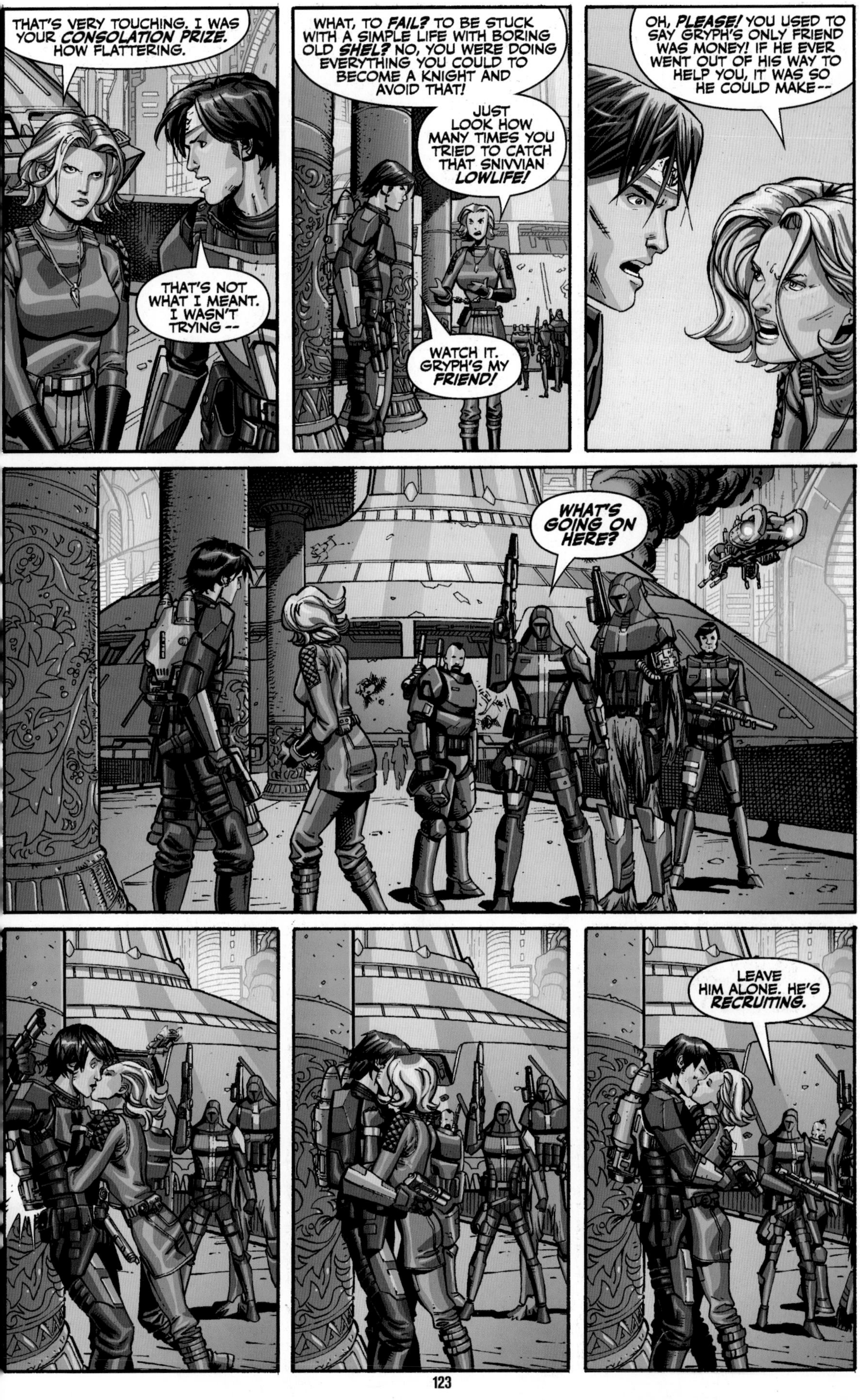

THAT'S VERY TOUCHING. I WAS YOUR *CONSOLATION PRIZE.* HOW FLATTERING.
THAT'S NOT WHAT I MEANT. I WASN'T TRYING --
WHAT, TO *FAIL?* TO BE STUCK WITH A SIMPLE LIFE WITH BORING OLD *SHEL?* NO, YOU WERE DOING EVERYTHING YOU COULD TO BECOME A KNIGHT AND AVOID THAT!
JUST LOOK HOW MANY TIMES YOU TRIED TO CATCH THAT SNIVVIAN *LOWLIFE!*
WATCH IT. GRYPH'S MY *FRIEND!*
OH, *PLEASE!* YOU USED TO SAY GRYPH'S ONLY FRIEND WAS MONEY! IF HE EVER WENT OUT OF HIS WAY TO HELP YOU, IT WAS SO HE COULD MAKE--
WHAT'S GOING ON HERE?
LEAVE HIM ALONE. HE'S *RECRUITING.*

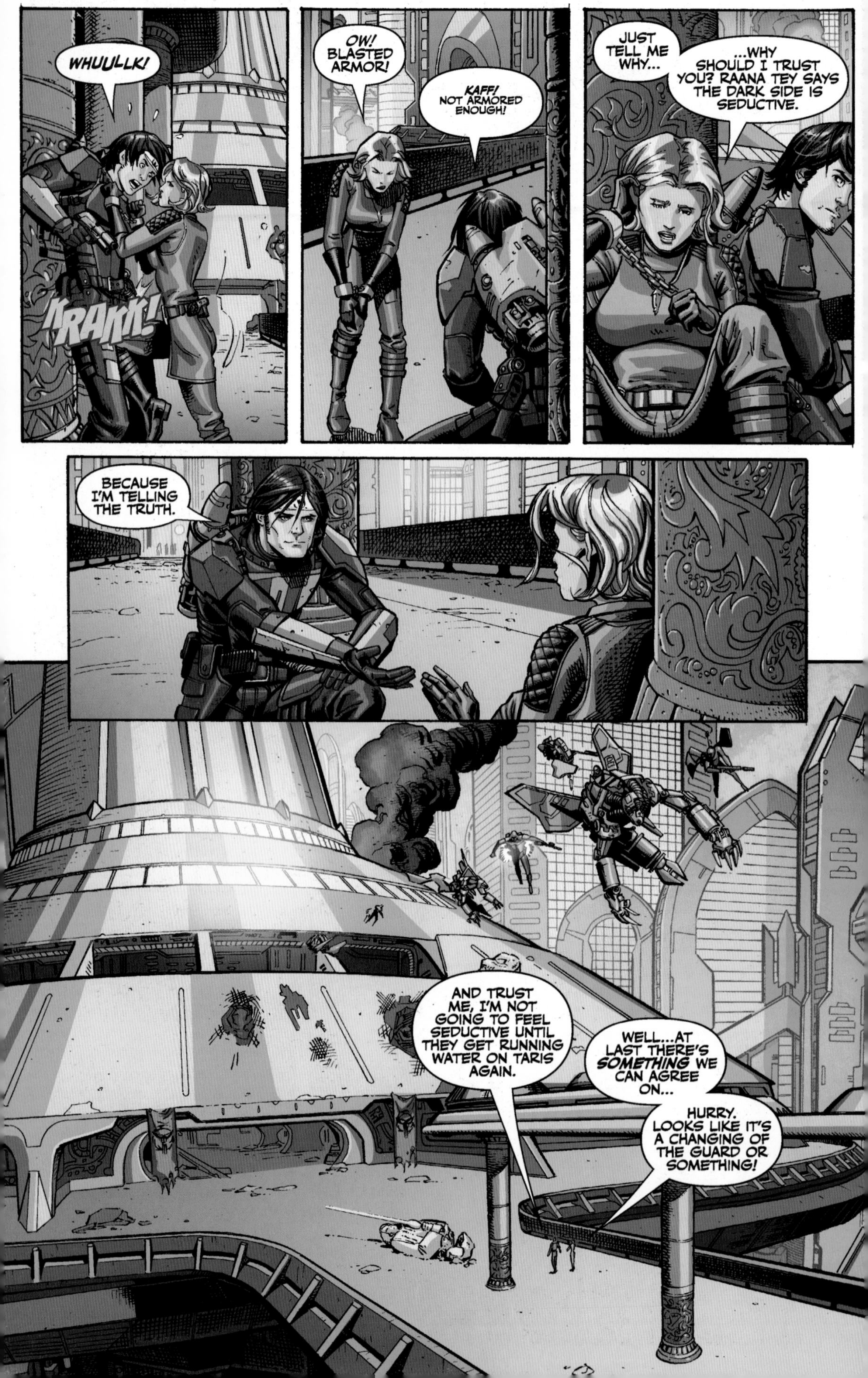
WHUULLK!
KRAKK!
OW! BLASTED ARMOR!
KAFF! NOT ARMORED ENOUGH!
JUST TELL ME WHY...
...WHY SHOULD I TRUST YOU? RAANA TEY SAYS THE DARK SIDE IS SEDUCTIVE.
BECAUSE I'M TELLING THE TRUTH.
AND TRUST ME, I'M NOT GOING TO FEEL SEDUCTIVE UNTIL THEY GET RUNNING WATER ON TARIS AGAIN.
WELL...AT LAST THERE'S SOMETHING WE CAN AGREE ON...
HURRY. LOOKS LIKE IT'S A CHANGING OF THE GUARD OR SOMETHING!

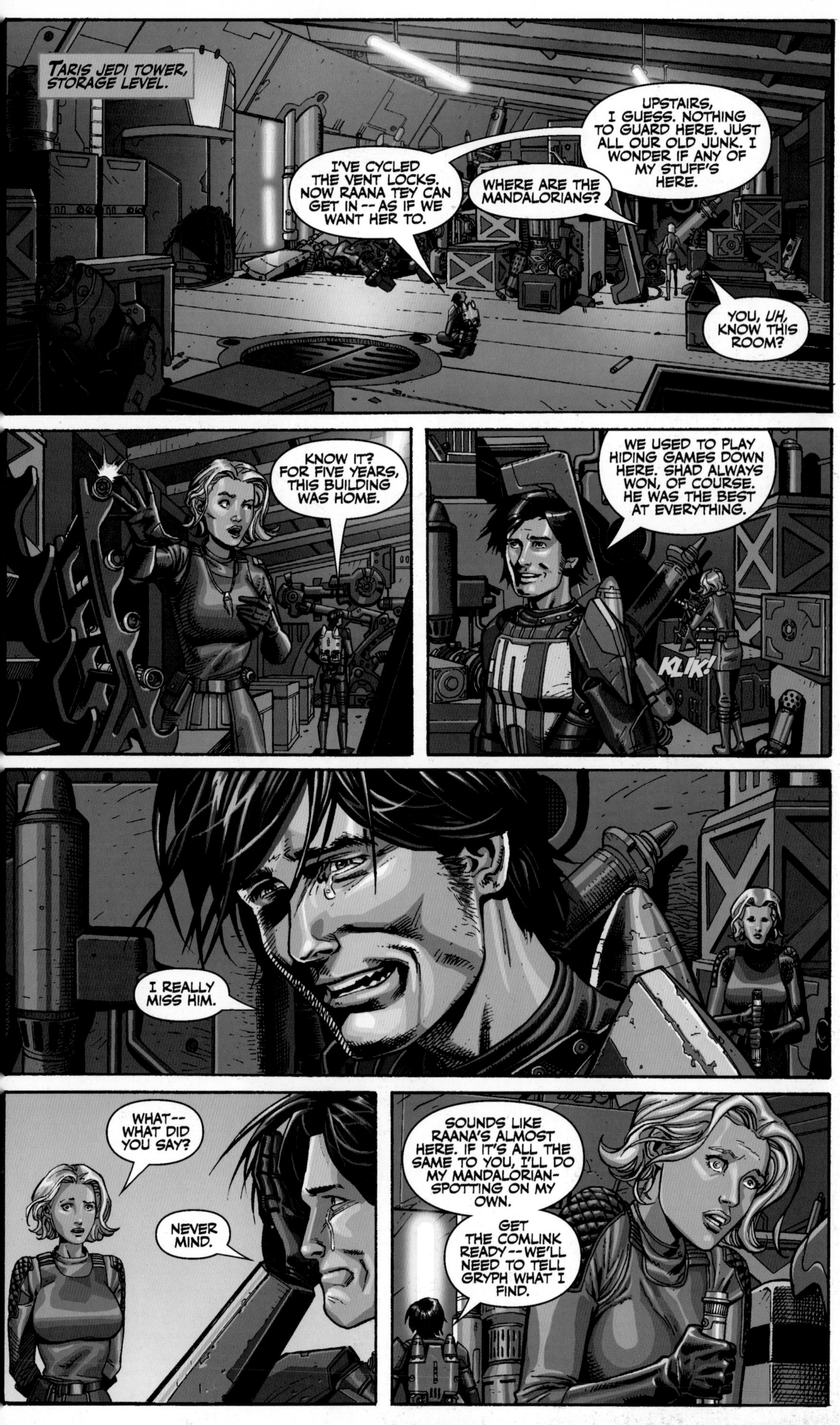
TARIS JEDI TOWER, STORAGE LEVEL.
I'VE CYCLED THE VENT LOCKS. NOW RAANA TEY CAN GET IN -- AS IF WE WANT HER TO.
WHERE ARE THE MANDALORIANS?
UPSTAIRS, I GUESS. NOTHING TO GUARD HERE. JUST ALL OUR OLD JUNK. I WONDER IF ANY OF MY STUFF'S HERE.
YOU, UH, KNOW THIS ROOM?
KNOW IT? FOR FIVE YEARS, THIS BUILDING WAS HOME.
WE USED TO PLAY HIDING GAMES DOWN HERE. SHAD ALWAYS WON, OF COURSE. HE WAS THE BEST AT EVERYTHING.
KLIK!
I REALLY MISS HIM.
WHAT-- WHAT DID YOU SAY?
NEVER MIND.
SOUNDS LIKE RAANA'S ALMOST HERE. IF IT'S ALL THE SAME TO YOU, I'LL DO MY MANDALORIAN-SPOTTING ON MY OWN.
GET THE COMLINK READY--WE'LL NEED TO TELL GRYPH WHAT I FIND.

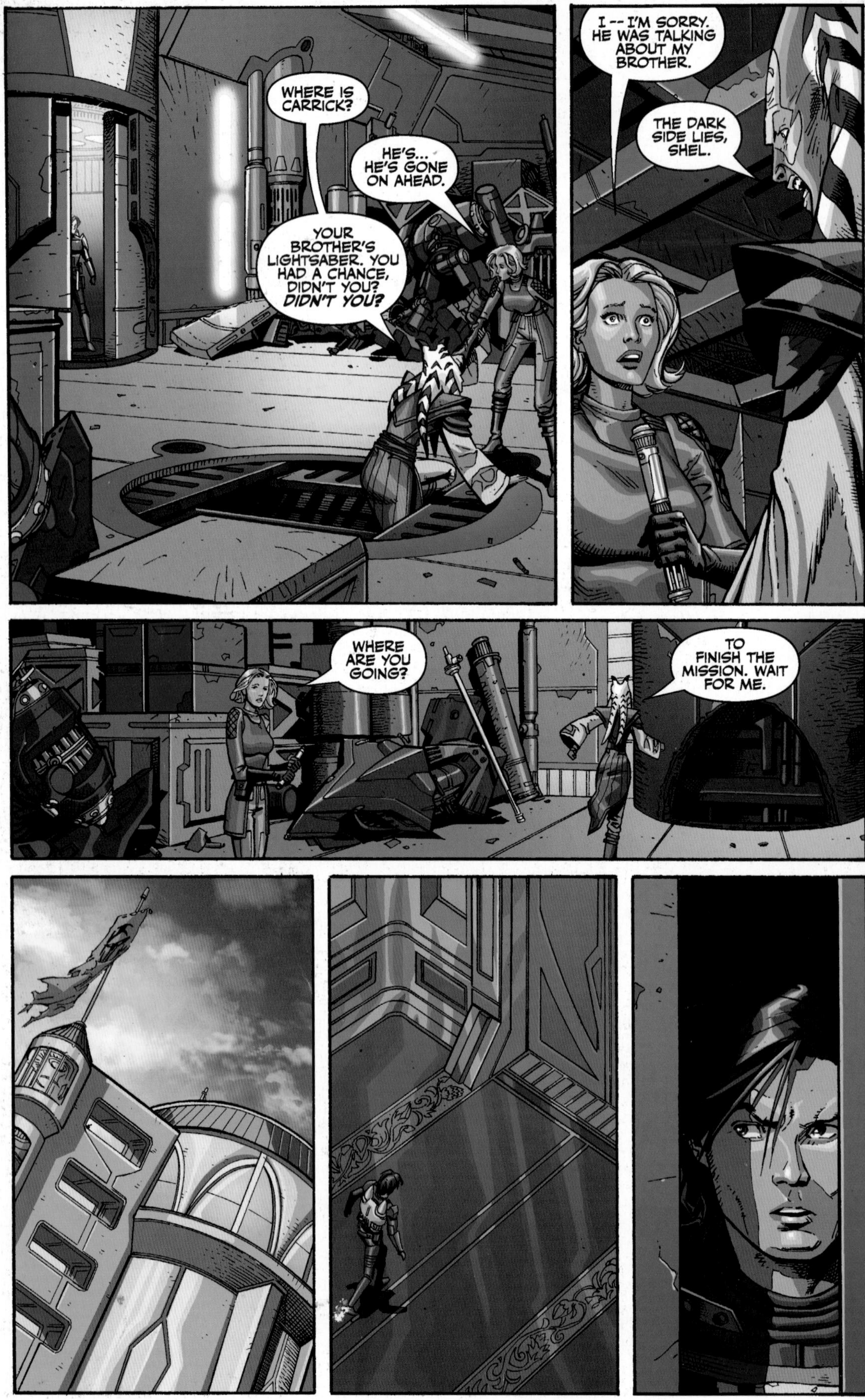
WHERE IS CARRICK?
HE'S... HE'S GONE ON AHEAD.
YOUR BROTHER'S LIGHTSABER. YOU HAD A CHANCE, DIDN'T YOU? DIDN'T YOU?
I -- I'M SORRY. HE WAS TALKING ABOUT MY BROTHER.
THE DARK SIDE LIES, SHEL.
WHERE ARE YOU GOING?
TO FINISH THE MISSION. WAIT FOR ME.

WHAT, DID YOU GET LEFT BEHIND?
I'M-- NEW.
YOU AND EVERYBODY ELSE. I SUPPOSE YOU LOST YOUR HELMET, WHILE YOU WERE AT IT. ROOKIES.
ARE YOU--ARE YOU *CASSUS FETT?*
COLOR-BLIND TOO, *HUH?* NO, CASSUS PULLED OUT AN HOUR AGO.
I THOUGHT THIS WAS HIS HEADQUARTERS.
WE'RE NOMADS. WE DON'T *HAVE* HEADQUARTERS. IF YOU DON'T MOVE AROUND, SOMEONE WILL FIND YOU.
THE LOCALS SURE DON'T KNOW THAT. CASSUS STUDIED THEIR STRONG POINTS IN THE LOWER CITY AND FIGURED OUT WHERE THEY'RE HOLED UP. THAT'S WHERE HE'S GONE.
AFTER THE RESISTANCE?
WHAT ARE YOU DOING HERE, AGAIN?
SORRY-- THIS IS A MISTAKE. I'VE GOT TO GO.
WAIT A MINUTE. WHAT ARE YOU DOING--?

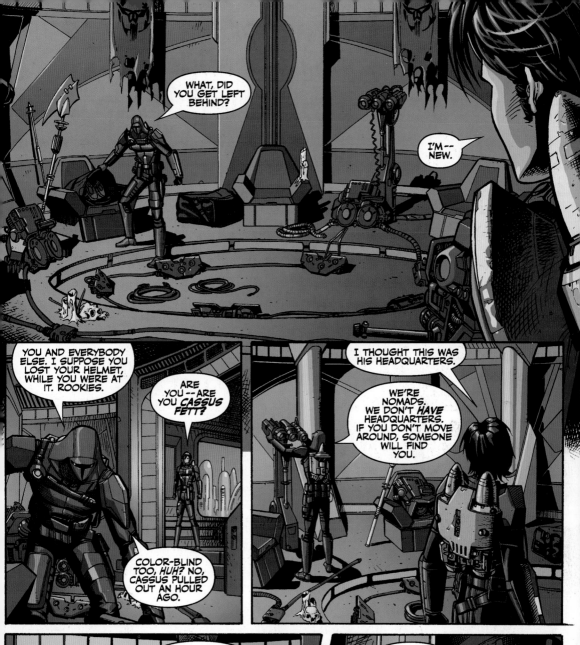

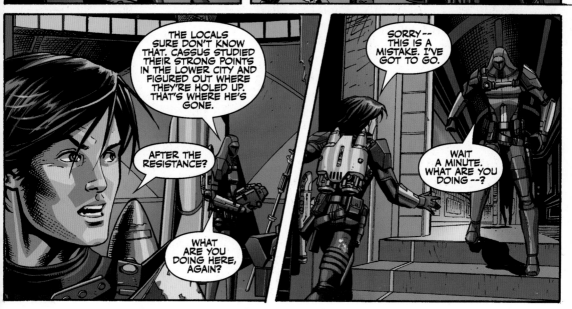

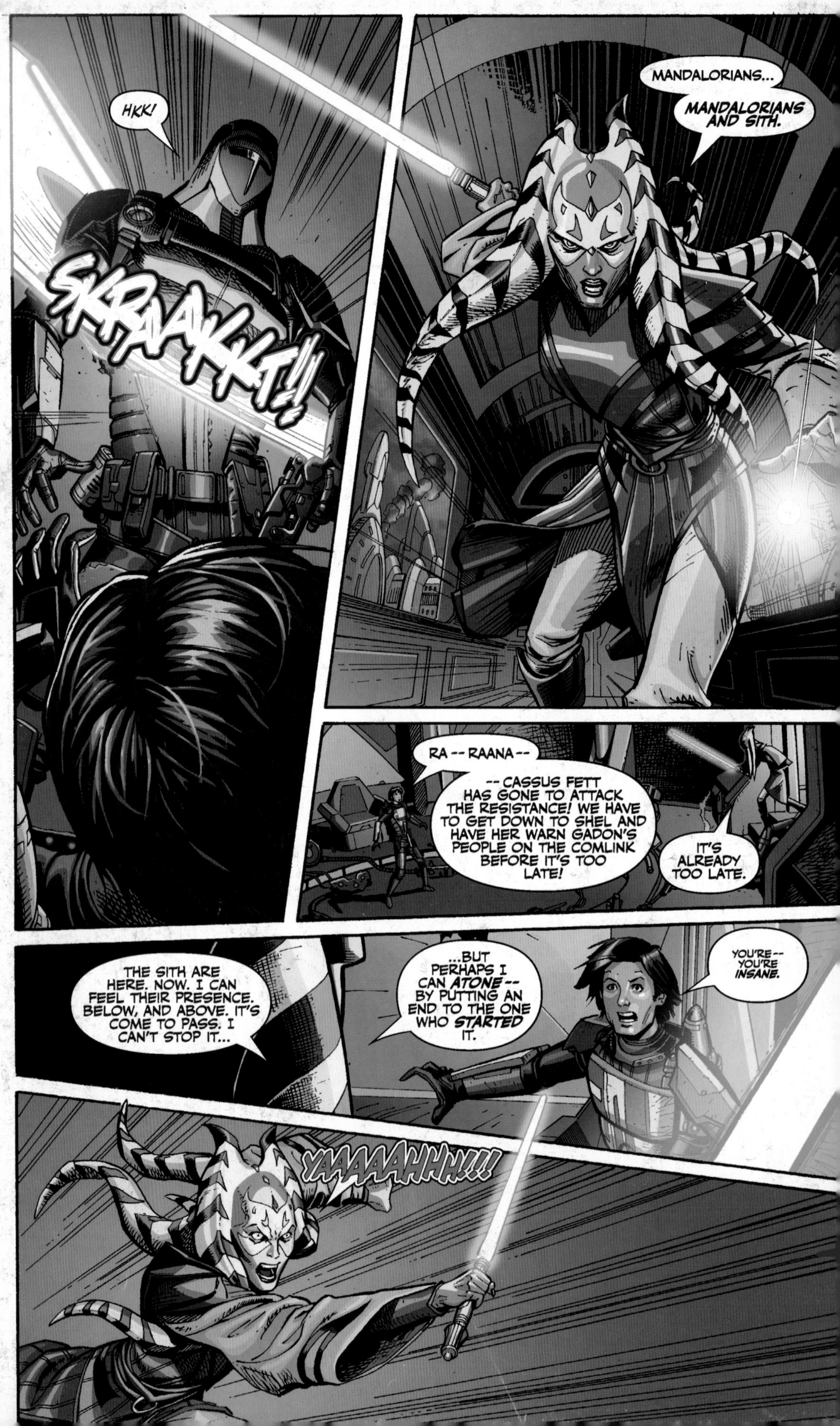
HKK!
SKRAKKT!!
MANDALORIANS...
MANDALORIANS AND SITH.
RA -- RAANA --
-- CASSUS FETT HAS GONE TO ATTACK THE RESISTANCE! WE HAVE TO GET DOWN TO SHEL AND HAVE HER WARN GADON'S PEOPLE ON THE COMLINK BEFORE IT'S TOO LATE!
IT'S ALREADY TOO LATE.
THE SITH ARE HERE. NOW. I CAN FEEL THEIR PRESENCE. BELOW, AND ABOVE. IT'S COME TO PASS. I CAN'T STOP IT...
...BUT PERHAPS I CAN ATONE -- BY PUTTING AN END TO THE ONE WHO STARTED IT.
YOU'RE -- YOU'RE INSANE.
YAAAAAHHH!!!

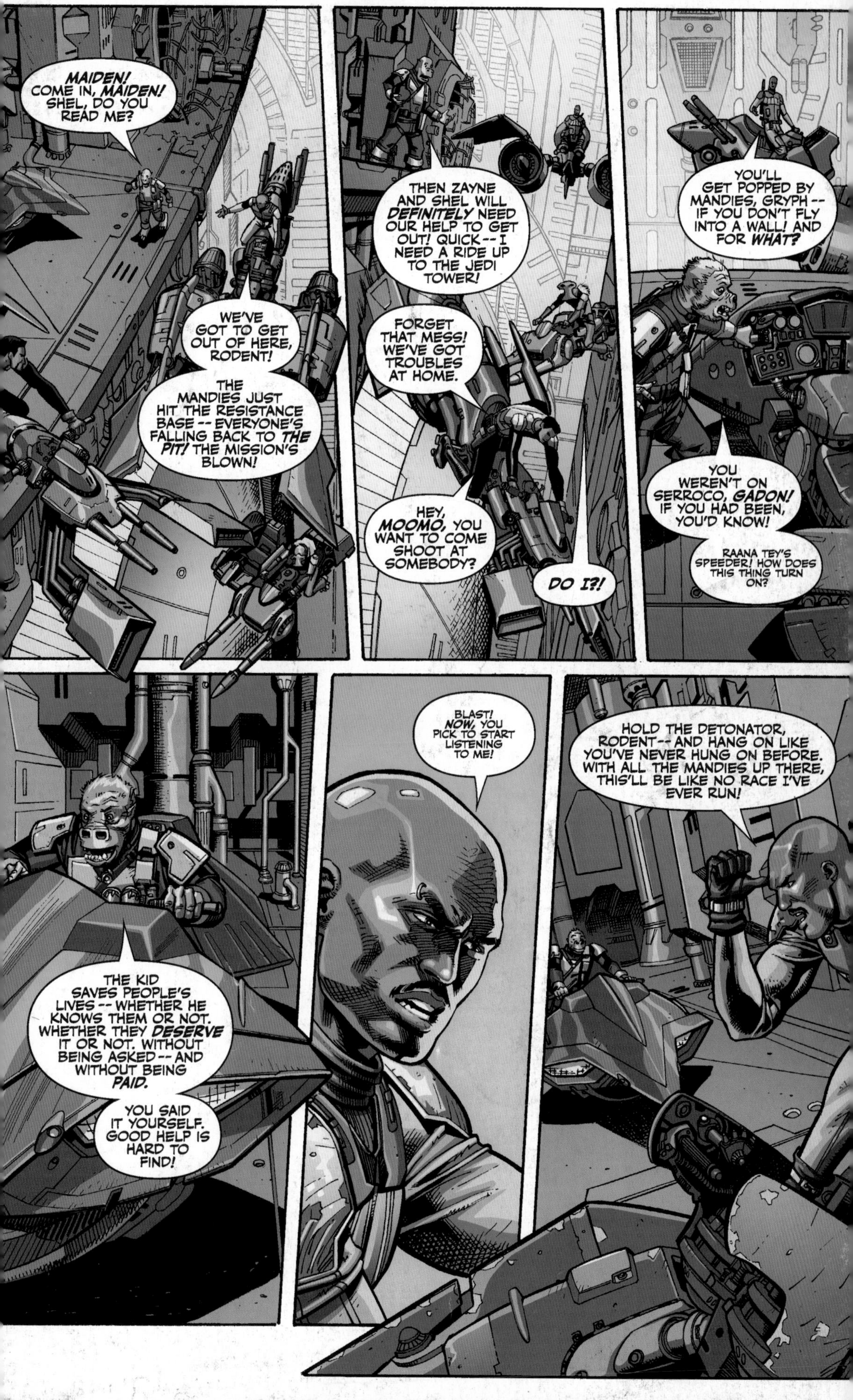
MAIDEN! COME IN, MAIDEN! SHEL, DO YOU READ ME?
WE'VE GOT TO GET OUT OF HERE, RODENT!
THE MANDIES JUST HIT THE RESISTANCE BASE -- EVERYONE'S FALLING BACK TO THE PIT! THE MISSION'S BLOWN!
THEN ZAYNE AND SHEL WILL DEFINITELY NEED OUR HELP TO GET OUT! QUICK -- I NEED A RIDE UP TO THE JEDI TOWER!
FORGET THAT MESS! WE'VE GOT TROUBLES AT HOME.
HEY, MOOMO, YOU WANT TO COME SHOOT AT SOMEBODY?
DO I?!
YOU'LL GET POPPED BY MANDIES, GRYPH -- IF YOU DON'T FLY INTO A WALL! AND FOR WHAT?
YOU WEREN'T ON SERROCO, GADON! IF YOU HAD BEEN, YOU'D KNOW!
RAANA TEY'S SPEEDER! HOW DOES THIS THING TURN ON?
THE KID SAVES PEOPLE'S LIVES -- WHETHER HE KNOWS THEM OR NOT. WHETHER THEY DESERVE IT OR NOT. WITHOUT BEING ASKED -- AND WITHOUT BEING PAID.
YOU SAID IT YOURSELF. GOOD HELP IS HARD TO FIND!
BLAST! NOW, YOU PICK TO START LISTENING TO ME!
HOLD THE DETONATOR, RODENT -- AND HANG ON LIKE YOU'VE NEVER HUNG ON BEFORE. WITH ALL THE MANDIES UP THERE, THIS'LL BE LIKE NO RACE I'VE EVER RUN!

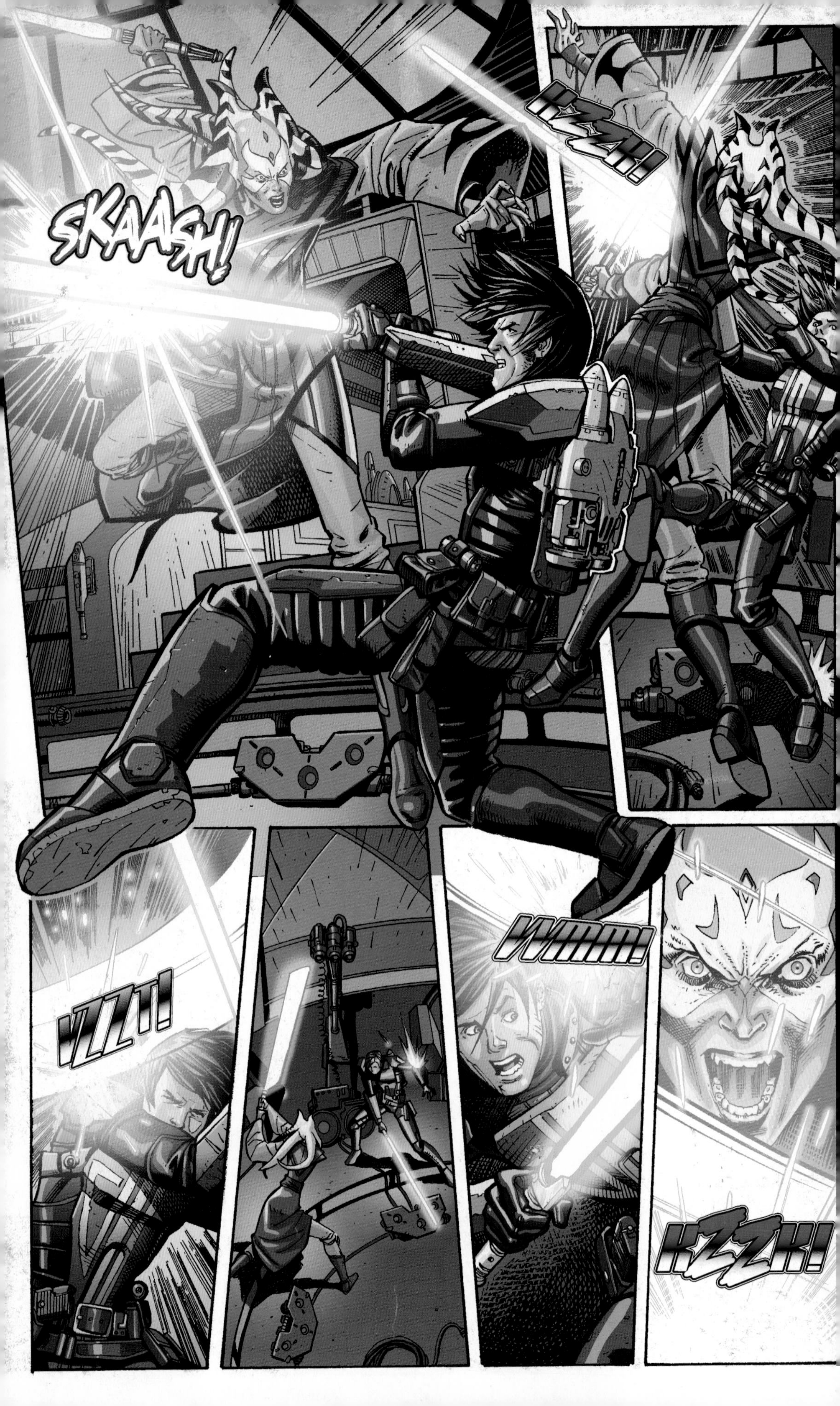

SKAASH!
KZZH!
VZZT!
VVMMM!
KZZH!

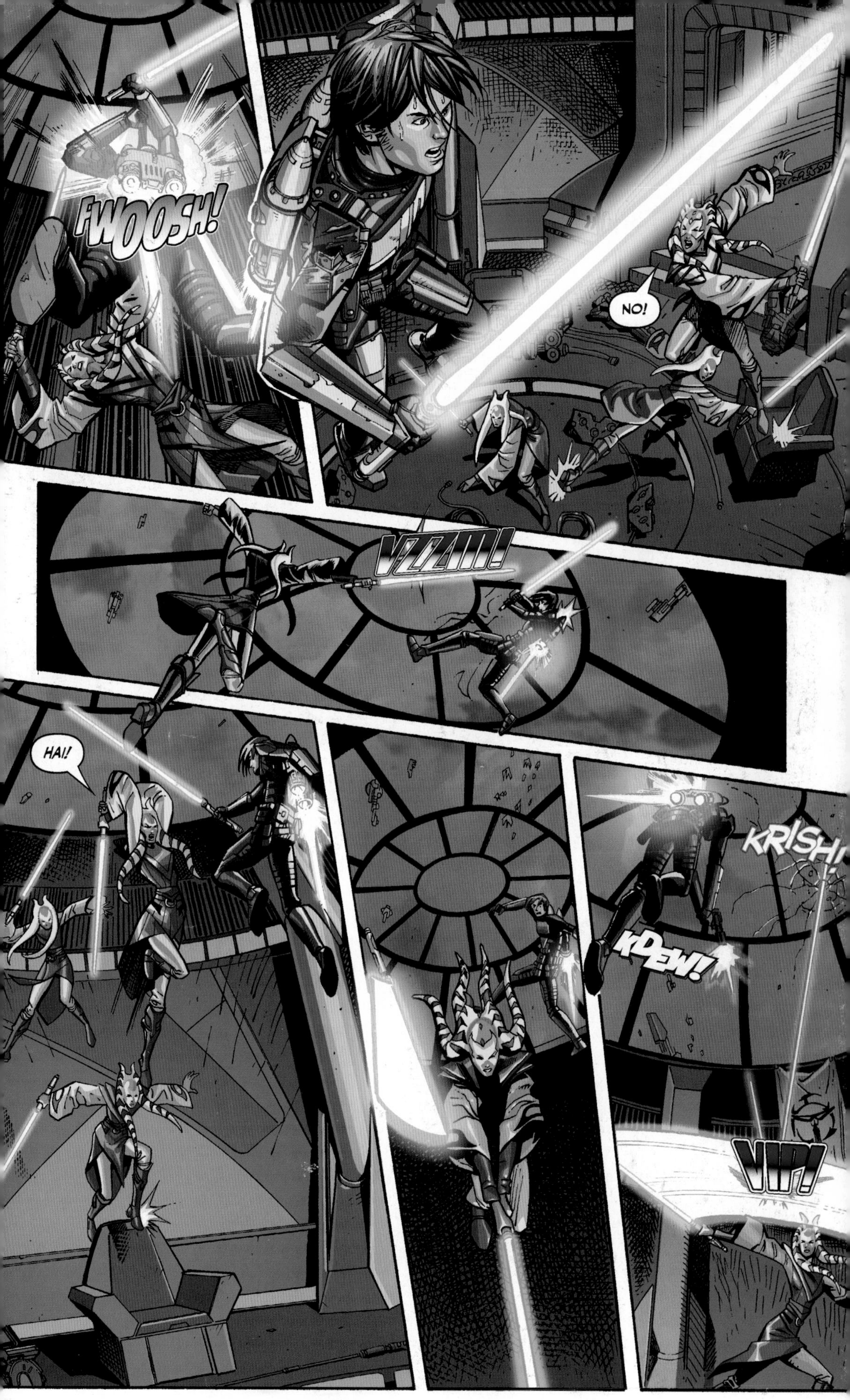
FWOOSH!
NO!
VZZM!
HA!
KRISH!
KDEW!
VIP!

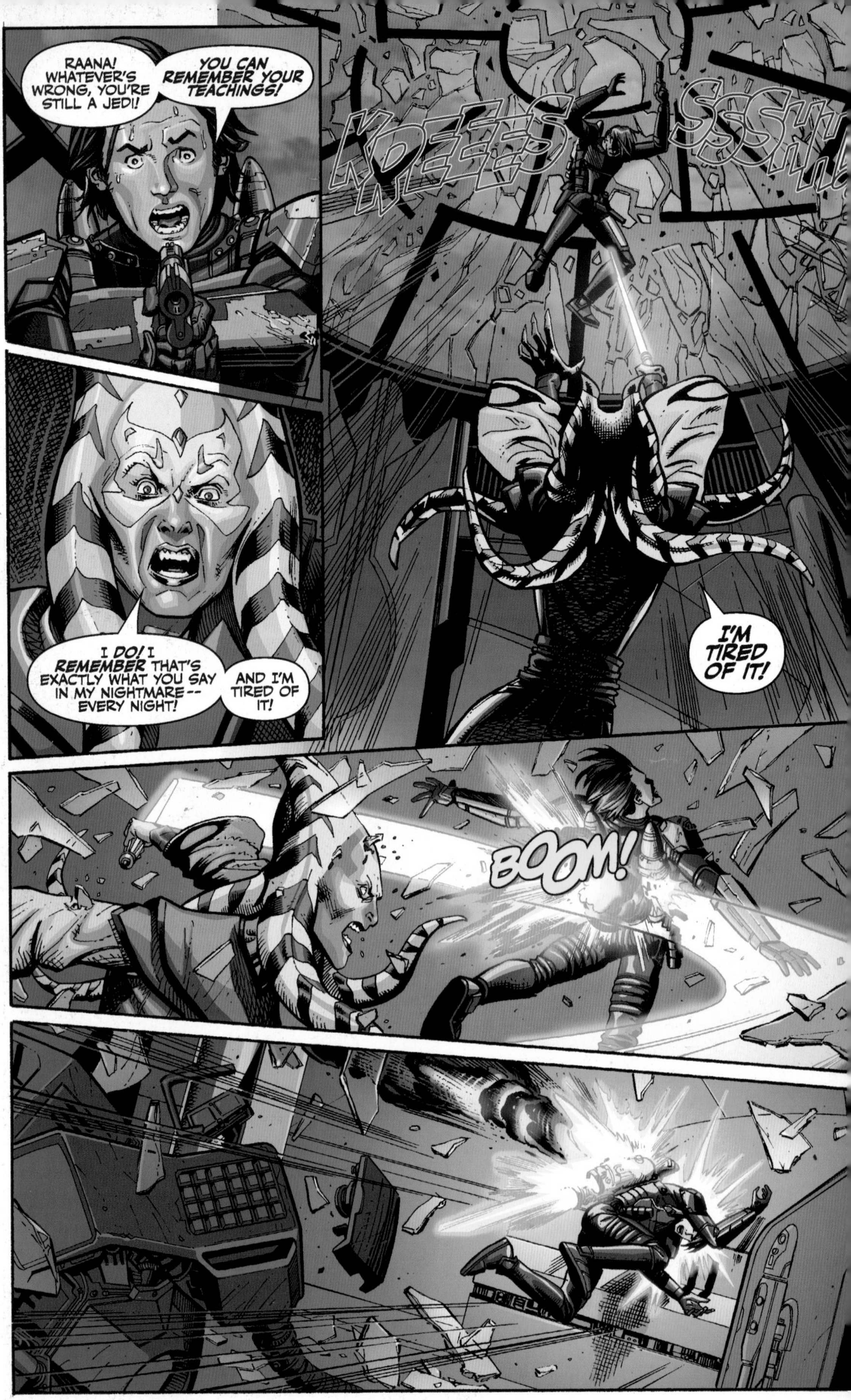
RAANA! WHATEVER'S WRONG, YOU'RE STILL A JEDI!
YOU CAN REMEMBER YOUR TEACHINGS!
I DO! I REMEMBER THAT'S EXACTLY WHAT YOU SAY IN MY NIGHTMARE-- EVERY NIGHT!
AND I'M TIRED OF IT!
I'M TIRED OF IT!
BOOM!

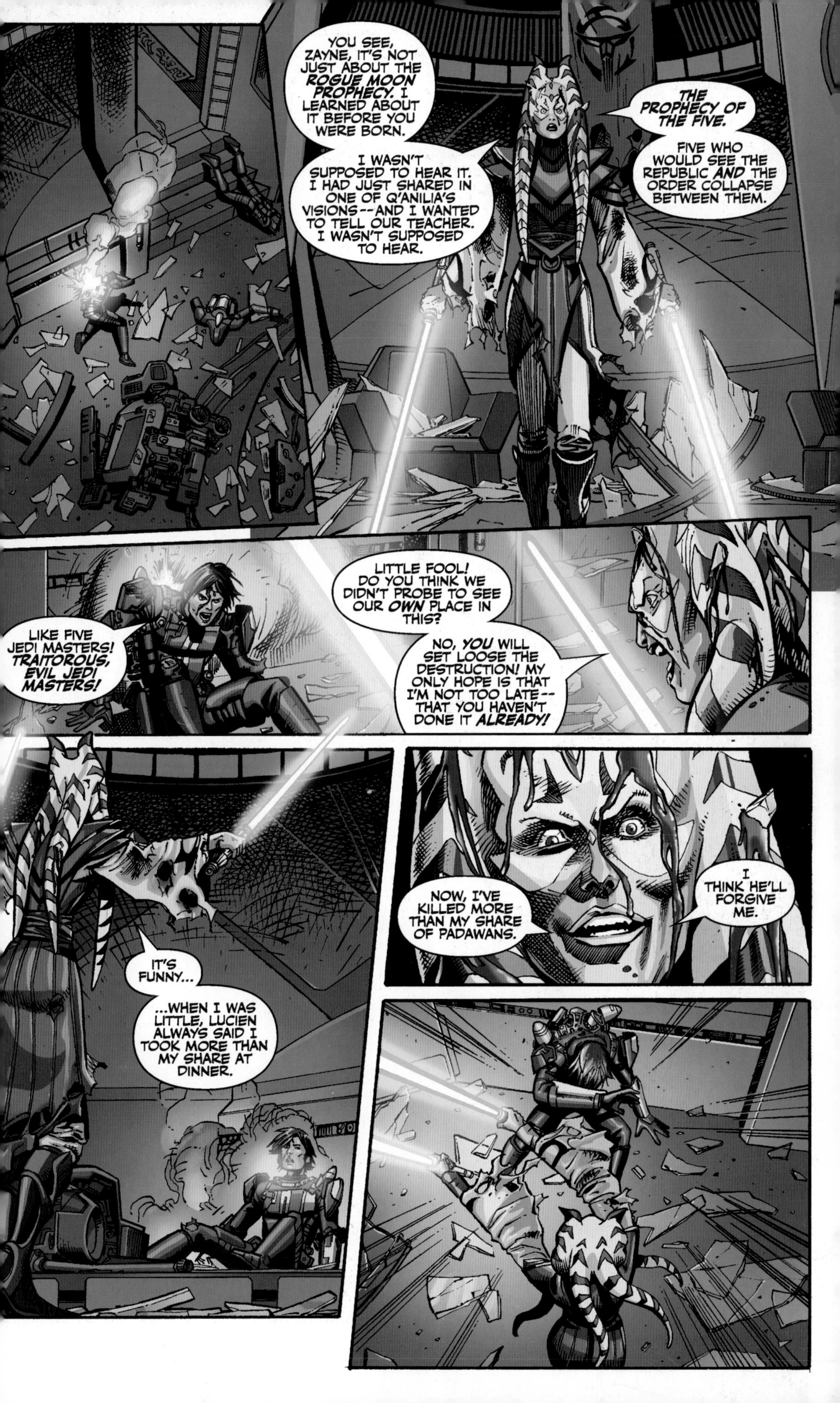
YOU SEE, ZAYNE, IT'S NOT JUST ABOUT THE ROGUE MOON PROPHECY. I LEARNED ABOUT IT BEFORE YOU WERE BORN.
I WASN'T SUPPOSED TO HEAR IT. I HAD JUST SHARED IN ONE OF Q'ANILIA'S VISIONS--AND I WANTED TO TELL OUR TEACHER. I WASN'T SUPPOSED TO HEAR.
THE PROPHECY OF THE FIVE.
FIVE WHO WOULD SEE THE REPUBLIC AND THE ORDER COLLAPSE BETWEEN THEM.
LIKE FIVE JEDI MASTERS! TRAITOROUS, EVIL JEDI MASTERS!
LITTLE FOOL! DO YOU THINK WE DIDN'T PROBE TO SEE OUR OWN PLACE IN THIS?
NO, YOU WILL SET LOOSE THE DESTRUCTION! MY ONLY HOPE IS THAT I'M NOT TOO LATE--THAT YOU HAVEN'T DONE IT ALREADY!
IT'S FUNNY...
...WHEN I WAS LITTLE, LUCIEN ALWAYS SAID I TOOK MORE THAN MY SHARE AT DINNER.
NOW, I'VE KILLED MORE THAN MY SHARE OF PADAWANS.
I THINK HE'LL FORGIVE ME.

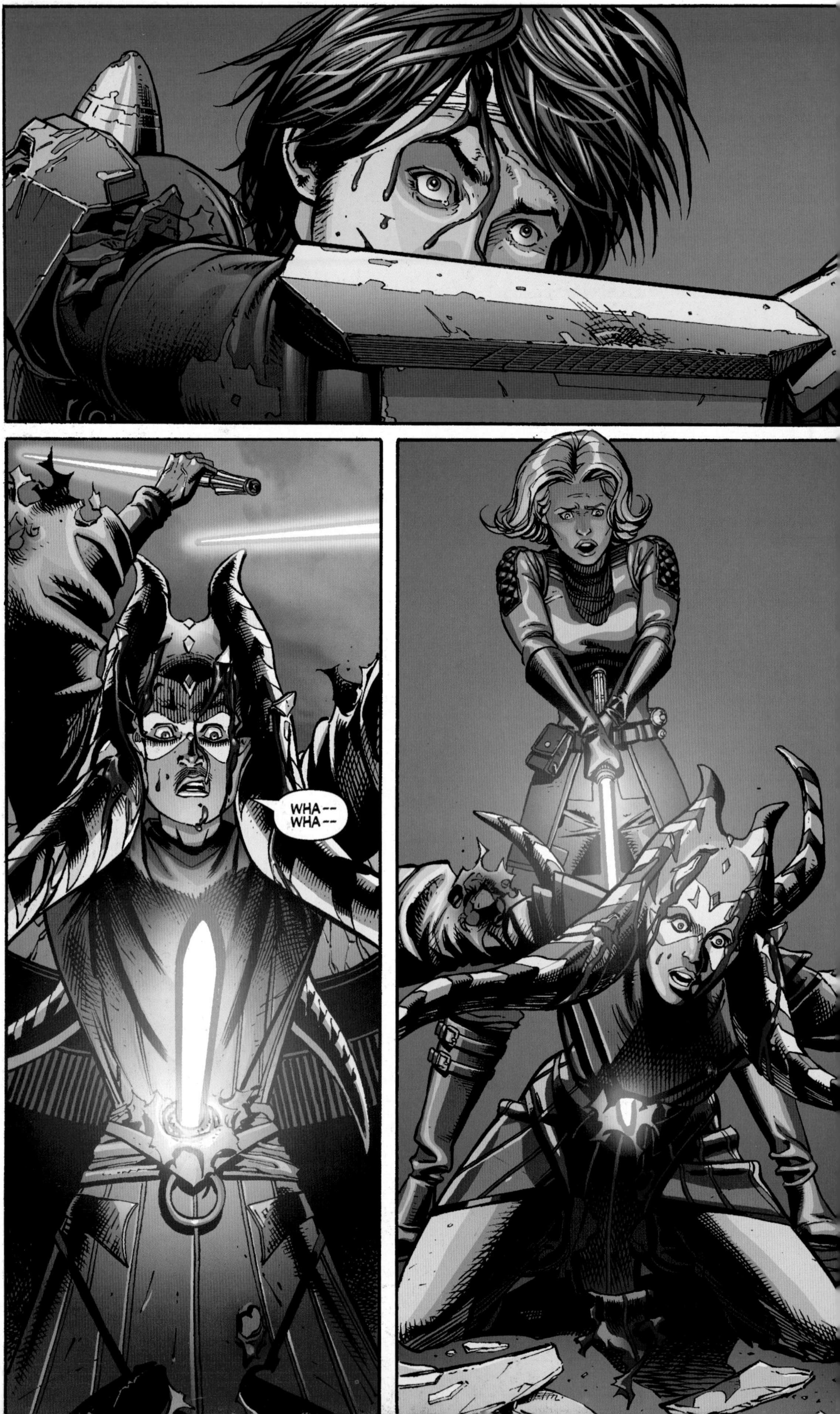
WHA--
WHA--

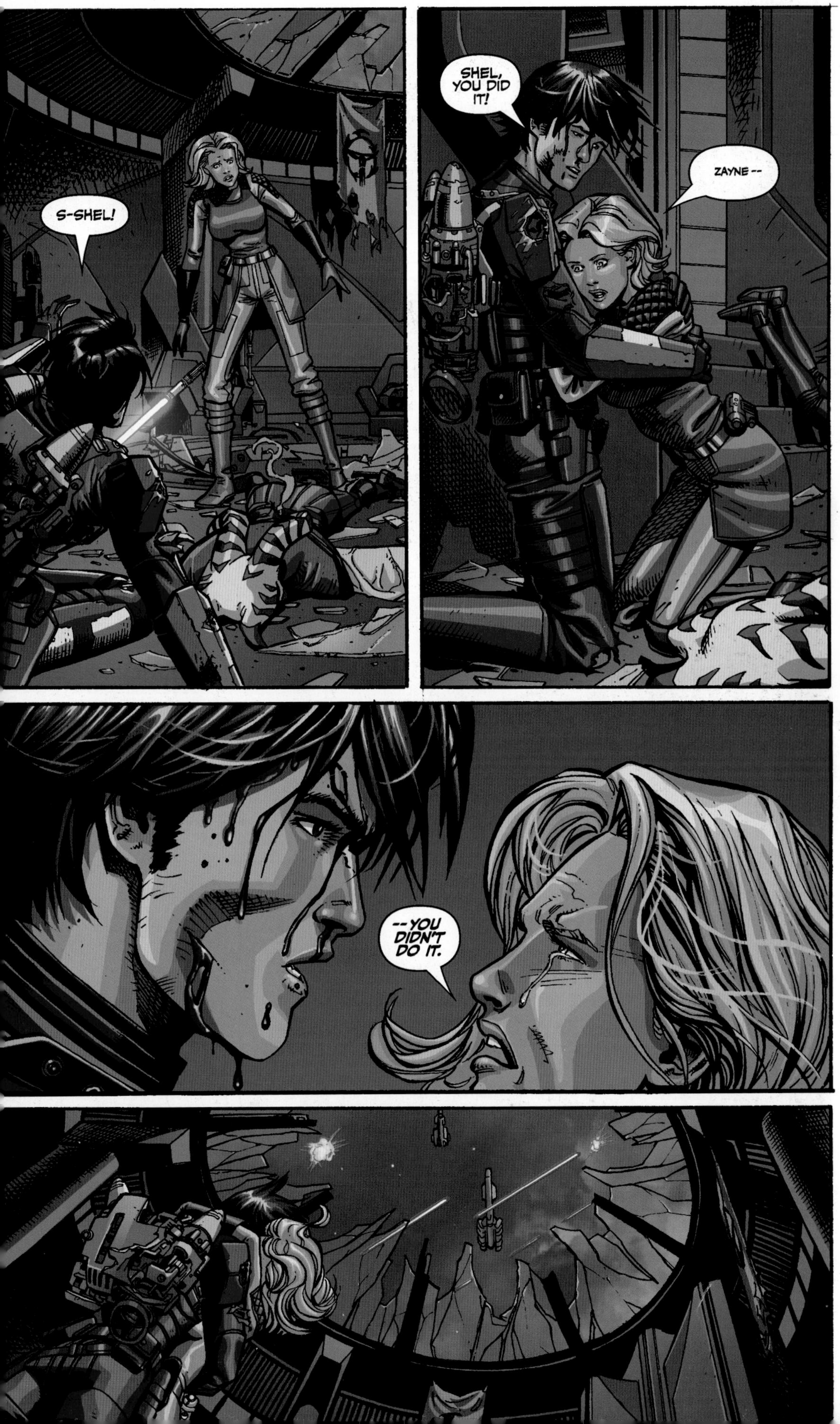
S-SHEL!
SHEL, YOU DID IT!
ZAYNE --
-- YOU DIDN'T DO IT.

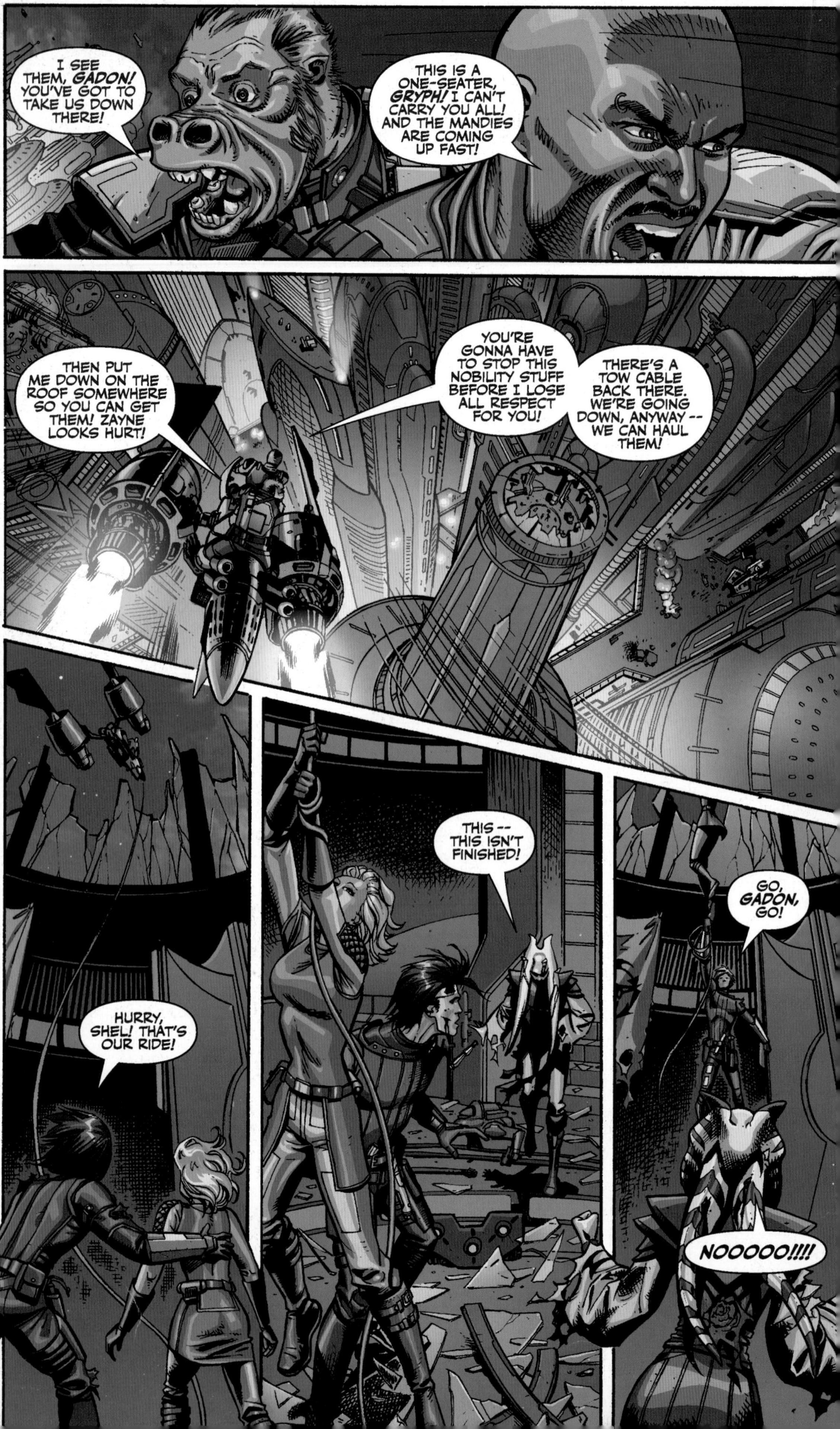

I SEE THEM, GADON! YOU'VE GOT TO TAKE US DOWN THERE!
THIS IS A ONE-SEATER, GRYPH! I CAN'T CARRY YOU ALL! AND THE MANDIES ARE COMING UP FAST!
THEN PUT ME DOWN ON THE ROOF SOMEWHERE SO YOU CAN GET THEM! ZAYNE LOOKS HURT!
YOU'RE GONNA HAVE TO STOP THIS NOBILITY STUFF BEFORE I LOSE ALL RESPECT FOR YOU!
THERE'S A TOW CABLE BACK THERE. WE'RE GOING DOWN, ANYWAY -- WE CAN HAUL THEM!
HURRY, SHEL! THAT'S OUR RIDE!
THIS -- THIS ISN'T FINISHED!
GO, GADON, GO!
NOOOOO!!!!

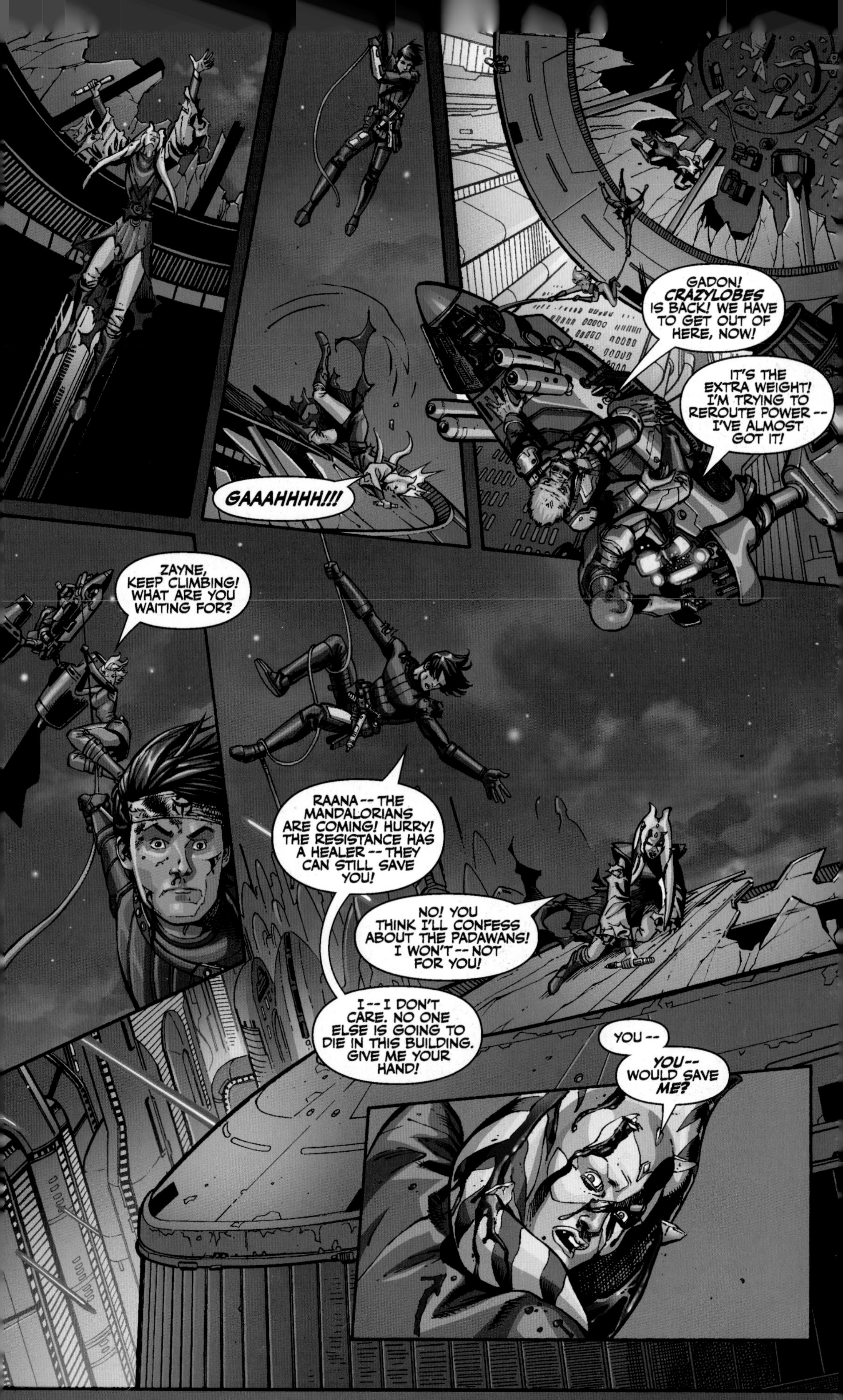
GADON! CRAZYLOBES IS BACK! WE HAVE TO GET OUT OF HERE, NOW!
IT'S THE EXTRA WEIGHT! I'M TRYING TO REROUTE POWER -- I'VE ALMOST GOT IT!
GAAAHHHH!!!
ZAYNE, KEEP CLIMBING! WHAT ARE YOU WAITING FOR?
RAANA -- THE MANDALORIANS ARE COMING! HURRY! THE RESISTANCE HAS A HEALER -- THEY CAN STILL SAVE YOU!
NO! YOU THINK I'LL CONFESS ABOUT THE PADAWANS! I WON'T -- NOT FOR YOU!
I -- I DON'T CARE. NO ONE ELSE IS GOING TO DIE IN THIS BUILDING. GIVE ME YOUR HAND!
YOU --
YOU -- WOULD SAVE ME?

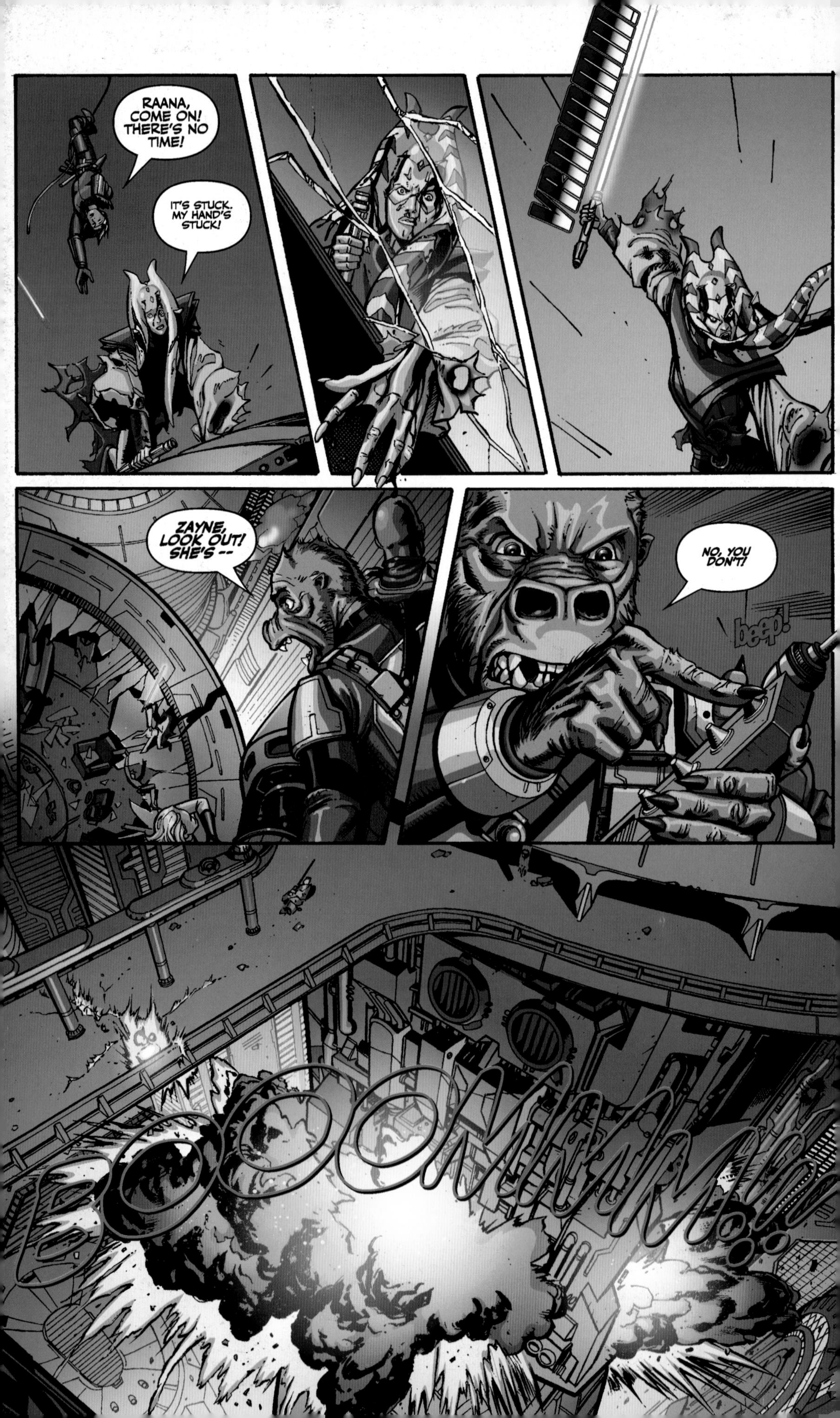
RAANA, COME ON! THERE'S NO TIME!
IT'S STUCK. MY HAND'S STUCK!
ZAYNE, LOOK OUT! SHE'S --
NO, YOU DON'T!
beep!

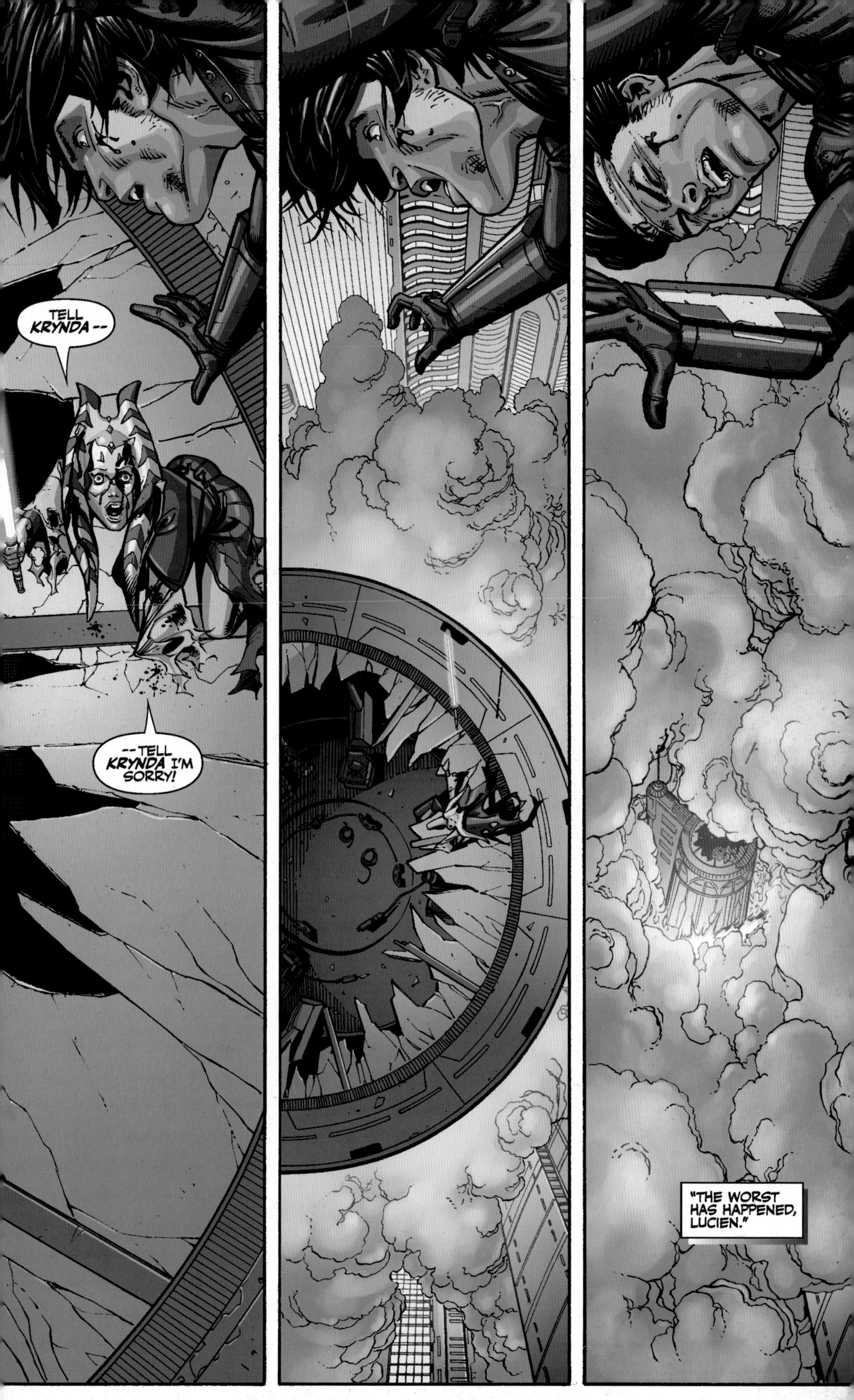

TELL KRYNDA --
--TELL KRYNDA I'M SORRY!
"THE WORST HAS HAPPENED, LUCIEN."

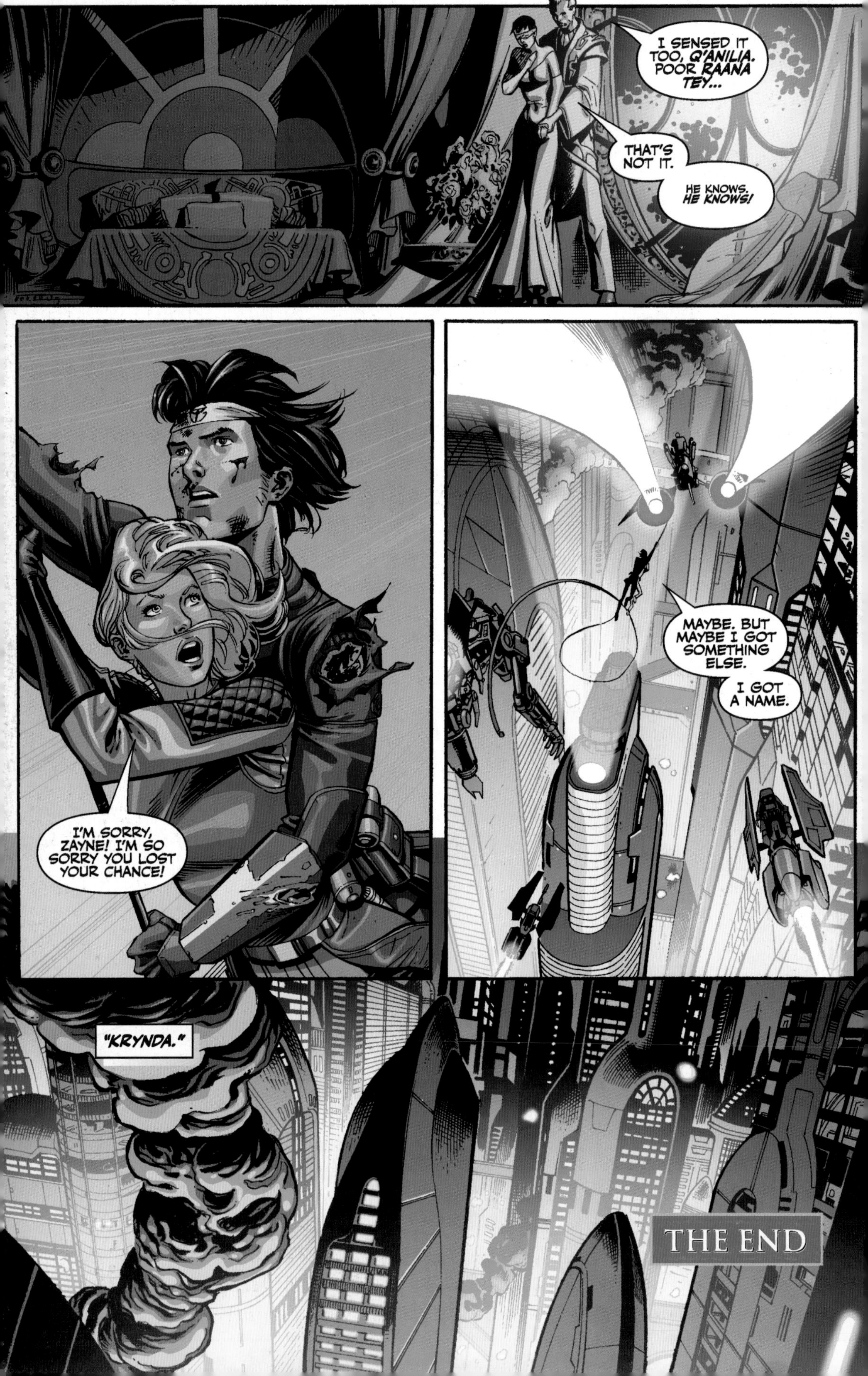
I SENSED IT TOO, Q'ANILIA. POOR RAANA TEY...
THAT'S NOT IT.
HE KNOWS. HE KNOWS!
I'M SORRY, ZAYNE! I'M SO SORRY YOU LOST YOUR CHANCE!
MAYBE. BUT MAYBE I GOT SOMETHING ELSE.
I GOT A NAME.
"KRYNDA."
THE END

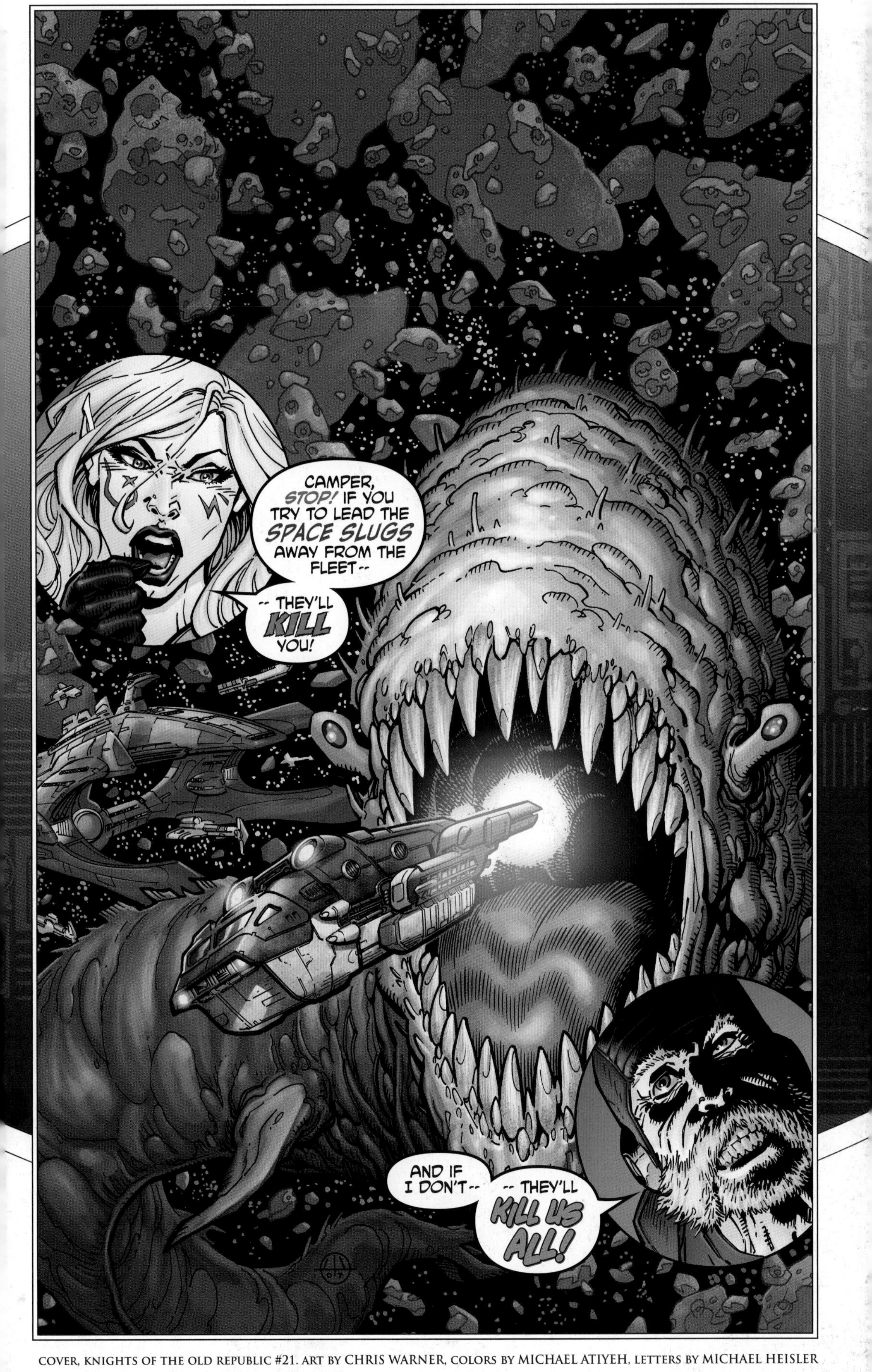
CAMPER, STOP! IF YOU TRY TO LEAD THE SPACE SLUGS AWAY FROM THE FLEET--
-- THEY'LL KILL YOU!
AND IF I DON'T--
-- THEY'LL KILL US ALL!

COVER, KNIGHTS OF THE OLD REPUBLIC #21. ART BY CHRIS WARNER, COLORS BY MICHAEL ATIYEH, LETTERS BY MICHAEL HEISLER

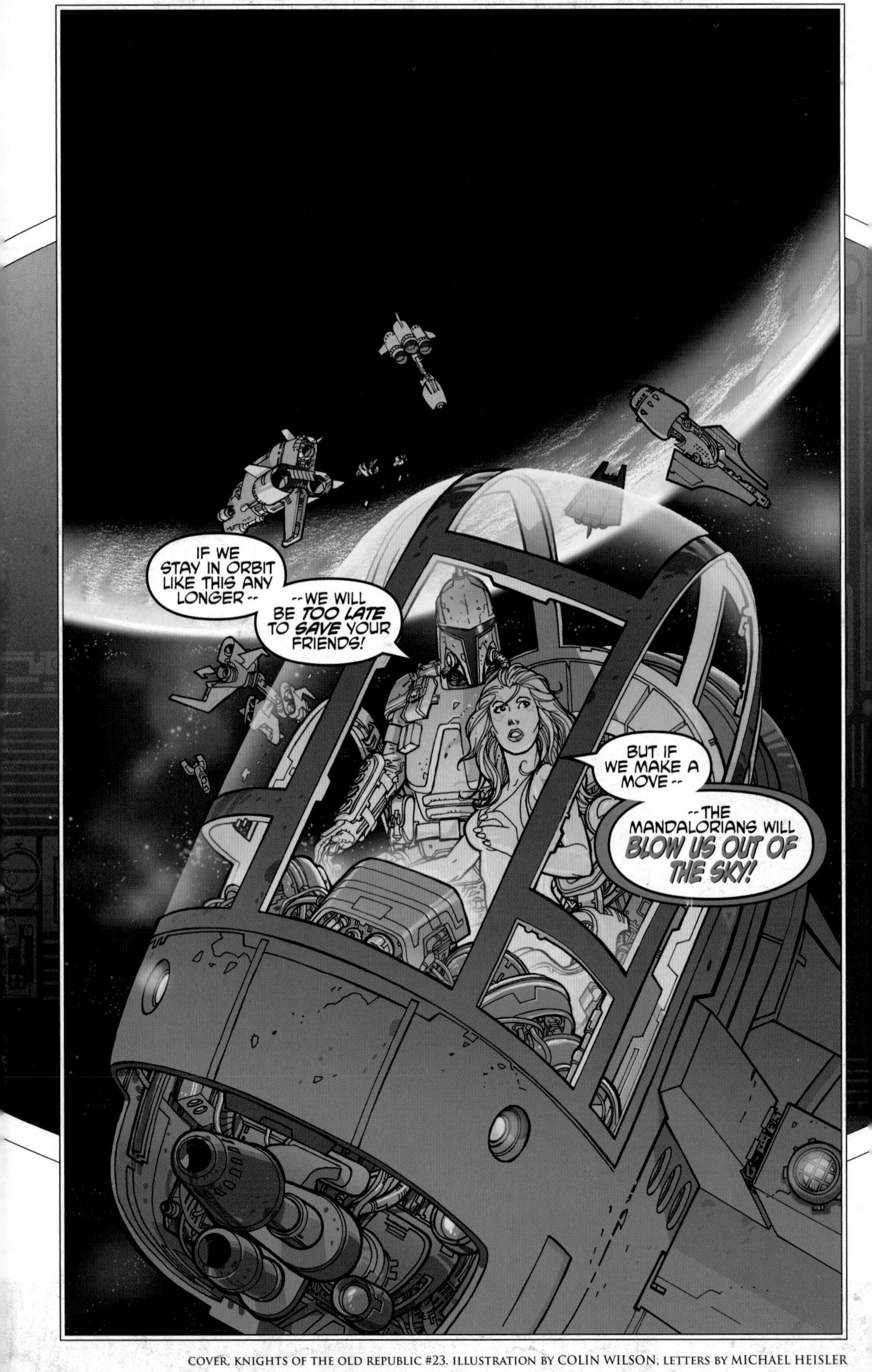
IF WE STAY IN ORBIT LIKE THIS ANY LONGER--
--WE WILL BE TOO LATE TO SAVE YOUR FRIENDS!
BUT IF WE MAKE A MOVE--
--THE MANDALORIANS WILL BLOW US OUT OF THE SKY!

COVER, KNIGHTS OF THE OLD REPUBLIC #23. ILLUSTRATION BY COLIN WILSON, LETTERS BY MICHAEL HEISLER

STAR WARS®
KNIGHTS OF THE OLD REPUBLIC

Volume 1: Commencement
ISBN: 978-1-59307-640-5

Volume 2: Flashpoint
ISBN: 978-1-59307-761-7

Volume 3: Days of Fear, Nights of Anger
ISBN: 978-1-59307-867-6

$18.95 each!

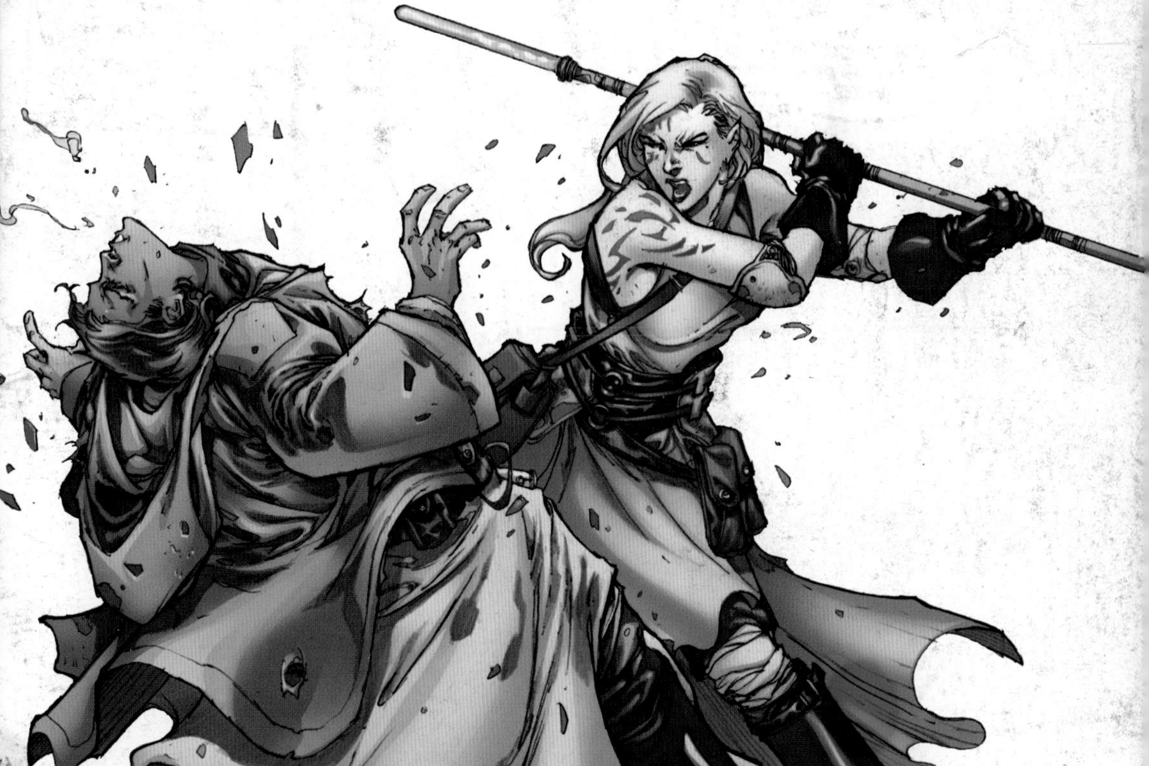

TO FIND A COMICS SHOP IN YOUR AREA, CALL 1-888-266-4226.
For more information or to order direct: *On the web: darkhorse.com *E-mail: mailorder@darkhorse.com
*Phone: 1-800-862-0052 Mon.-Fri. 9 A.M. to 5 P.M. Pacific Time.

DARK HORSE COMICS

STAR WARS GRAPHIC NOVEL TIMELINE (IN YEARS)

Tales of the Jedi—5,000–3,986 BSW4
Knights of the Old Republic—3,964 BSW4
Jedi vs. Sith—1,000 BSW4
Jedi Council: Acts of War—33 BSW4
Prelude to Rebellion—33 BSW4
Darth Maul—33 BSW4
Episode I: The Phantom Menace—32 BSW4
Outlander—32 BSW4
Emissaries to Malastare—32 BSW4
Jango Fett: Open Seasons—32 BSW4
Twilight—31 BSW4
Bounty Hunters—31 BSW4
The Hunt for Aurra Sing—30 BSW4
Darkness—30 BSW4
The Stark Hyperspace War—30 BSW4
Rite of Passage—28 BSW4
Jango Fett—27 BSW4
Zam Wesell—27 BSW4
Honor and Duty—24 BSW4
Episode II: Attack of the Clones—22 BSW4
Clone Wars—22–19 BSW4
Clone Wars Adventures—22–19 BSW4
General Grievous—20 BSW4
Episode III: Revenge of the Sith—19 BSW4
Dark Times—19 BSW4
Droids—3 BSW4
Boba Fett: Enemy of the Empire—2 BSW4
Underworld—1 BSW4
Episode IV: A New Hope—SW4
Classic Star Wars—0–3 ASW4
A Long Time Ago . . .—0–4 ASW4
Empire—0 ASW4
Rebellion—0 ASW4
Vader's Quest—0 ASW4
Boba Fett: Man with a Mission—0 ASW4
Jabba the Hutt: The Art of the Deal—1 ASW4
Splinter of the Mind's Eye—1 ASW4
Episode V: The Empire Strikes Back—3 ASW4
Shadows of the Empire—3–5 ASW4
Episode VI: Return of the Jedi—4 ASW4
X-Wing Rogue Squadron—4–5 ASW4
Mara Jade: By the Emperor's Hand—4 ASW4
Heir to the Empire—9 ASW4
Dark Force Rising—9 ASW4
The Last Command—9 ASW4
Dark Empire—10 ASW4
Boba Fett: Death, Lies, and Treachery—11 ASW4
Crimson Empire—11 ASW4
Jedi Academy: Leviathan—13 ASW4
Union—20 ASW4
Chewbacca—25 ASW4
Legacy—130 ASW4

Old Republic Era
25,000 – 1000 years before
Star Wars: A New Hope

Rise of the Empire Era
1000 – 0 years before
Star Wars: A New Hope

Rebellion Era
0 – 5 years after
Star Wars: A New Hope

New Republic Era
5 – 25 years after
Star Wars: A New Hope

New Jedi Order Era
25+ years after
Star Wars: A New Hope

Legacy Era
130+ years after
Star Wars: A New Hope

Infinities
Does not apply to timeline

Sergio Aragonés Stomps Star Wars
Star Wars Tales
Star Wars Infinities
Tag and Bink
Star Wars Visionaries

BSW4 = before *Episode IV: A New Hope*. ASW4 = after *Episode IV: A New Hope*.